Edgewood Public Montessori LMC
Okemos, MI

Endangered
Species
2nd EDITION

Endangered Species

2nd EDITION

VOLUME 2
Arachnids,
Birds,
Crustaceans,
Insects, and
Mollusks

Sonia Benson,
Rob Nagel

Detroit • New York • San Diego • San Francisco • Cleveland • New Haven, Conn. • Waterville, Maine • London • Munich

Endangered Species, 2nd Edition

Sonia Benson and Rob Nagel

Project Editors
Julie L. Carnagie, Allison McNeill

Editorial
Diane Sawinski, Sarah Hermsen

Permissions
Margaret Chamberlain

Imaging and Multimedia
Robyn Young

Product Design
Michelle DiMercurio, Kate Scheible

Composition
Evi Seoud

Manufacturing
Rita Wimberley

©2004 by U•X•L. U•X•L is an imprint of The Gale Group, Inc., a division of Thomson Learning, Inc.

U•X•L® is a registered trademark used herein under license. Thomson Learning™ is a trademark used herein under license.

For more information, contact:
The Gale Group, Inc.
27500 Drake Rd.
Farmington Hills, MI 48331-3535
Or you can visit our Internet site at
http://www.gale.com

ALL RIGHTS RESERVED
No part of this work covered by the copyright hereon may be reproduced or used in any form or by any means—graphic, electronic, or mechanical, including photocopying, recording, tap-ing, Web distribution, or information storage retrieval systems—without the written permission of the publisher.

For permission to use material from this product, submit your request via Web at http://www.gale-edit.com/per-missions, or you may download our Permissions Request form and submit your request by fax or mail to:

Permissions Department
The Gale Group, Inc.
27500 Drake Rd.
Farmington Hills, MI 48331-3535

Permissions Hotline:
248-699-8006 or 800-877-4253, ext. 8006
Fax: 248-699-8074 or 800-762-4058

Volume 1 cover photograph reproduced by permission of Photo Researchers, Inc. Volume 2 cover photograph reproduced by permission of the Cincinnati Zoo. Volume 3 cover photograph reproduced by permission of Photo Researchers, Inc.

While every effort has been made to ensure the reliability of the information presented in this publication, The Gale Group, Inc. does not guarantee the accuracy of the data contained herein. The Gale Group, Inc. accepts no payment for listing; and inclusion in the publication of any organization, agency, institution, publication, service, or individual does not imply endorsement by the editors or publisher. Errors brought to the attention of the publisher and verified to the satisfaction of the publisher will be corrected in future editions.

LIBRARY OF CONGRESS CATALOGING-IN-PUBLICATION DATA

Benson, Sonia.
    Endangered species / Sonia Benson ; Julie L. Carnagie, project editor. — 2nd ed.
    p. cm.
    Rev. ed. of: Endangered species / Rob Nagel. ©1999.
    Summary: Entries on more than 200 extinct, endangered, vulnerable, and threatened animals and plants describe the individual species, its habitat and current distribution, and efforts to protect and preserve it. Includes bibliographical references.
    ISBN 0-7876-7618-7 (set : hardcover) — ISBN 0-7876-7619-5 (vol. 1) — ISBN 0-7876-7620-9 (vol. 2) — ISBN 0-7876-7621-7 (vol. 3)
    1. Endangered species—Juvenile literature. [1. Endangered species—Encyclopedias.] I. Carnagie, Julie. II. Nagel, Rob. Endangered species. III. Title.
QL83.N35 2003
333.95'42—dc22
                                                        2003016691

Printed in the United States of America
10 9 8 7 6 5 4 3 2 1

Contents

VOLUME 2: Arachnids, Birds, Crustaceans,
Insects, and Mollusks

VOLUME 3: Amphibians, Fish, Plants, and Reptiles

Fish

Plants

Reader's Guide

Endangered Species, 2nd Edition, presents information on endangered and threatened mammals, birds, reptiles, amphibians, fish, mollusks, insects, arachnids, crustaceans, and plants. Its 240 entries were chosen to give a glimpse of the broad range of species currently facing endangerment. While well-publicized examples such as the American bison, northern spotted owl, and gray wolf are examined, so, too, are less conspicuous—yet no less threatened—species such as the Australian ant, Cape vulture, freshwater sawfish, and Peebles Navajo cactus.

The entries are spread across three volumes and are divided into sections by classes. Within each class, species are arranged alphabetically by common name.

Each entry begins with the species's common and scientific names. A fact box containing classification information—phylum (or division), class, order, and family—for that species follows. The box also lists the current status of the species in the wild according to the International Union for Conservation of Nature and Natural Resources (IUCN) and the U.S. Fish and Wildlife Service (which administers the Endangered Species Act). Finally, the box lists the country or countries where the species currently ranges.

Locator maps outlining the range of a particular species are included in each entry to help users find unfamiliar countries or locations. In most entries, a color photo provides a more concrete visualization of the species. Sidebar boxes containing interesting and related information are also included in some entries.

Each entry is broken into three sections:

- The information under the subhead **Description and Biology** provides a general description of the species. This includes physical dimensions, eating and reproductive habits, and social behavior.

- The information under the subhead **Habitat and Current Distribution** describes where the species is found today, its preferred habitat, and, if available, recent estimates of its population size.

- The information under the subhead **History and Conservation Measures** relates, if possible, the history of the species and the factors currently threatening it. Conservation efforts to save the species, if any are underway, are also described.

Beginning each volume of *Endangered Species,* 2nd Edition, is an overview of the history and current state of endangerment and its causes and a discussion of the International Union for Conservation of Nature and Natural Resources (IUCN–The World Conservation Union) that includes a brief history of the organization, its current focus, and a brief explanation of the status categories in which the IUCN places imperiled species. The final section focuses on the Endangered Species Act, briefly examining its passage, purpose, implementation, status categories, and current state.

Each volume ends with a Where to Learn More section composed of books, periodicals, Internet addresses, and environmental organizations. The book listing is annotated. The environmental organizations list—a selected catalog of organizations focusing on endangered species—contains mailing addresses, telephone numbers, Internet addresses (if available), and a brief description of each organization.

Finally, the volumes conclude with a cumulative index providing access to all the species discussed throughout *Endangered Species,* 2nd Edition.

The scope of this work is neither definitive nor exhaustive. No work on this subject can be. The information presented is as current as possible, but the state of endangered species, sadly, changes almost daily.

A note about the 2nd Edition

Since the publication of *Endangered Species* in 1999, the endangered or threatened status of many of the species included in these volumes has changed. Through the efforts of conservationists and legislators, some of these species have recovered or were upgraded to a less threatened status. The Przewalski's horse, for example, was considered extinct in the wild in 1996 by the IUCN, but a program to reintroduce horses bred in captivity into their historical habitat was unexpectedly successful. By 2000, 84 Przewalski's horses had been reintroduced and 114 foals (baby horses) had been born in the wild. In the early 2000s, a population of around 142 Przewalski's horses roamed freely, and the animals appear to be doing better each year they spend in the wild. Other species have declined to the very brink of extinction. Some—like the scimitar-horned oryx—have dramatically fallen on the IUCN Red List. The status of the scimitar-horned oryx fell from endangered to critically endangered in 1996 to extinct in the wild in 1999. It is likely that, with a captive-bred population now being prepared for reintroduction to the wild, the scimitar-horned oryx will be upgraded on the Red List in the near future. There are also new stories in many of the existing entries. Chimpanzees and gorillas, for one sad example among many, began making the news in 2003 when a scientific study found that their populations had been reduced by nearly one-half since the 1980s and that an Ebola virus is currently ravaging the populations.

Endangered Species cannot cover all threatened species worldwide, but 40 new species have been included in the 2nd Edition to ensure that the situations of species worldwide—as it stands five years after the first publication—are represented. Conservationists today are facing the same concerns as five years ago, many with more urgency and some new twists. The issues range from a worldwide decline in the amphibian and reptile populations to declining fish species that seem unable to recover from overfishing; from the effects of inbreeding in populations that have become very tiny to the lack of appropriate habitats in which to release the new captive-bred populations. Many of the new entries chronicle the enormous efforts of scientists to save species on the brink of extinction. For instance, the Chatham Islands robin population had dwindled to five birds in 1981, with only one female, "Old Blue," remaining. Through a breeding-in-captivity program, that species now has 259 members, but all of them are direct descendants of Old Blue and her mate, Old Yellow. And sometimes these efforts may not be enough: There were only three Po'oulis (honeycreepers) left in 2003, and because their ranges did not overlap, they had no chance of mating in the wild. Scientists were preparing to take these last remaining members of the species into custody as the only hope for saving the species.

Acknowledgments

Special thanks are due for the invaluable comments and suggestions provided by the *Endangered Species* advisors:

Valerie Doud, Science Teacher, Peru Junior High School, Peru, Indiana

Melba Holland, Earth Science/Science Department Head, Slaton Junior High School, Slaton, Texas

Bonnie L. Raasch, Media Specialist, C. B. Vernon Middle School, Marion, Iowa

The editors of *Endangered Species* also graciously thank Tom Romig and Julie Carnagie for their commitment to this project and for their patience and understanding during its completion. It is a continuing privilege and pleasure to work with the U•X•L family.

Comments and Suggestions

We welcome your comments on *Endangered Species* and suggestions for species to be included in future editions of *Endangered Species*. Please write: Editors, *Endangered Species*, U•X•L, 27500 Drake Rd., Farmington Hills, Michigan 48331–3535; call toll free: 1–800–877–4253; fax: 248–699–8097; or send e-mail via www.gale.com.

Endangerment and Its Causes: An Overview

Living organisms have been disappearing from the face of Earth since the beginning of life on the planet. Most of the species that have ever lived on Earth are now extinct. Extinction and endangerment can occur naturally as a normal process in the course of evolution. It can be the result of a catastrophic event, such as the collision of an asteroid with Earth. Scientists believe an asteroid struck the planet off Mexico's Yucatán Peninsula some 65,000,000 years ago, bringing about the extinction of almost 50 percent of the plant species and 75 percent of the animal species then living on Earth, including the dinosaurs. Widespread climate changes, disease, and competition among species can also result in natural extinction. To date, scientists believe there have been five great natural extinction episodes in Earth's history.

Since humans became the dominant species on the planet, however, the rate at which other species have become extinct has increased dramatically. Especially since the seventeenth century, technological advances and an ever-expanding human population have changed the natural world as never before. At present, scientists believe extinctions caused by humans are taking place at 100 to 1,000 times nature's normal rate between great extinction episodes. Species are disappearing faster than they can be created through evolution. In fact, some biologists estimate that in the early 2000s three or more plant and animal species become extinct each day.

Because scientists have described and named only a small percentage of Earth's species, it is impossible to measure the total number of species endangered or going extinct. Just 1,400,000 species—out of an estimated 10,000,000 to 100,000,000—have been described to date.

Scientists do know that humans are endangering species and the natural world primarily in three ways: habitat destruction, commercial exploitation of animals and plants, and the transplantation of species from one part of the world to another.

Habitat destruction

The destruction of habitats all over the world is the primary reason species are becoming extinct or endangered. Houses, highways, dams, industrial buildings, and ever-spreading farms now dominate landscapes formerly occupied by forests, prairies, deserts, scrublands, and wetlands. Since the beginning of European settlement in America, over 65,000,000 acres of wetlands have been drained. One million acres alone vanished between 1985 and 1995.

Habitat destruction can be obvious or it can be subtle, occurring over a long period of time without being noticed. Pollution, such as sewage from cities and chemical runoff from farms, can change the quality and quantity of water in streams and rivers. To species living in a delicately balanced habitat, this disturbance can be as fatal as the clear-cutting of a rain forest.

As remaining habitats are carved into smaller and smaller pockets or islands, remaining species are forced to exist in these crowded areas, which causes further habitat destruction. These species become less adaptable to environmental change; they become more vulnerable to extinction. Scientists believe that when a habitat is cut by 90 percent, one-half of its plants, animals, insects, and microscopic life-forms will become extinct.

Commercial exploitation

Animals have been hunted by humans not only for their meat but for parts of their bodies that are used to create medicines, love potions, and trinkets. Overhunting has caused the extinction of many species and brought a great many others to the brink of extinction. Examples include species of whales, slaughtered for their oil and baleen. The rhinoceroses of Africa are critically endangered, having been killed mainly for their horns. Sharks' fins, cruelly cut off of the live animal, are used in Asia as an aphrodisiac, and 75 shark species are now endangered.

International treaties outlaw the capture and trade of many endangered or threatened species. These laws, however, are difficult to enforce. The smuggling of endangered species is a huge business. In the early 2000s, the illegal trade in wildlife products was estimated at $15 billion a year worldwide—second only to the value of the international illegal drug trade.

Introduced species

Native species are those that have inhabited a given biological landscape for a long period of time. They have adapted to the environment, climate, and other species in that locale. Introduced or exotic species are those that have been brought into that landscape by humans, either accidentally or intentionally.

In some cases, these introduced species may not cause any harm. They may, over time, adapt to their new surroundings and fellow species, becoming "native." Most often, however, introduced species seriously disrupt ecological balances. They compete with native species for food and shelter. Often, they prey on the native species, who lack natural defenses against the intruders. In the last 500 years, introduced insects, cats, pigs, rats, and others have caused the endangerment or outright extinction of hundreds of native species.

Endangered Species Fact Boxes and Classification: An Explanation

Each entry in *Endangered Species,* 2nd Edition, begins with the common name of a species, followed by its scientific name. Underneath is a shaded fact box. This box contains the classification information for that species: phylum (or division), class, order, and family. It also lists the current status of that species in the wild according to the International Union for Conservation of Nature and Natural Resources (IUCN; see page xxiii) and the Endangered Species List compiled under the Endangered Species Act (ESA; see page xxvii). (Note: For a listing of species whose status has changed since the publication of the first edition, see page xxxi.) Finally, the box lists the country or countries where the species is currently found and provides a locator map for the range of the species.

Classification

Biological classification, or taxonomy, is the system of arranging plants and animals in groups according to their similarities. This system, which scientists around the world currently use, was developed by eighteenth-century Swedish botanist (a person specializing in the study of plants) Carolus Linnaeus. Linnaeus created a multilevel system or pyramid-like structure of nomenclature (naming) in which living organisms were grouped according to the number of physical traits they had in common. The ranking of the system, going from general to specific, is: kingdom, phylum (or division for plants), class, order, and family. The more specific the level (closer to the top of the pyramid), the more traits shared by the organisms placed in that level.

Scientists currently recognize five kingdoms of organisms: Animalia (animals, fish, humans); Plantae (plants, trees, grasses); Fungi (mushrooms, lichens); Protista (bacteria, certain algae, other one-celled organisms having nuclei); and

Monera (bacteria, blue-green algae, other one-celled organisms without nuclei).

Every living organism is placed into one of these kingdoms. Organisms within kingdoms are then divided into phylums (or divisions for plants) based on distinct and defining characteristics. An example would be the phylum Chordata, which contains all the members of the kingdom Animalia that have a backbone. Organisms in a specific phylum or division are then further divided into classes based on more distinct and defining characteristics. The dividing continues on through orders and then into families, where most organisms probably have the same behavioral patterns.

To further define an organism, Linnaeus also developed a two-part naming system—called binomial nomenclature—in which each living organism was given a two-part Latin name to distinguish it from other members in its family. The first name—italicized and capitalized—is the genus of the organism. The second name—italicized but not capitalized—is its species. This species name is an adjective, usually descriptive or geographic. Together, the genus and species form an organism's scientific name.

How similar organisms are separated by their scientific names can be seen in the example of the white oak and the red oak. All oak trees belong to the genus *Quercus*. The scientific name of white oak is *Quercus alba* (*alba* is Latin for "white"), while that of the red oak is *Quercus rubra* (*rubra* is Latin for "red").

Since each species or organism has only one name under binomial nomenclature, scientists worldwide who do not speak the same languages are able to communicate with each other about species.

International Union for Conservation of Nature and Natural Resources (IUCN–The World Conservation Union)

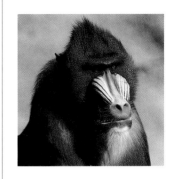

The IUCN is one of the world's oldest international conservation organizations. It was established in Fountainbleau, France, on October 5, 1947. It is a worldwide alliance of governments, government agencies, and nongovernmental organizations. Working with scientists and experts, the IUCN tries to encourage and assist nations and societies around the world to conserve nature and to use natural resources wisely. At present, IUCN members represent 74 governments, 105 government agencies, and more than 700 nongovernmental organizations.

The IUCN has six volunteer commissions. The largest and most active of these is the Species Survival Commission (SSC). The mission of the SSC is to conserve biological diversity by developing programs that help save, restore, and manage species and their habitats. One of the many activities of the SSC is the production of the *IUCN Red List of Threatened Animals* and the *IUCN Red List of Threatened Plants.*

These publications, which have provided the foundation for *Endangered Species,* present scientifically based information on the status of threatened species around the world. Species are classified according to their existence in the wild and the current threats to that existence. The categories differ slightly between animals and plants.

IUCN Red List categories

The *IUCN Red List of Threatened Animals* places threatened animals into one of nine categories:

- **Extinct:** A species that no longer exists anywhere around the world.

- **Extinct in the wild:** A species that no longer exists in the wild, but exists in captivity or in an area well outside its natural range.

- **Critically endangered:** A species that is facing an extremely high risk of extinction in the wild in the immediate future.

- **Endangered:** A species that is facing a high risk of extinction in the wild in the near future.

- **Vulnerable:** A species that is facing a high risk of extinction in the wild in the medium-term future.

- **Lower risk: Conservation dependent:** A species that is currently the focus of a conservation program. If the program is halted, the species would suffer and would qualify for one of the threatened categories above within a period of five years.

- **Lower risk: Near threatened:** A species that does not qualify for Conservation Dependent status, but is close to qualifying for Vulnerable status.

- **Lower risk: Least concern:** A species that qualifies for neither Conservation Dependent status or Near Threatened status.

- **Data deficient:** A species on which there is little information to assess its risk of extinction. Because of the possibility that future research will place the species in a threatened category, more information is required.

The *IUCN Red List of Threatened Plants* places threatened plants into one of six categories:

- **Extinct:** A species that no longer exists anywhere around the world.

- **Extinct/Endangered:** A species that is considered possibly to be extinct in the wild.

- **Endangered:** A species that is in immediate danger of extinction if the factors threatening it continue.

- **Vulnerable:** A species that will likely become endangered if the factors threatening it continue.

- **Rare:** A species with a small world population that is currently neither endangered nor threatened, but is at risk.

- **Indeterminate:** A species that is threatened, but on which there is not enough information to place it in the appropriate category of Extinct, Endangered, Vulnerable, or Rare.

The IUCN issues its Red List assessments of animal and plant endangerment periodically. The Red List of 2000 revised the previous 1996 list. The trends shown in the 2000 report were not encouraging. In 2002, the IUCN listed 11,167 threatened species worldwide. Of these, 3,521 were vertebrates, 1,932 were invertebrates, and 5,714 were plants. The majority of these species were listed as vulnerable. From 1996 to 2000, the number of endangered species rose. Notably, the number of critically endangered mammals rose from 169 to 180, and the number of critically endangered birds rose from 168 to 182. Among mammals, there were dramatic population declines in amphibians, reptiles, and primates, among other groups. At the same time there was an upward shift in levels of endangerment.

Endangered Species Act

The Endangered Species Act (ESA) was passed by the U.S. Congress in 1973 and was reauthorized in 1988. The purpose of the ESA is to recover species around the world that are in danger of human-caused extinction. There are three basic elements to the ESA program: the creation of a list of endangered animals and plants (the Endangered Species List), the formulation of recovery plans for each species on the list, and the designation of critical habitat for each species listed. Through this program, the act seeks to provide a means of conserving those species and their ecosystems.

The U.S. Fish and Wildlife Service (USFWS), a part of the Department of Interior, is the federal agency responsible for listing (or reclassifying or delisting) endangered and threatened species on the Endangered Species List. The National Marine Fisheries Service is responsible for many species that live in the oceans. The decision to list a species is based solely on scientific factors. Once a species is placed on the list, the USFWS is required to develop a plan for its recovery and to designate "critical habitat" for the species. Critical habitat is an area that has been deemed essential to the physical and biological needs of the species, either in their original range or an area similar to it. The designated critical habitat must provide appropriate space for population growth and normal behavior so that a species may recover. The critical habitat designation does not prohibit human activity or create a refuge for the species. Once it has been established, however, any federal agencies planning to build on that land (a highway, for example) must seek the permission of the USFWS. Any other activities requiring federal permits must go through the USFWS as well. Private landowners are not affected, except that the designation alerts the public to the importance of the area in the species' survival. The ESA explicitly states that the economic interests of the human community must be given ample consideration in designating critical habitats and requires the balancing of species protection with economic development.

When a species is placed on the Endangered Species List, it is positioned in one of two categories:

- **Endangered:** A species that is in danger of extinction throughout all or a significant part of its range.
- **Threatened:** A species that is likely to become endangered in the foreseeable future.

The ESA outlaws the buying, selling, transporting, importing, or exporting of any listed species. Most important, the act bans the taking of any listed species within the United States and its territorial seas. "Taking" is defined as harassing, harming, pursuing, hunting, shooting, wounding, cutting, trapping, killing, removing, capturing, or collecting. The taking of listed species is prohibited on both private and public lands.

Violators of the ESA are subject to heavy fines. Individuals can face up to $100,000 in fines and up to one year's imprisonment. Organizations found in violation of the act may be fined up to $200,000.

In 2003 there were 1,253 species on the Endangered Species List. This total included 517 animals and 746 plants.

In the 30 years since its passage, the ESA has been continually targeted by its many opponents. Some of those opponents believe the ESA prohibits human progress, placing the rights of other species ahead of the rights of humans. There are many interest groups who lobby against the ESA: building and real estate development associations oppose ESA because it could present some federal impediments to the large financial gains to be made in constructing new communities or facilities; loggers, farmers, fishers, hunters, fur traders, and others whose means of making a living are affected are also heavily represented in anti-ESA activism. Politicians, even those who nominally support the ESA, do not often find it politically advantageous to provide the necessary support and funding to rescue little-known animals or to oppose large and powerful companies.

On May 28, 2003, the USFWS announced a moratorium (suspension of activity) on designating critical habitat for endangered species—a required step under the ESA. The Department of the Interior said that its critical habitat program had run out of money. Of all the 1,253 endangered species to date, only 426 had critical habitats, and since 2000, those had shrunk in size considerably. Large conservation groups had repeatedly taken the government to court for its failure to designate critical habitat for a listed endangered species. The courts continuously upheld the requirement under the ESA for the USFWS to designate critical habitat for a species once it had been listed on the Endangered Species List.

Spokespeople from the Department of the Interior contend that the critical habitation designation system is unreasonably expensive and that it is not effective in saving endangered species. They also argue that the cost of these lawsuits over critical habitat designation is depleting the budget for protecting species. Many environmental groups, however, argue that critical habitat designation, flawed though the program may be, has been effective in the recovery of many species. Since habitat loss is considered to be the largest factor in the recovery of endangered species, the limited power of the program to protect habitats often represents the only hope for many species. Many endangered species, even if their populations could be increased, are simply running out of places where they can survive in the wild.

In the early 2000s, the issue of endangered species has increasingly become one of the arenas in which U.S. political divisions are playing out very dramatically. In the meantime, some of the species included in *Endangered Species,* 2nd Edition, are losing the last few acres or streams or caves or hillsides they require to survive; others stand only a few individual animals away from extinction.

Changes in Status from First Edition

Key: OFF = Delisted because of recovery; LR–CD = Lower Risk, Conservation Dependent; LR–NT = Lower Risk, Near Threatened; TH = Threatened; R = Rare; VU = Vulnerable; EN = Endangered; CE = Critically Endangered; EXEN = Extinct/Endangered (plants); EW = Extinct in the Wild

Species That Moved to a Less Threatened Status, 1998–2003

Mammals
Horse, Przewalski's: EW to OFF (IUCN)

Wolf, gray: LR–CD to OFF (IUCN); EN to TH (ESA)

Birds
Albatross, short tailed: EN to VU (IUCN)

Egret, Chinese egret: EN to VU (IUCN)

Falcon, American peregrine: EN to OFF (ESA)

Ground–dove, purple–winged: CE to EN (IUCN)

Kakapo: EW to CE (IUCN)

Kestrel, Mauritius: EN to VU (IUCN)

Lovebird, black-cheeked: EN to VU (IUCN)

Pelican Dalmatian: VU to LR–CD (IUCN)

Vireo, black-capped: EN to VU (IUCN)

Woodpecker, ivory-billed: EW to CE (IUCN)

Plants
Aloe, spiral Aloe: EN to OFF (IUCN)

Cactus, agave living–rock: EN to VU (IUCN)

Cactus, Peebles Navajo: VU to OFF (IUCN)

Cinquefoil, Robbins': EN to OFF (IUCN); EN to OFF (ESA)

Palm, Argun: EXEN to CE (IUCN)

Reptiles
Caiman, black: EN to LR–CD (IUCN)

Species That Moved to a More Threatened Status, 1998–2004

Mammals
Addax: EN to CE (IUCN)

Camel, bactrian: EN to CE (IUCN)

Jaguar: LR–NT to NT (IUCN)

Mandrill: LR–NT to VU (IUCN)

Monkey, woolly spider: EN to CE (IUCN)

Orangutan: VU to EN (IUCN)

Oryx, scimitar-horned: CE to EW (IUCN)

Tapir, Central American: VU to EN (IUCN)

Arachnids
No-eyed big-eyed cave wolf spider: No status to EN (ESA)

Birds
Booby, Abbott's: VU to CE (IUCN)

Crane, Siberian: EN to CE (IUCN)

Murrelet, Marbled : LR to VU (IUCN)

Parrot, Imperial Parrot: VU to EN (IUCN)

Penguin, yellow-eyed : VU to EN (IUCN)

Fish
Coelacanth: EN to CE (IUCN)

Plants
Cypress, Saharan: EN to CE(IUCN)

Fir, Baishan: EN to CE (IUCN)

Palm, Carossier: EN to CE (IUCN)

Rosewood, Brazilian: R to VU(IUCN)

Torreya, Florida: EN to CE(IUCN)

Reptiles
Leatherback Sea Turtle: EN to CE (IUCN)

Changes in Status from First Edition

Words to Know

A

Adaptation: A genetically determined characteristic, or inherited trait, that makes an organism better able to cope with its environment.

Alpine: Relating to mountainous regions.

Arid: Land that receives less than 10 inches (250 millimeters) of rainfall annually and has a high rate of evaporation.

B

Biodiversity: The entire variety of life on Earth.

Brackish: A mixture of freshwater and saltwater; briny water.

Browse: A method of grazing in which an animal eats the leaf and twig growth of shrubs, woody vines, trees, and cacti.

C

Canopy: The uppermost spreading branchy layer of a forest.

Carapace: A shell or bony covering on the back of animals such as turtles, lobsters, crabs, and armadillos.

Carnivore: An animal that eats mainly meat.

Carrion: Dead and decaying flesh.

Cetacean: An aquatic mammal that belongs to the order Cetacea, which includes whales, dolphins, and porpoises.

Chaparral: An ecological community of shrubby plants adapted to long, dry summers and natural forest fire cycles, generally found in southern California.

CITES: Abbreviation for Convention on International Trade in Endangered Species of Wild Fauna and Flora; an international agreement by 143 nations to prohibit trade of endangered wildlife.

Clear-cutting: The process of cutting down all the trees in a forest area.

Clutch: The number of eggs produced or incubated at one time.

Competitor: A species that may compete for the same resources as another species.

Conservation: The management and protection of the natural world.

Critical habitat: A designated area considered necessary for the protection and preservation of a species that has been listed under the Endangered Species Act in the United States. The area, either within or near the species' historical range, must provide an environment for normal behavior and reproduction so that the species may recover. The critical habitat designation does not prohibit human activity or create a refuge for the species. Once it has been established, though, any federal agencies planning to build or conduct activities within that area must seek the permission of the USFWS. The designation also serves to alert the public to the importance of the area in the species' survival.

D

Deciduous: Shedding seasonally; a tree whose leaves fall off annually or a forest made up of trees that shed their leaves annually, for example.

Deforestation: The loss of forests as they are rapidly cut down to produce timber or to make land available for agriculture.

Desertification: The gradual transformation of productive land into that with desertlike conditions.

Diurnal: Active during the day.

Domesticated: Animals trained to live with or be of use to humans.

E

Ecosystem: An ecological community, including plants, animals, and microorganisms, considered together with their environment.

Endangered: Species in danger of extinction in the foreseeable future.

Endangered Species Act (ESA): The legislation, passed by the U.S. Congress in 1973, which protects listed species.

Endangered Species List: The list of species protected under the Endangered Species Act.

Endemic species: A species native to, and found only in, a certain region.

Estivate: To hibernate (or sleep) through the summer.

Estuary: The place where freshwater enters the sea (e.g., at a river mouth).

Extinction: A species or subspecies is extinct when no living members exist.

Extirpated species: A species that no longer survives in the regions that were once part of its range.

F

Fauna: The animal life of a particular region, geological period, or environment.

Feral: An animal that has escaped from domestication and has become wild.

Fledge: When birds grow the feathers needed for flight.

Flora: The plants of a particular region, geological period, or environment.

G

Gene: The basic biological unit of heredity that determines individual traits. Part of the DNA molecule, the gene is transmitted from parents to children during reproduction, and contains information for making particular proteins, which then make particular cells.

Gestation: Pregnancy.

H

Habitat: The environment in which specified organisms live.

Herbivore: An animal that eats mainly plants.

Historic range: The areas in which a species is believed to have lived in the past.

I

Inbreeding: The mating or breeding of closely related individuals, usually within small communities. Inbreeding occurs when both parents have at least one common ancestor.

Introduced species: Flora or fauna not native to an area, but introduced from a different ecosystem.

IUCN: Abbreviation for International Union for the Conservation of Nature and Natural Resources; publishes *IUCN Red List of Threatened Animals* and *IUCN Red List of Threatened Plants*.

L

Larval: The immature stage of certain insects and animals, usually of a species that develops by complete metamorphosis.

Lichen: A plantlike composite consisting of a fungus and an alga.

M

Marsupial: Mammals, such as the kangaroo and the opossum, whose young continue to develop after birth in a pouch on the outside of the mother's body.

Metamorphosis: A change in the form and habits of an animal during natural development.

Migrating: The act of changing location periodically, usually moving seasonally from one region to another.

Molting: The process of shedding an outer covering, such as skin or feathers, for replacement by a new growth.

N

Native species: The flora or fauna indigenous or native to an ecosystem, as opposed to introduced species.

Nocturnal: Most active at night.

O

Old-growth forest: A mature forest dominated by long-lived species (at least 200 years old), but also including younger trees; its complex physical structure includes multiple layers in the canopy, many large trees, and many large dead standing trees and dead logs.

P

Perennial: A plant that lives, grows, flowers, and produces seeds for three or more continuous years.

Poaching: Illegally taking protected animals or plants.

Pollution: The contamination of air, water, or soil by the discharge of harmful substances.

Population: A group of organisms of one species occupying a defined area and usually isolated from similar groups of the same species.

Predator: An animal that preys on others.

Prehensile: Adapted for grasping or holding, especially by wrapping around something.

Pupal: An intermediate, inactive stage between the larva and adult stages in the life cycle of many insects.

R

Rain forest: A dense evergreen forest with an annual rainfall of at least 100 inches (254 cm); may be tropical (e.g., Amazon) or temperate (e.g., Pacific Northwest).

Range: The area naturally occupied by a species.

Recovery: The process of stopping or reversing the decline of an endangered or threatened species to ensure the species' long-term survival in the wild.

Reintroduction: The act of placing members of a species in their original habitat.

Reserve: An area of land set aside for the use or protection of a species or group of species.

Rhizomatous plant: A plant having an underground horizontal stem that puts out shoots above ground and roots below.

S

Savanna: A flat, treeless tropical or subtropical grassland.

Scrub: A tract of land covered with stunted or scraggly trees and shrubs.

Slash-and-burn agriculture: The process whereby a forest is cut down and all trees and vegetation are burned to create cleared land.

Species: A group of individuals related by descent and able to breed among themselves but not with other organisms.

Steppe: Vast, semiarid grass-covered plains found in southeast Europe, Siberia, and central North America.

Subspecies: A population of a species distinguished from other such populations by certain characteristics.

Succulent: A plant that has thick, fleshy, water-storing leaves or stems.

Sustainable development: Methods of farming or building human communities that meet the needs of the current generation without depleting or damaging the natural resources in the area or compromising its ability to meet the needs of future generations.

T

Taproot: The main root of a plant growing straight downward from the stem.

Territoriality: The behavior displayed by an individual animal, a mating pair, or a group in vigorously defending its domain against intruders.

Troglobyte: A species that lives only in caves.

Tropical: Characteristic of a region or climate that is frost free with temperatures high enough to support—with adequate precipitation—plant growth year round.

Tundra: A relatively flat, treeless plain in alpine, arctic, and antarctic regions.

U

Underbrush: Small trees, shrubs, or similar plants growing on the forest floor underneath taller trees.

Urban sprawl: The spreading of houses, shopping centers, and other city facilities through previously undeveloped land.

U.S. Fish and Wildlife Service (USFWS): A federal agency that oversees implementation of the Endangered Species Act.

V

Vulnerable: A species is vulnerable when it satisfies some risk criteria, but not at a level that warrants its identification as Endangered.

W

Wetland: A permanently moist lowland area such as a marsh or a swamp.

Endangered Species

2nd EDITION

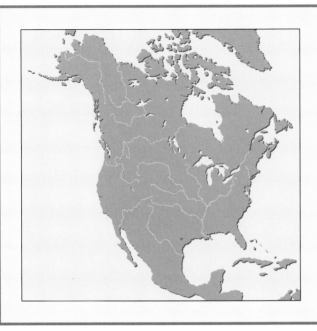

HARVESTMAN, BEE CREEK CAVE
Texella reddelli

PHYLUM: Arthropoda
CLASS: Arachnida
ORDER: Opiliones
FAMILY: Phalangodidae
STATUS: Endangered, ESA
RANGE: USA (Texas)

Harvestman, Bee Creek Cave

Texella reddelli

Description and biology

Harvestmen are eyeless spiders. They are often called daddy longlegs because they have small rounded or oval bodies to which four pairs of long, slender legs are attached. The Bee Creek Cave harvestman's body is orange or light yellowish–brown in color and measures only 0.07 to 0.1 inch (0.17 to 0.25 centimeter) long.

This harvestman is a slow–moving, predatory species. It grasps its prey with its pedipalps (pronounced PEH–de–palps; a pair of specialized appendages or limbs located near its mouth). Its diet includes tiny, hopping insects called collembolans.

Biologists (people who study living organisms) have no information on the mating habits of this species. Young Bee Creek Cave harvestmen are white to yellowish–white in color.

The Bee Creek Cave harvestman is a slow–moving, predatory, eyeless spider that inhabits underground caves in Texas.

Habitat and current distribution

Bee Creek Cave harvestmen inhabit underground caves in limestone rock in the Edwards Plateau region in Travis County, Texas. In these caves, the harvestmen are usually found under rocks in total darkness or in dim twilight. The species requires stable temperatures, high humidity, and a steady supply of small invertebrates on which to feed.

History and conservation measures

The primary threat to the Bee Creek Cave harvestman and other cave invertebrates (animals with no backbone) in its range is the loss of its habitat. Residential and urban areas continue to grow in this region. As a result, many caves have been paved over or filled in. Because the caves are formed by seeping water, any change or alteration in the flow of that water can change the environment of a cave. To meet the needs of these newly populated areas, much of this water has been diverted. Some caves have become dry while others have become flooded. Pollution from populated areas has also seeped into the groundwater, and the water in many caves has become contaminated.

Conservation efforts are underway to protect the habitat of the Bee Creek Cave harvestman and other endangered species. A protected area measuring approximately 7,000 acres (2,800 hectares) has been proposed.

**SPIDER, NO–EYED
BIG–EYED WOLF**
Adelocosa anops

PHYLUM: Arthropoda

CLASS: Arachnida

ORDER: Araneae

FAMILY: Lycosidae

STATUS: Endangered, IUCN
Endangered, ESA

RANGE: USA (Hawaii)

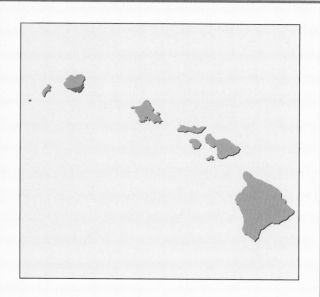

Spider, no-eyed big-eyed wolf

Adelocosa anops

Description and biology

The no–eyed big–eyed wolf spider, also known as the Kauai cave wolf spider, is a troglobite—a species that lives only in caves. It has a body length of 0.39 to 0.78 inch (0.99 to 1.98 centimeters). Its head and thorax (body segment between head and abdomen) are fused or united. This body part is called the cephalothorax (pronounced se–fa–la–THOR–ax), and it is light brown or orange. The spider's bristly legs are also orange in color. The abdomen is dull white.

All other spiders belonging to this family have large, well–developed eyes. The no–eyed big–eyed wolf spider is so–named because it is blind. To capture prey, wolf spiders do not spin webs like other spiders; most actively stalk and over-take other small invertebrates (animals with no backbone). The sightless no–eyed big–eyed wolf spider crawls slowly through the cracks and crevices in caves, finding its prey through its senses of touch, smell, and taste. It has large fangs with which to inject and subdue its prey with its venom (poison). The spider's usual food is the Kauai cave amphipod, a tiny crustacean that lives in the same caves as the cave wolf spider. The two species have a predator/prey relationship: the amphipod gets its nutrients from the rotting vegetation on the moist rocks of the humid cave environment, and the spider then feeds on the amphipod.

Females of this species lay only 15 to 30 eggs in a clutch (number of eggs produced or incubated at one time). They carry the egg sac inside their mouths until the eggs hatch. At that time, fully developed and unusually large infant spiders emerge. The newborn offspring stay with their mother for a few days, riding on her back, until they are ready to hunt on their own. The life span of an adult no–eyed big–eyed wolf spider is at least six months.

Habitat and current distribution

The no–eyed big–eyed wolf spider inhabits only the deep areas of Koloa caves, located on the southeast coast of Kauai Island in the Hawaiian Islands. The spider is found in the caves as well as in small cavities attached to the cave that humans cannot reach.

In its extremely limited cave ecosystem (all living things and their environment), the spider requires specific conditions. The humidity in the cave must be a constant 100 percent, the air must be stagnant (still), and the air temperature must be between 75° and 80°F (24° and 27°C). The caves must also have the right type of woody vegetation for the spider's prey, the Kauai cave amphipod, to eat. The no–eyed big–eyed wolf spider is known to exist only in six caves in the Koloa area.

History and conservation measures

The no–eyed big–eyed wolf spider, along with its prey, the Kauai cave amphipod, was discovered in the beginning of the 1970s and for decades was known to exist in only four caves. Two more caves with populations of the species were found in 2002. The species is limited to a small and very specific area and has become endangered because of the deterioration of its habitat. The caves in which these spiders live are in a very popular and developed resort area of Hawaii. Tourism and urban growth are constant pressures. Water is already scarce in the area, and natural water sources have been diverted to meet the needs of tourist facilities and urban areas. Without a constant supply of seeping water, the caves inhabited by the spider will dry out.

Runoff from urban areas can pollute the groundwater with pesticides and other toxic (poisonous) chemicals. Runoff from nearby farms has already ruined the largest lava cave in the area: it became covered with waste residue from sugar cane production. Human visitors can also destroy these caves by trampling, littering, smoking, vandalizing, and altering the climate by merely entering the caves.

After the no–eyed big–eyed wolf spider was given endangered status under the Endangered Species Act (ESA) in 2000, a federal court ruled that the U.S. Fish and Wildlife Service (USFWS) should determine a critical habitat area for the spider—an area considered necessary to the conservation of the species that requires special management and protection. Critical habitat designation does not create a wildlife refuge and does not ban human activities in the area. Rather, it ensures that all federal agencies check with the USFWS about any activities they authorize in the area. On April 9, 2003, the USFWS designated 272 acres (110 hectares) in southern Kauai as critical habitat. One year earlier, the agency had proposed that 4,193 acres (1,698 hectares) should be designated as critical habitat, but changed the proposal because it would have been very costly to private landowners in Hawaii.

SPIDER, TOOTH CAVE
Neoleptoneta myopica

PHYLUM: Arthropoda
CLASS: Arachnida
ORDER: Araneae
FAMILY: Leptonetidae
STATUS: Data deficient, IUCN
Endangered, ESA
RANGE: USA (Texas)

Spider, Tooth Cave

Neoleptoneta myopica

Description and biology

The Tooth Cave spider is a very small, slender spider species. It measures just 0.06 inch (0.16 centimeter) long. Pale cream in color, it has relatively long legs. Because it lives in a dark cave environment, it has small, undeveloped eyes. A delicate predator, it feeds on tiny invertebrates (animals with no backbone).

Biologists (people who study living organisms) have no information on the spider's reproductive habits.

Habitat and current distribution

Tooth Cave spiders inhabit underground caves in limestone rock in the Edwards Plateau region in Travis County, Texas. In these caves, the spiders are usually found hanging from cave walls or ceilings by a single tangle or sheet web. In order to live, they require stable temperatures, high humidity, and a ready supply of small invertebrates on which to feed.

The Tooth Cave spider is a very small, slender spider that feeds on tiny invertebrates (animals with no backbone).

History and conservation measures

Not much is known about Tooth Cave spiders or other endangered cave invertebrates in the region because scientific studies were not undertaken there until the early 1960s.

The main threat to this spider is the loss of its habitat. Residential and urban areas continue to grow in this region. As a result, many caves have been paved over or filled in. Because the caves are formed by seeping water, any change or alteration in the flow of that water can change the environment of a cave. To meet the needs of these newly populated areas, much of this water has been diverted. Some caves have become dry while others have become flooded. Pollution from populated areas has also seeped into the groundwater, and the water in many caves has become contaminated.

Conservation efforts are underway to protect the habitat of the Tooth Cave spider and other endangered species. A protected area measuring approximately 7,000 acres (2,800 hectares) has been proposed.

TARANTULA, RED–KNEED
*Euathlus smithi (also
Brachypelma smithi)*

PHYLUM: Arthropoda

CLASS: Arachnida

ORDER: Araneae

FAMILY: Theraphosidae

STATUS: Lower risk; near
threatened, IUCN

RANGE: Mexico

Tarantula, red-kneed

Euathlus smithi (also Brachypelma smithi)

Description and biology

The red–kneed tarantula is one of the biggest spiders in
the world, with a body length from 2.5 to 4 inches (6.4 to
10.2 centimeters) and a leg span of 4 to 7 inches (10.2 to 18
centimeters). It can weigh up to 2.5 ounces (71 grams). The
tarantula's body is dark brown and covered in tiny hairs. The
joints (knees) on its eight legs are bright orange and red, which
is the basis for its name. It has two claws on the end of each
of its legs for climbing and gripping. Although the red–kneed
tarantula has eight eyes set above its mouth to give it forward
and backward vision, it has very poor eyesight. It uses its sensitive leg hairs to feel its way about.

The red–kneed tarantula lives in a burrow it has dug out
underground and lined with its spun silk. Its diet consists of
centipedes and millipedes, beetles, crickets, grasshoppers, small
frogs, lizards, and sometimes mice. It hunts at night, locating
its prey by means of a special sensitivity to its sounds and

vibrations. The tarantula sits quietly, hidden in the dark, and then springs upon its victim. It grasps the prey with its two pedipalps (special appendages located near the mouth), and enfolds it with its eight legs and then bites it, injecting its venom. Tarantulas cannot digest food inside their own bodies; the venom they inject must serve two purposes. First, it stuns the prey into submission, and then it begins to digest the animal, turning its insides to liquid proteins and fats. The tarantula then sucks out the predigested liquid.

In late summer, male tarantulas look for females to mate. The male enters a female's burrow and then uses his pedipalps to inject sperm into the female's reproductive tract. He has to be very careful, though, because the female may attempt to kill and eat him. After mating, the female spins a web and lays anywhere from 50 to 700 eggs upon it. She then wraps the eggs in the silk ball and carries them between her fangs to incubate (keep warm until ready to hatch) for several weeks. Male tarantulas usually live about 8 years, while a female may live between 20 and 30 years.

Despite people's fears, red–kneed tarantulas are not as dangerous as they look. Although their bites are painful, they are generally not any more powerful than a bee sting. When threatened, red–kneed tarantulas display their red bristles and sometimes rub their back legs in order to drop hairs on their enemy. The hairs can cause rashes and even blindness. Even humans handling these spiders get rashes from their hairs. Generally, though, the red–kneed tarantula is not aggressive to humans. For this reason and because of its beautiful coloration, this tarantula became prized as a pet and has been one of the favored spiders for use in movies.

Habitat and current distribution

Red–kneed tarantulas can be found in deserts and rain forests. They are known to occur in southwestern Mexico along the Sierra Madre mountain range along the Pacific coast in the Mexican states extending from Jalisco (pronounced hah–LEES–coe) and Colima down to Oaxaca (pronounced wah–HAH–cah).

History and conservation measures

The friendliness to humans, brilliant coloring, and long life of the red–kneed tarantula have made the species very popular among spider collectors. Up until 1985, thousands of these tarantulas were imported from Mexico and then sold as pets. After years of this trade, the population of spiders in the wild declined, and in 1985 the Convention on International Trade in Endangered Species (CITES) banned the exportation and importation of red–kneed tarantulas that have been caught in the wild. Only red–kneed tarantulas bred in captivity can be traded legally. This is the only species of tarantula to be protected under CITES. Destruction of its habitat in Mexico is also responsible for decline in this species' population.

ALBATROSS, SHORT–TAILED
Diomedea albatrus

PHYLUM: Chordata
CLASS: Aves
ORDER: Procellariiformes
FAMILY: Diomedeidae
STATUS: Vulnerable, IUCN
Endangered, ESA
RANGE: China, Japan, Russia,
Taiwan, USA (Alaska, California,
Hawaii, Oregon, Washington)

Albatross, short-tailed
Diomedea albatrus

Description and biology

Albatrosses are ocean birds that spend most of their time gliding over the open sea. They come ashore only to nest. The short–tailed albatross, also known as the Stellar's albatross, is a large bird with a 7–foot (2–meter) wingspan. It has a white body, neck, and head. Its wings and the tip of its tail are dark brown. The bird feeds on fish, shrimp, and squid.

Like other albatrosses, the short–tailed albatross has an elaborate courtship ritual that includes dancing, stamping, and special greeting calls. After mating, the male and female pair build a crude nest in a clump of tall grass on the slope of a volcano, and the female lays a single white egg. Both parents guard and incubate (sit on or brood) the egg for two to three months until it hatches. Both parents then feed the chick, often by regurgitating (vomiting) partially digested food directly into its beak. The young albatross leaves the nest at about five months of age but does not reach full maturity for eight to nine years. Short–tailed albatrosses mate for life. The couples return to the same nest sites year after year.

Habitat and current distribution

The short–tailed albatross mates and nests only on the volcanic island of Torishima, one of the Izu Islands south of Tokyo, Japan. The bird's guano (excrement) enriches the volcanic soil of Torishima, which in turns helps the growth of the tall grass clumps used as nesting sites.

In the late 1940s, biologists (people who study living organisms) estimated that there were fewer than 50 adult short–tailed albatrosses. By 2000, there were an estimated 1,200 birds in the wild.

The short–tailed albatross became endangered due to hunters looking to collect its feathers.

DID YOU KNOW?

Short–tailed albatrosses can remain in flight over the ocean for as long as five years without landing. By expertly using the winds and air currents, they can fly without flapping their wings for long periods of time, and they can sleep while in flight. They land only for nesting, and they remain on land only long enough to produce and raise one chick. Albatrosses are not comfortable on land. Although they are skillful at flying, taking off and landing are not easy for them. They are particularly easy prey for hunters because they simply remain at their nests when the hunters approach.

History and conservation measures

In the nineteenth century, the short–tailed albatross had a population that numbered in the hundreds of thousands or millions. It nested on islands throughout the northwestern Pacific Ocean. Its range extended along the entire western coast of North America, where Native Americans hunted it for food.

By the early twentieth century, its population had been quickly reduced by hunters seeking the bird's beautiful snowy–white breast feathers. In 1903, the Japanese government outlawed the hunting of the birds for their feathers, but the practice continued. Between the late 1800s and early 1900s, it is estimated that feather hunters killed 5 million of the birds in about 17 years. In 1929, only 1,400 birds remained in existence. In 1939, there was a volcanic eruption on Torishima, which buried much of the habitat. By the end of World War II (1939–45), the short–tailed albatross was feared extinct. Then, in 1951, a tiny colony of ten birds was discovered on Torishima.

Japanese biologists (people who study living organisms) and conservationists (people who work to protect the natural world) worked hard to save the short–tailed albatross. The Japanese island breeding habitat is protected, and it has been improved with new plantings and the elimination of feral animals (domestic animals that have become wild). Other islands are being prepared as potential habitats for the species, in an effort to relocate them and save them from future volcanic eruptions on Torishima. Efforts have been made to reduce pollution in the ocean. Commercial fishers in Alaska are being educated about the birds so that they will stop accidentally catching them.

The short–tailed albatross has made a significant recovery, moving from endangered to vulnerable status on the International Union for the Conservation of Nature and Natural Resources (IUCN) Red List. The species remains in jeopardy, however, because its main breeding habitat is volcanic. An eruption could destroy most of the albatross's habitat.

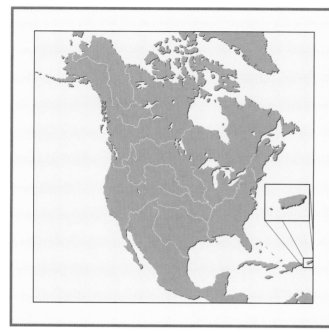

**BLACKBIRD,
YELLOW–SHOULDERED**
Agelaius xanthomus

PHYLUM: Chordata
CLASS: Aves
ORDER: Passeriformes
FAMILY: Icteridae
STATUS: Endangered, IUCN
Endangered, ESA
RANGE: Puerto Rico

Blackbird, yellow-shouldered

Agelaius xanthomus

Description and biology

The rare yellow–shouldered blackbird is similar to its North American relative the red–winged blackbird. Its body is 7 to 9 inches (18 to 23 centimeters) long and dark gray in color. A distinctive yellow patch on its shoulder gives the bird its common name. Females are smaller than males. The bird eats mainly insects that it forages from plants and the leaves, branches, and bark of trees.

The birds nest in colonies and defend the immediate territory around their nests. Unlike many other blackbird species, the yellow–shouldered blackbird is monogamous (has just one mate for life). Mating usually takes place in April or May. The female lays 2 to 3 eggs and incubates (sits on or broods) them for 12 to 14 days before they hatch. After the nestlings are born, the female and male both share in gathering food.

Habitat destruction is the leading cause of the decline of yellow–shouldered blackbirds.

There are two subspecies of yellow–shouldered blackbird: the Puerto Rico yellow–shouldered blackbird (*Agelaius xanthomus xanthomus*) and the Mona yellow–shouldered blackbird (*Agelaius xanthomus monensis*). Both subspecies are considered endangered.

Habitat and current distribution

Puerto Rico yellow–shouldered blackbirds nest in coconut palms and mangroves, most often on offshore islets (very small islands) around Puerto Rico. Approximately 400 of the birds exist on and around the island.

Mona yellow–shouldered blackbirds are found on Mona Island, which lies between Puerto Rico and Hispaniola (the island divided between Haiti on the west and the Dominican Republic on the east). These birds nest on the ledges or in the crevices of sheer coastal cliffs. Their population numbers between 400 and 900.

History and conservation measures

The Puerto Rico yellow–shouldered blackbird was once abundant throughout coastal areas of Puerto Rico. It was found in various habitats, including freshwater wetlands, open woodlands, and fields. In the 1970s, its population was estimated at over 2,000.

Biologists (people who study living organisms) believe habitat destruction—mainly the draining of almost all the wetland areas in its range—was the initial cause of the bird's decline. The Puerto Rico yellow–shouldered blackbird continues to be threatened by mongooses, rats, and other mammals that eat its eggs. A more recent threat is the shiny cowbird. This bird, introduced to the region in the 1950s, slyly lays its eggs in the blackbird's nest. When the female blackbird returns, she broods on both her eggs and the cowbird's eggs. After the eggs hatch, the larger cowbirds dominate the smaller blackbirds, eating more of their food and often pushing them out of the nest.

The Mona yellow–shouldered blackbird is also currently threatened by habitat destruction (caused by increasing human development of Mona Island) and the shiny cowbird.

Controlling the cowbird population in the region and developing protected areas such as Puerto Rico's Boquerón Commonwealth Forest are measures conservationists have undertaken to help the yellow–shouldered blackbird recover.

BOOBY, ABBOTT'S
Sula (or papasula) abbotti

PHYLUM: Chordata
CLASS: Aves
ORDER: Pelecaniformes
FAMILY: Sulidae
STATUS: Critically endangered, IUCN
Endangered, ESA
RANGE: Christmas Island

Booby, Abbott's
Sula (or papsula) abbotti

Description and biology

Booby is the common name for a large seabird that inhabits tropical waters. Those members of the same family that inhabit northern waters are called gannets. The Abbott's booby measures 31 inches (79 centimeters) long and weighs about 3 pounds (1.4 kilograms). It has a wingspan of almost 6 feet (1.8 meters). The female is slightly larger than the male. This booby is black and white in color and has a saw–toothed bill that is gray in males and pink in females. During greeting and courtship, the bird emits a distinctive deep, loud call.

The Abbott's booby is the only member of its family that builds its large, bulky nest at the top of a tall tree instead of on the ground. Females of the species lay one very large white egg between May and June. They incubate (sit on or brood) the egg for 42 to 55 days before it hatches. Both mother and father care for the chick, which is quite helpless for the first three weeks. It grows slowly and does not take its first flight until it is five or six months old. After about one year, the chick finally flies out to open sea.

Like other boobies and gannets, the Abbott's booby feeds on fish and squid. The bird dives after its prey from great heights and will often chase it underwater. Air sacs under the booby's skin help soften the impact when it hits the water; they also help the bird to float. The average life span for the Abbott's booby is 25 to 30 years.

Habitat and current distribution

The Abbott's booby nests only on Christmas Island (territory of Australia), a tiny island in the Indian Ocean lying roughly 200 miles (320 kilometers) south of the island of Java (part of Indonesia). Biologists (people who study living organisms) estimate that about 2,000 male–female pairs currently exist.

The Abbott's booby nests only on Christmas Island, a tiny island in the Indian Ocean lying roughly 200 miles south of the island of Java.

The birds prefer to build their nests at the top of very tall rain forest trees on the island's western plateau. They generally feed at sea northwest of the island.

History and conservation measures

Boobies were so–named because of their rather dull facial expression and their extreme tameness. They are easily approached by humans, a factor that led to their early decline. When sailors and early settlers on the island began hunting Abbott's boobies, they merely walked up to the birds and clubbed them to death.

The main threat to the Abbott's booby for decades has been deforestation. In order to mine underground phosphate (mineral salt) deposits, humans on Christmas Island have clear–cut a vast majority of mature trees in the booby's habitat. Since 1987, mining activities have been limited to those areas already cleared of trees. Attempts have been made to reforest some areas and to establish a national park where the Abbott's booby would be protected, but replanting a rain forest takes a long time and the species reproduces at a very slow rate.

A new threat to the booby is the yellow crazy ant (*Anoplolepis gracilipes*). The ant, which is native to Africa, was introduced to Christmas Island early in the twentieth century and it became widespread. The crazy ants have wiped out the red crab population of Christmas Island. The red crab was essential to the ecosystem because it ate weed seedlings and leaves, keeping the balance in the rain forest. Scientists predict that unless the yellow crazy ant is eliminated, it will cause a rapid reduction in the population of Abbott's boobies over the next three generations.

BULLFINCH, AZORES
Pyrrhula murina

PHYLUM: Chordata
CLASS: Aves
ORDER: Passeriformes
FAMILY: Fringillidae
STATUS: Endangered, IUCN
Endangered, ESA
RANGE: Azores, Portugal

Bullfinch, Azores
Pyrrhula murina

Description and biology

The Azores (pronounced uh–ZOAR–ays) bullfinch, known locally as "piolo" (pronounced pee–OH–low) is the only endemic (native to, and occurring only in one place) land bird on the Azores archipelago, a group of nine islands plus some small islets in the North Atlantic Ocean about 800 miles (1,290 kilometers) off the coast of Portugal. The Azores bullfinch is in many ways like the common bullfinch that lives on the European continent. The mainland bullfinch, however, has a bright red breast and gray back set off by a coal–black head, while the Azores bullfinch is dull in its coloring. Unlike the mainland birds, male and female Azores bullfinches are nearly identical in color. They can be identified by white bars on their wing. They are small in size, at about 6.25 inches (16 centimeters) long. Male Azores bullfinches are larger than females.

The Azores bullfinch lives in the laurel (a kind of ever-green tree) forests of the Azores. The bird's diet consists mainly of seeds. It eats seeds of herbal plants in summer, seeds of fruits in the fall, and seeds of trees and ferns in the winter. In the spring it eats flower buds. Because of this variety in its diet, the Azores bullfinch needs a good supply of specific plants in its area.

Azores bullfinches live in inaccessible (difficult to get to) forests and wildlife biologists (scientists who study living organisms) do not know a lot about their habits.

Habitat and current distribution

The Azores bullfinch can be found in dense Azores laurel forests. Within the Azores archipelago, the bird is limited to a fairly small area in the Pico da Varda area of eastern São Miguel, consisting of the Pico da Varda and Pico Verde mountains and the Ribeira do Guilherme valley. This area is virtually impenetrable (not possible to enter) for humans. There are about 120 male–female pairs of Azores bullfinches in existence today.

History and conservation measures

In the nineteenth century, there was an abundance of Azores bullfinches. Farmers viewed them as pests in their orchards and killed them whenever possible. The Azores government joined in the effort to eliminate the birds in order to help the farmers with their crops, and actually paid rewards to local citizens who brought in bird beaks to prove they had killed the bullfinches. The campaign to get rid of the birds was highly successful. By the beginning of the twentieth century, the Azores bullfinch had become quite rare.

For the few remaining Azores bullfinches, the introduction of foreign plants has caused another decline in population. The new plants have invaded the forests and overwhelmed the native plants. This forces the Azores bullfinches into smaller and smaller areas where the native vegetation they eat and live in still exists.

In 1995, a local forestry program funded by the European Union was established to restore and expand laurel forests in the Azores in an effort to increase the population of the Azores bullfinch. A laurel forest on the slopes around the Pico da Vara summit was designated a natural forest reserve.

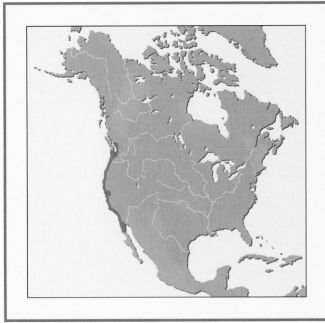

CONDOR, CALIFORNIA
Gymnogyps californianus

PHYLUM: Chordata
CLASS: Aves
ORDER: Falconiformes
FAMILY: Cathartidae
STATUS: Critically endangered, IUCN
Endangered, IUCN
RANGE: USA (reintroduced in Arizona and California)

Condor, California
Gymnogyps californianus

Description and biology

The California condor, or California vulture, is the largest bird in North America and one of the largest flying birds in the world. It measures 45 to 55 inches (114 to 140 centimeters) long and weighs between 20 and 25 pounds (9 and 11 kilograms). It has a wingspan of up to 9.5 feet (2.9 meters), and its plumage (covering of feathers) is a dull gray–black. A diamond–shaped white patch appears on the underside of its wings. The bird's neck and head are bare, and its skin color ranges from gray to orange–red.

Like all vultures, the California condor feeds mainly on carrion (decaying flesh of dead animals), preferring the carcasses of deer, cattle, or sheep. It will also attack and eat rodents, fish, and birds. When searching for food, the condor covers vast distances, sometimes as much as 140 miles (225 kilometers). It soars at speeds of 35 to 55 miles (56 to 88 kilometers) per hour on warm thermal updrafts at altitudes up to 15,000 feet (4,570

The California condor is now the rarest bird in North America.

meters). When not eating, the condor spends much of its time bathing and preening (smoothing feathers).

California condors do not begin breeding until they are between five and eight years old. Once paired, a male and female condor mate for life. Mating takes place during the winter, with the female laying one large egg. Both parents incubate (sit on or brood) the egg for 50 to 56 days until it hatches. The young condor fledges (develops flying feathers) within six months, but may remain dependent on its parents for more than a year. Because of this, male and female pairs usually breed once every two years.

Habitat and current distribution

California condors prefer to nest in caves or on rocky cliffs in mountainous terrain and to roost (rest or sleep) on tall, exposed trees and rocky outcrops. They feed on nearby open grasslands or savannas.

The last 9 wild California condors were taken into captivity in 1987, making a total of 27 condors in the world, all in captivity. Five years later, eight captive–bred birds were released into the wild in California at the Sespe Condor Sanctuary in the Los Padres National Forest. In December 1996, six young California condors were released in the Vermillion Cliffs, a remote part of the Glen Canyon National Recreation Area in northern Arizona. Other releases have occurred in Lion Canyon and Castle Crags, two remote regions of the Los Padres National Forest in Santa Barbara County, California; and in the Ventana Wilderness Sanctuary near Big Sur on the coast of northern California. From the 27 condors that were taken into captivity in 1987, the population of condors in 2000 was 155 condors; 56 of them were living in the wild.

History and conservation measures

Currently one of the rarest birds in North America, the California condor ranged over the entire continent for thousands of years. It fed on the remains of large Ice Age mammals such as mammoths and camels. Around 8000 B.C. , when these mammals became extinct, the number of condors began to decline. By the time Europeans began colonizing North America in the seventeenth century, the bird's range was already reduced to the western coast and mountains. In the nineteenth century, the condor population rapidly declined as settlers moved west. By the mid–twentieth century, the birds numbered less than 100 and were restricted to a small area in central California. By the mid–1980s, only five breeding pairs remained in the wild.

Many factors have led to the California condor's decline in modern times. Because it feeds on the remains of other animals, it is susceptible to poisoning. Poisons ingested by animals become highly concentrated in the predators that eat them. Many condors have died from eating the remains of animals that had ingested pesticides or that had been deliberately poisoned by farmers and ranchers. Others have perished by ingesting lead bullets from the carrion of animals shot by hunters. Condors have also been hunted themselves and have had their eggs stolen from their nests by collectors. As is the case with many other endangered species, the condor's habitat and feeding range has been reduced by human development.

Beginning in 1986, researchers decided to remove the remaining California condors from the wild and place them in captive–breeding programs. The condors bred well in captivity. In the early 1990s, researchers started reintroducing captive–bred condors into the wild. Most of the birds released have slowly adapted to their new environment. In April 2002, the first baby condor born in the wild hatched from its shell in Ventura County. On May 1, 2002, the last wild condor to be taken into captivity back in 1987, a 22–year–old bird, was released back to the wilderness in Los Padres National Forest after spending 15 years in captivity and becoming the father of 16 baby condors. Scientists hoped that the released condors could remember enough about life in the wild to show the ropes to released condors that had been born in captivity.

The goal of the condor reintroduction program is to establish separate condor populations in the wild of at least 150 birds each. Despite its initial success, the program remains controversial. In hopes that the condors will stay in their sanctuary and not eat poisoned animals, biologists (people who study living organisms) often leave deer and cattle carcasses for the birds to eat. Some scientists and researchers believe this prevents the condors from surviving entirely on their own.

In addition to the San Diego Wild Animal Park and the Los Angeles Zoo, California condors are also kept in captivity at the World Center for Birds of Prey in Boise, Idaho.

CORMORANT, GALÁPAGOS
Phalacrocorax harrisi

PHYLUM: Chordata
CLASS: Aves
ORDER: Pelecaniformes
FAMILY: Phalacrocoracidae
STATUS: Endangered, IUCN
RANGE: Ecuador (Galápagos Islands)

Cormorant, Galápagos
Phalacrocorax harrisi

Description and biology

The Galápagos cormorant, also known as the flightless cormorant, is the only one of the world's 29 cormorant species that is flightless. It is a large bird, measuring about 35 to 40 inches (89 to 100 centimeters) long and weighing anywhere from 5 to 9 pounds (2.5 to 4 kilograms)—making it the heaviest bird in the cormorant family. Males are larger than females. Its feathers are dark brown or black and they are much thicker and softer—and more like hair—than the feathers of other cormorants. The eyes are a bright turquoise and the bill is long with a hook at the end. This cormorant's wings are mere stubs; the part of the breastbone that would normally support the flight muscles in a bird that can fly is very small in the flightless cormorant. On the other hand, the Galápagos cormorant's short black legs are heavier and

The Galápagos cormorant is a
large, flightless bird that lives in
limited parts of the coastline of
the Galápagos Islands
off Ecuador.

more powerful than those of other cormorants. With them,
the large bird propels itself through the water with powerful
kicks. It is an excellent diver and a fast, efficient swimmer.

The Galápagos cormorant feeds underwater. Its diet is
made up of small fish, eels, squid, and octopus. When hunting, the cormorant swims with its body almost entirely sub-
merged in the water. Only its head and neck remain above
the surface. When it spots its prey, the bird dives in a
jack–knife movement using powerful kicks to shoot through
the water. The cormorant stays within 330 miles (100 meters)
of the shore when it swims.

Galápagos cormorants have a very elaborate courtship routine. Starting in the water, the male and female swim around
one another in a kind of dance with their heads held in a
snakelike manner. They then go to shore, where they continue their routine. When the initial dance is over, the two
birds build a nest of seaweed. Often the nest is situated within
a colony of nests made by a dozen or more other Galápagos
cormorant couples on hard–to–reach sheltered rocky beaches

or in lagoons. The male then begins to bring little additions for the nest to the female— "gifts" of more seaweed, dead starfish, or bits of litter, such as plastic bags, bottle caps, or rope. The female will add these gifts to the nest. Two or three eggs are laid, usually in the spring, summer, and fall. The incubation period—in which both parents take turns sitting on the eggs to keep them warm—lasts about 35 days. Both parents initially take care of the young, but if there is enough food, the female will leave the male with the offspring (he will stay with the young for about nine months), and go off to find another mate. The female can breed as many as three times in one year.

Habitat and current distribution

The Galápagos cormorant lives in limited parts of the coastline of the Galápagos Islands off Ecuador, primarily in cold currents off the shores of the Fernandina Island and off the northwest shore of the Isabela Island. The total population is estimated at around 1,000 individual birds, but this population dips and recovers in years when the weather changes, such as in El Niño years.

History and conservation measures

Because there were originally no natural enemies of the Galápagos cormorant within its habitat, the bird had no need to fly and the species eventually lost the ability to do so. Instead, it developed its swimming skills. Humans eventually brought cats, dogs, and pigs onto the islands, and feral (domestic animals that have escaped into the wild) populations developed. Suddenly the cormorant had predators on the islands. The birds were particularly ill–equipped to protect themselves, since they had no fear of their enemies and they lacked the means to fly away from danger. Feral dogs in particular drastically reduced the population. In recent times, however, feral dogs have been eliminated from the cormorants' habitat.

DID YOU KNOW?

In 1835, a young naturalist (someone who observes nature to find its laws) named Charles Darwin visited the Galápagos Islands aboard the British ship HMS *Beagle.* There, as he collected specimens of the abundant plant and animal life, he began to get the idea for his theory of evolution when he noticed that similar species were found on separate islands. The islands, with their thousands of species, were a wonderful place for the study of plant and animal life. With no aboriginal inhabitants, they had been left undisturbed by humans until the seventeenth century. Even today, most animals on the islands lack the instinct of fear because there were no natural predators before humans arrived. Although the islands were used by pirates and hunters during the seventeenth and eighteenth centuries, and small colonies were established there by Ecuador in the nineteenth century, most of the islands' current human population of 18,000 came later in the twentieth century. Recognizing the extraordinary natural abundance of the Galápagos Islands, the Ecuador government established 97 percent of the islands' area as a national park in 1959. In 1986, the waters around the islands were placed under protection as well. Despite an active resource management campaign under the Charles Darwin Foundation, the islands have human–related conservation problems stemming from feral animals, introduced plants, and illegal fisheries.

Although the tourist populations that pour into the Galápagos Islands are not usually able to make their way into the remote habitats of the flightless cormorants, their presence has further reduced the population. Sea–cucumber fisheries (sea cucumbers are sea animals prized as food in many Asian markets) have been established in the waters off of the islands. Pollution of many kinds has reached the islands, including an oil slick from the oil tanker *Jessica* that ran aground off the island of San Cristobal in 2001, spilling hundreds of thousands of gallons of fuel into the waters. Net fishing around the islands has been responsible for the deaths of individual birds that get caught in the nets, as well as the depletion of their food from the waters.

The Galápagos cormorant population has always responded to changes in climate with a change in its numbers. A routine climate change, El Niño, occurs every two to seven years, with a change in winds that causes a rise in water temperatures. This causes the death of many South American fish. During El Niño of 1982–83, the worst ever recorded, Galápagos cormorants stopped breeding and the population was reduced by 49 percent. Within one year, however, the population had recovered. Although the population has the capacity to bounce back after a seasonal climate change, it may not be able to bounce back if more than one change in environment occurs. The oil slick on top of an El Niño, for example—or the more permanent climate changes due to global warming that may take place in the early twenty–first century—would threaten the already reduced population with extinction.

In 1977, the Charles Darwin Research Station began carefully observing the populations of Galápagos cormorants and continues to provide necessary data for the continued efforts to protect the birds and their habitat.

CRANE, SIBERIAN
Grus leucogeranus

PHYLUM: Chordata
CLASS: Aves
ORDER: Gruiformes
FAMILY: Gruidae
STATUS: Critically endangered, IUCN
Endangered, ESA
RANGE: Afghanistan, China, India, Iran, Mongolia, Pakistan, Russia

Crane, Siberian
Grus leucogeranus

Description and biology

The Siberian crane, also known as the Siberian white crane, is a beautiful and rare wading bird. It has long, reddish pink legs, a reddish orange face, and a snowy white body with black markings on its wings. An average Siberian crane stands 47 to 55 inches (119 to 140 centimeters) high. While young cranes eat insects, frogs, and small rodents, adults feed mainly on the roots and tubers (swollen underground stems) of aquatic plants.

Male and female Siberian cranes mate in early spring. Their courtship ritual includes rhythmic dances and flutelike calls. Very territorial, male–female pairs often build their nests 15 miles (24 kilometers) apart from other pairs. Female Siberian cranes lay 2 eggs, and both parents take part in incubating (sitting on or brooding) them for about 30 days. The chicks leave the nest soon after hatching, but remain with their

The main threat to Siberian cranes is hunting along their migration route.

parents until they fledge (develop flying feathers) at two to four months. Usually only one chick survives infancy.

Habitat and current distribution

The Siberian crane currently breeds in only two areas: one in northeastern Siberia (between the Yana and Kolyma Rivers, the other in western Siberia on the lower reaches of the Ob River. The northeastern region features the majority of the cranes, about 3,000 breed there. In winter, they migrate to Boyang (Poyang) Lake in southeast China. The Ob River population, which numbers less than 20, divides and migrates in winter to two different sites: the Keoladeo Ghana Bird Sanctuary in Bharatpur, India, and the lowlands in northern Iran near the Caspian Sea.

The birds prefer to breed in marshy and lightly wooded tundra areas. In winter, they inhabit freshwater wetlands and shallow ponds.

History and conservation measures

Siberian cranes once nested throughout much of Siberia. Because the birds are seldom seen during migration, their wintering grounds remained a mystery until 1981, when the Boyang Lake site was discovered.

The major threat to the Siberian crane is hunting by humans along its migration path in Afghanistan and Iran. Habitat loss also puts the bird at risk. Wetlands along its migration routes and in its wintering regions have been drained by humans to create farmland and other developed land. In China, in addition to drainage for farmland, the wintering area in the mud flats around Lake Poyang are threatened by construction of the massive Three Gorges Dam on the Yangtze River. Oil exploration and development is damaging the habitat in the breeding grounds in Siberia.

Programs have been established in the United States, Germany, and Russia to transfer eggs produced by Siberian cranes in captivity to wild sites, such as the breeding grounds around the Ob River. In the wild, the eggs are hatched in electric incubators. Human keepers then care for the chicks until they fledge (acquire the ability to fly). To keep the cranes as isolated from humans as possible, the keepers dress in crane costumes.

CRANE, WHOOPING
Grus americana

PHYLUM: Chordata
CLASS: Aves
ORDER: Gruiformes
FAMILY: Gruidae
STATUS: Endangered, IUCN
Endangered, ESA
RANGE: Canada, Mexico, USA

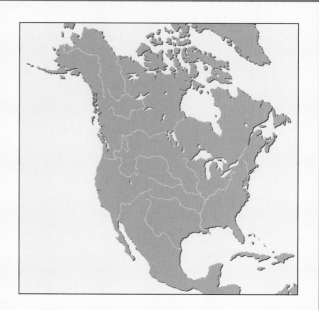

Crane, whooping

Grus americana

Description and biology

The whooping crane is so named because of its whooping, trumpet–like call. The tallest North American bird, it stands 5 feet (1.5 meters) tall and weighs almost 16 pounds (7.2 kilograms). It has an average wingspan of 7.5 feet (2.3 meters). This marsh or wetland bird has a snowy–white body, white wings marked with black tips, long dark legs, black feet, a red face, and a long, pointed yellow bill. Its diet consists of crabs, crayfish, frogs, rodents, insects, berries, and small birds.

The courtship behavior of whooping cranes is among the most unusual in nature. Their dance consists of strutting, leaping, head bobbing, wing flapping, and loud calls. Once a pair decides to mate, they mate for life. The pair requires a range of 300 to 400 acres (120 to 160 hectares) in order to find enough food and nesting sites.

In late spring, after building a nest on the ground among vegetation, a female whooping crane lays 2 light tan to green eggs. Both parents incubate (sit on or brood) the eggs for about 30 days before they hatch. The chicks' feathers are cinnamon colored. They will not develop their white adult plumage (covering of feathers) until their second summer. Of the two chicks born, only one will survive to adulthood. The first–hatched chick (born one to two days ahead of the other) usually attacks and drives away the younger chick from the nest.

Migrating whooping cranes often fly in groups of 10 birds or fewer.

Habitat and current distribution

Whooping cranes are migratory (they relocate on a seasonal basis) birds. They summer in the Wood Buffalo National Park in Northwest Territories, Canada. They begin migrating south in September in flocks of less than 10 birds. In November, they arrive at their winter home in the Aransas National Wildlife Refuge in Texas on the coast of the Gulf of Mexico. In April, they make the 2,600–mile (4,200–kilometer) trip back to Canada. About 300 whooping cranes currently exist in the wild and another 118 in captivity.

The birds prefer to build their nests in wetlands and marshes. In winter, they inhabit coastal lagoons and fresh and brackish (mixture of freshwater and salt water) marshes.

History and conservation measures

Scientists believe the whooping crane population was probably always small. They estimate that no more than 1,400 of the birds inhabited North America in 1870. Despite their small population, whooping cranes were found on the Great Plains and on both coasts of the United States. Before the American West was settled, they nested from Illinois to southern Canada and wintered from the Carolinas to Mexico.

By 1941, however, fewer than 20 whooping cranes existed in the world. Several factors contributed to their rapid decline. Many died as a result of hunting—for their meat or for sport. Others died from disease. The vast majority succumbed to habitat destruction. Over the past two centuries, more than half of all the wetlands that existed in the United States have been drained and filled in to create farmland, roads, and land suitable for homes and businesses.

Because each whooping crane couple requires a certain amount of territory, which they will defend from other whooping cranes, the population cannot grow unless they begin to use a different wintering ground. The Aransas Reserve in Texas is big enough only to sustain a population of about 200 cranes. It is surrounded by developed communities, so it cannot be made larger.

In 1967, the U.S. Fish and Wildlife Service (USFWS) began a whooping crane recovery program. Part of that program involved wildlife biologists (people who study living organisms) removing one of the two eggs from the birds' nests and placing them in the nests of sandhill cranes, which are closely related to whooping cranes. At first, the plan was successful. The sandhill cranes became "foster parents," incubating the eggs and then raising the whooping crane chicks as their own. However, when these whooping cranes grew to adulthood, they believed they were sandhill cranes and would not mate with other whooping cranes.

Biologists then began raising the captured eggs in captivity. Successful breeding programs were established in Maryland, Wisconsin, and Alberta, Canada. Beginning in 1993, captive–reared, nonmigratory whooping cranes were reintroduced to the wild on the Kissimmee Prairie in Florida. In the early 2000s, programs were initiated that taught the reintroduced cranes to migrate by leading them in ultra–light aircraft.

To protect existing migratory whooping cranes, the USFWS's recovery program includes the conservation of wetlands and other suitable habitat.

CROW, HAWAIIAN
Corvus hawaiiensis

PHYLUM: Chordata
CLASS: Aves
ORDER: Passeriformes
FAMILY: Corvidae
STATUS: Critically endangered, IUCN
Endangered, ESA
RANGE: USA (Hawaii)

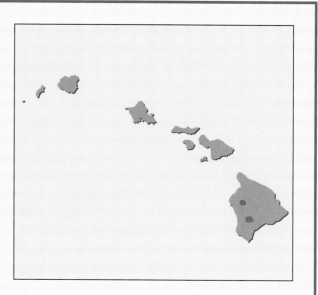

Crow, Hawaiian
Corvus hawaiiensis

Description and biology

The Hawaiian crow, called 'alala in Hawaiian, is a large, dark brown bird with a thick, strong beak. An average adult measures 19 inches (48 centimeters) long. The bird's diet consists mainly of fruit, but also includes insects, rodents, small lizards, and even some small birds. Rats and mongooses are its main predators.

Hawaiian crows build their nests high in ohia (lehua) trees (trees in the myrtle family with bright red flowers and hard wood). They use these same nests year after year. Females lay one to five eggs between March and June.

Habitat and current distribution

The Hawaiian crow prefers to inhabit high–elevation rain forests or dry forests that contain many fruit–producing plants and shrubs. The bird is currently restricted to the western side of the island of Hawaii at elevations between 3,400 and 5,000

Although hunting and habitat loss are partially responsible for the Hawaiian crow's endangered status, its main threat is its low breeding ability. Only one chick per nest survives in the wild.

feet (1,035 and 1,525 meters). In the early 1990s, biologists (people who study living organisms) counted only 11 Hawaiian crows in the wild. A captive population of 10 exists in the Olinda Endangered Species Breeding Facility on the island of Maui.

History and conservation measures

The Hawaiian crow was found throughout the island of Hawaii until the 1930s. Many factors may have led to the bird's present critically endangered state, including hunting, habitat loss, and poor breeding success.

The Hawaiian crow's population was reduced initially by hunting, which was finally outlawed in 1931. Then, the bird lost much of its original habitat as forests were cut down on the island to create farmland or land suitable for housing. With farms came cattle, goats, and pigs, which eventually began eating the Hawaiian crow's natural food sources. Mongooses and rats, as well as disease, further reduced its numbers.

The most significant factor in the bird's decline, however, has been its naturally low breeding ability. Only about one chick per nest survives infancy in the wild. This problem also occurs in captive breeding programs. At the Olinda facility, only two chicks were born in 1989 and 1990. Without high population numbers in the wild to overcome this problem, the Hawaiian crow will not be able to survive.

CURLEW, ESKIMO
Numenius borealis

PHYLUM: Chordata
CLASS: Aves
ORDER: Charadriiformes
FAMILY: Scolopacidae
STATUS: Critically endangered, IUCN
Endangered, ESA
RANGE: Argentina, Brazil, Canada, Chile, French Guiana, Guyana, Paraguay, Suriname, USA, Uruguay

Curlew, Eskimo

Numenius borealis

Description and biology

Curlews are large shorebirds. The Eskimo curlew is the smallest of the American curlews. It averages 11.5 to 14 inches (29 to 35.5 centimeters) in length. The feathers on its back are dark brown while those on its breast are lighter. Its throat is almost white in color. The upper part of its breast and the underside of its wings are marked with dark brown streaks. Its legs are gray and its eyes are dark brown.

Because of the fat layer it builds up for winter migration, the Eskimo curlew is also called the prairie pigeon or the doughbird. Its 2–inch (5–centimeter) black, curved bill is rich in nerve endings. When the bird sticks its bill in the ground to feed, these nerves detect vibrations caused by underground insects and worms. It also feeds on snails and berries.

Nerves at the end of the Eskimo curlew's bill help it to detect food, such as insects and worms, that live underground.

Eskimo curlews begin breeding in May and June. A female lays 3 to 4 green–brown eggs in a nest of straw and leaves. The nest is hidden in a hollow in the ground. She then incubates (sits on or broods) the eggs for 18 to 30 days. After hatching, the young chicks are cared for by both parents until they fledge (develop flying feathers).

Habitat and current distribution

During breeding season, Eskimo curlews inhabit arctic tundra. In winter, they are found in the pampas (partly grassy, partly arid plain) of central Argentina. While migrating northward, they inhabit the tall grass prairies of the Mississippi valley.

Since the 1980s, there have been no confirmed sightings of Eskimo curlews. Many wildlife biologists (scientists who study living organisims) consider the species to be extinct. If there are any Eskimo curlews remaining in the wild, the population is extremely low.

History and conservation measures

At the beginning of the nineteenth century, Eskimo curlews numbered in the millions. But intense hunting of the bird as it migrated quickly reduced its population. The conversion of pampas and prairies into farmland also reduced its habitat and food supply. By the early twentieth century, it was thought to be extinct.

After sightings of Eskimo curlew flocks were reported in Canada and the United States in the 1980s, a recovery program was developed. Soon after, however, the sightings stopped.

PHYLUM: Chordata
CLASS: Aves
ORDER: Anseriformes
FAMILY: Anatidae
STATUS: Vulnerable, IUCN
Endangered, ESA
RANGE: USA (Hawaii)

Duck, Laysan

Anas laysanensis

Description and biology

The Laysan duck is a relative of the more well–known mallard duck. An average Laysan duck measures 16 inches (41 centimeters) long. Its plumage (covering of feathers) ranges in color from light to dark brown. A white patch surrounds the duck's eyes and extends to its ear openings. The male (called a drake) has a green bill, while the female (simply called a duck) has a brown one. Both sexes have a purplish–green patch surrounded by white and black feathers on their secondary wing.

Relatively tame, the Laysan duck flies only short distances on the island it inhabits. Nocturnal (active at night), it feeds in lagoons on insect larvae and small crustaceans (group of animals including lobsters, crabs, and shrimp).

The breeding season for Laysan ducks lasts from February to August. After building a nest on the ground within clumps of grass, a female Laysan duck lays at least 3 pale green eggs.

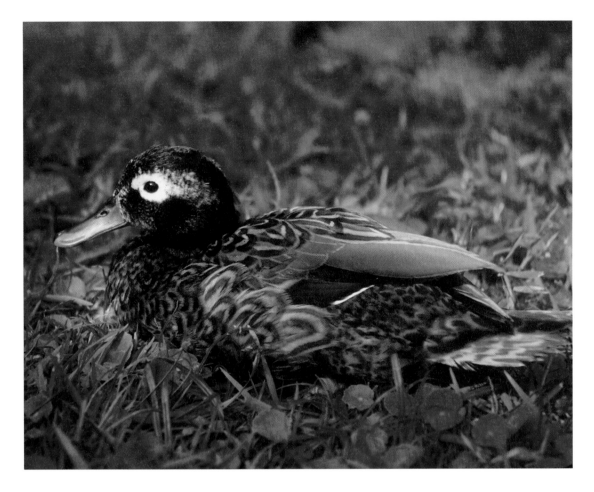

Although the incubation for Laysan duck eggs is unknown, it is probably between 28 to 30 days.

Male and female Laysan ducks have different bill colors. The male has a green bill, while the female has a brown one.

Habitat and current distribution

Laysan ducks are found only on Laysan Island, which is an islet (very small island) of the Hawaiian Islands, located about 750 miles (1,200 kilometers) northwest of Niihau Island. The ducks prefer to inhabit the island's lagoons and marshes. Biologists (people who study living organisms) estimate the Laysan duck population to be 500.

History and conservation measures

The Laysan duck population declined for two reasons. The first was human hunting for food and sport. The second—and more serious—was habitat destruction. At the beginning of the twentieth century, rabbits were brought to Laysan Island. They quickly consumed most of the vegetation on the island, destroying the ducks' nesting grounds. By the time the rabbits were eliminated from the island in the 1920s, the ducks had become almost extinct.

As vegetation on the island recovered, so did the Laysan duck population. By the late 1950s, it had grown to almost 600. The current stable population of 500 seems to be the number the island's habitat can comfortably support.

Laysan Island is a part of the Hawaiian Islands National Wildlife Refuge. Human access to the island is strictly prohibited. Recent efforts to introduce the duck to other nearby islands have failed. Because its limited, fragile habitat cannot tolerate changes, the Laysan duck will always be considered threatened or vulnerable.

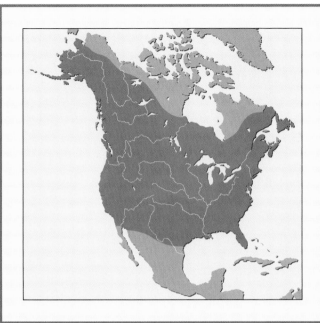

EAGLE, BALD
Haliaeetus leucocephalus

PHYLUM: Chordata
CLASS: Aves
ORDER: Falconiformes
FAMILY: Accipitridae
STATUS: Threatened, ESA
RANGE: Canada, USA

Eagle, bald
Haliaeetus leucocephalus

Description and biology

Eagles, members of the same family as hawks and Old World vultures, are found throughout the world. The bald eagle is the only eagle unique to North America. An average bald eagle measures 32 to 40 inches (81 to 107 centimeters) long, weighs between 6 and 16 pounds (2.7 and 7.3 kilograms), and has a wingspan up to 7.5 feet (2.3 meters). Females are generally larger than males. The color of the plumage (covering of feathers) on the body is brown. The distinctive white head and tail feathers appear after the eagle is four to seven years old. The bird has black talons, a yellow beak, and pale eyes. Its diet is composed mainly of fish, although it will eat ducks, rodents, snakes, and anything else it can catch.

Bald eagles are solitary birds that mate for life. Once paired, a male and female eagle build a large nest in the top of a large tree near a river, lake, marsh, or other wetland area.

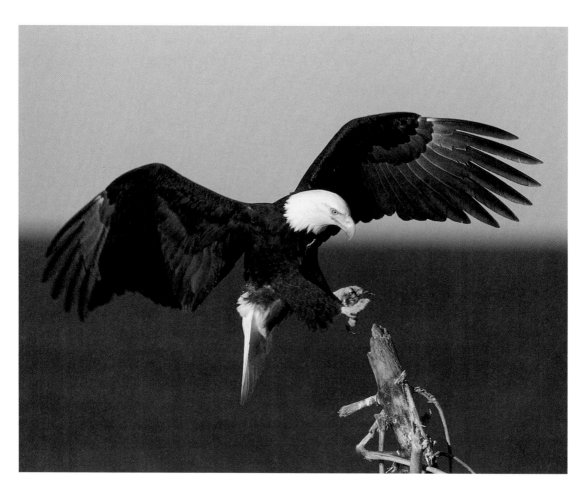

Once the most notable symbol for endangered species in North America, conservation efforts have been successful in restoring the bald eagle population.

The birds may use and add to this nest year after year. Some older nests measure 10 feet across. Bald eagles range over great distances, but usually nest within 100 miles (161 kilometers) of where they were raised.

A female bald eagle usually lays 2 to 3 eggs once a year. She then incubates (sits on or broods) them for 35 days until they hatch. The young eagles, called eaglets, fledge (develop flying feathers) within three months and leave the nest about a month afterward. Because of disease, bad weather, and lack of food, many eaglets do not survive their first year. Those that do survive may live 30 years or longer in the wild.

Habitat and current distribution

Bald eagles prefer to inhabit secluded forests with tall, mature trees and flowing water. Northern eagles usually migrate south during winter to open water areas where food is abundant.

The bald eagle ranges over most of the North American continent, from Alaska and Canada down to northern Mexico. Biologists (people who study living organisms) believe between 80,000 and 110,000 bald eagles currently exist.

History and conservation measures

Since ancient times, eagles have served as symbols of royal power, appearing on coins, flags, and standards. In 1782, the United States Congress adopted the bald eagle as the country's national emblem. However, this majestic bird began to disappear from the countryside as settlers carved out more and more of the American wilderness in the nineteenth and early twentieth centuries. As their habitat shrank, so did their food supply. In addition, they were often shot by farmers and ranchers in the mistaken belief that they were pests or a threat to livestock.

By 1940, the number of bald eagles was so low that Congress passed the Bald Eagle Protection Act. This act made it illegal to kill, harass, possess (without a permit), or sell bald eagles. Nonetheless, the eagle population continued to decline, especially after World War II (1939–45). The reason was the rampant spraying of the powerful pesticide DDT (dichloro-diphenyltrichloroethane).

Farmers, foresters, and others used DDT to kill weeds, insects, rodents, and other pests that harmed agricultural crops. However, DDT does not dissolve in water and does not break down chemically in the environment. After being sprayed on cropland, it is washed (through rain and other precipitation) into nearby streams, rivers, and lakes. The DDT residue is absorbed by aquatic plants and small animals, which are then eaten by fish. In turn, the fish are consumed by bald eagles. At each step higher in the food chain, the DDT residue becomes more concentrated in the fatty tissues of the contaminated animals.

Contaminated bald eagles (and other birds) began laying eggs that had weak shells. The eggs often broke during incubation or did not hatch at all, and the eagle population quickly fell. By the early 1960s, only about 400 pairs of nesting bald eagles existed in the lower 48 states. In some areas, they had disappeared completely.

In 1962, marine biologist and writer Rachel Carson published *Silent Spring*. The book documented the dangers of pesticides, particularly that of DDT. In large part because of this famous book, DDT was banned for most uses in the United States in 1972.

This ban, coupled with efforts to protect bald eagle habitat, brought the bird back from certain extinction. By 1981, the nesting population in the lower 48 states had doubled. In July 1995, the U.S. Fish and Wildlife Service officially downlisted the bald eagle on the Endangered Species List from endangered to threatened throughout the nation. On July 6, 1999, the agency officially proposed to delist the bald eagle—that is, to remove it from the endangered species list.

Habitat destruction and illegal hunting still threaten the bald eagle, primarily in the southern part of its range. Most wildlife experts agree, though, that the bald eagle's recovery is encouraging.

EAGLE, PHILIPPINE
Pithecophaga jefferyi

PHYLUM: Chordata
CLASS: Aves
ORDER: Falconiformes
FAMILY: Accipitridae
STATUS: Critically endangered, IUCN
Endangered, ESA
RANGE: Philippines

Eagle, Philippine

Pithecophaga jefferyi

Description and biology

The Philippine eagle, also known as the monkey–eating eagle, is one of the rarest and most endangered birds of prey in the world. A huge and powerful bird, it measures 34 to 40 inches (86 to 102 centimeters) long. Its wings are short and its tail is long.

The eagle hunts for monkeys from treetops or by gliding over the forest canopy. It also feeds on large birds and small deer. Its home range can vary greatly, from 5 to 40 square miles (13 to 104 square kilometers).

Habitat and current distribution

The Philippine eagle is found on the Philippine islands of Leyte, Luzon, Mindanao, and Samar. Its primary habitat is rain forest. Biologists (people who study living organisms) estimate that less than 200 Philippine eagles currently exist.

The Philippine eagle is one of the most endangered birds of prey on Earth. Biologists estimate that fewer than 200 of the birds currently exist.

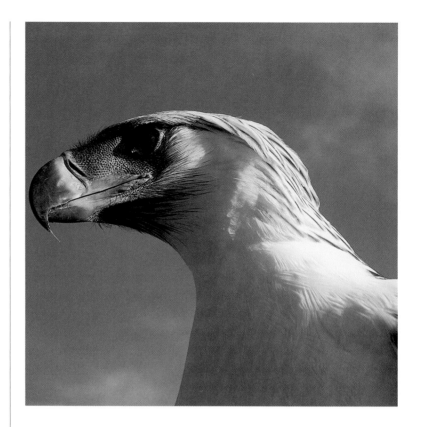

History and conservation measures

Hunting and trapping were the initial causes for the Philippine eagle's decline. While these threats are still very real, deforestation has become an even greater threat. The forests of the Sierra Madre Mountains on the northeast coast of Luzon provide the largest remaining habitat. Unless conservation measures are undertaken, logging of the forests will continue and the Philippine eagle's habitat will be destroyed.

Captive–breeding programs for the Philippine eagle have been established. In 1992, the first chick was hatched in captivity.

EGRET, CHINESE
Egretta eulophotes

PHYLUM: Chordata
CLASS: Aves
ORDER: Ciconiiformes
FAMILY: Ardeidae
STATUS: Vulnerable, IUCN
Endangered, ESA
RANGE: Brunei, China, Indonesia,
Japan, Malaysia, North Korea,
Philippines, Russia, Singapore,
South Korea, Taiwan, Thailand,
Vietnam

Egret, Chinese
Egretta eulophotes

Description and biology

Egret is the common name for herons that develop long, drooping plumes during breeding season. The Chinese egret is a tall wading bird with long legs, a long neck, and a long, pointed bill. It measures 25 to 27 inches (63.5 to 68.5 centimeters) long. Its plumage (covering of feathers) is pure white in color. A crest of white long feathers forming a showy plume develops along the top and back of its head and neck.

The Chinese egret feeds alone or in small groups. It wades in shallow water to catch fish, shrimp, and crabs. Male and female egrets mate for life. After building a nest in a tree or in low vegetation, the female lays 2 to 5 eggs and incubates (sits on or broods) them for approximately 30 days until they hatch.

Habitat and current distribution

This species of egret breeds on offshore islands along the western coast of North Korea and the eastern coast of China.

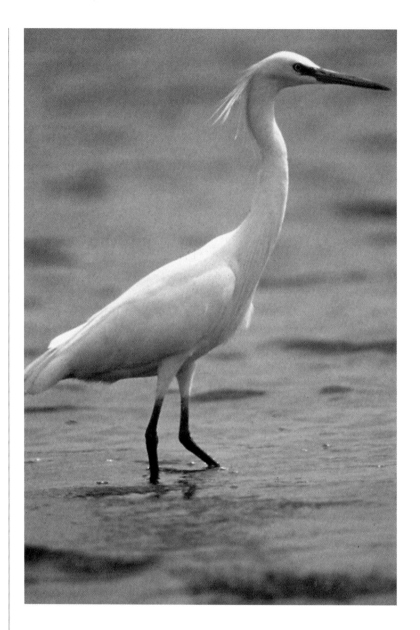

The Chinese egret prefers to inhabit estuaries, bays, tidal mudflats, and lagoons where it can feed in shallow water.

In winter, the bird migrates south to the Philippines and Malaysia. Biologists (people who study living organisms) estimate the total Chinese egret population to be composed of 960 male–female pairs. During the 1990s, a significant population of the species created a new breeding site in Russia on Furugelm Island in the Peter the Great Bay, about 372 miles (600 kilometers) from Korea. By 1999, 40 pairs had built their nests on Furugelm Island. These birds left behind their former nesting sites in Korean islands, where a huge airport had crowded them and avid birdwatchers had overrun their territory.

Along coasts, the Chinese egret prefers to inhabit estuaries, bays, tidal mudflats, and lagoons where it can feed in shallow water.

History and conservation measures

The Chinese egret was once plentiful and wide–ranging. Like many egret species, it was hunted almost to the point of extinction in the nineteenth century when the fashion industry increased its demand for feathers. The egret, bearing its beautiful white plume during breeding season, was a tempting and easy target for hunters. Although hunting was finally outlawed at the beginning of the twentieth century, Chinese egrets have never fully recovered.

The surviving Chinese egrets are threatened by the loss of their habitat as wetlands are drained to create farmland, particularly rice fields. The collection of their eggs, though prohibited, continues. However, the population of the egrets that has taken up residence on Furugelm Island has a much safer place to live, which is hopeful for the survival of the species.

FALCON, AMERICAN
PEREGRINE
Falco peregrinus anatum

PHYLUM: Chordata
CLASS: Aves
ORDER: Falconiformes
FAMILY: Falconidae
STATUS: Delisted, recovered, ESA
RANGE: Canada, Mexico, USA

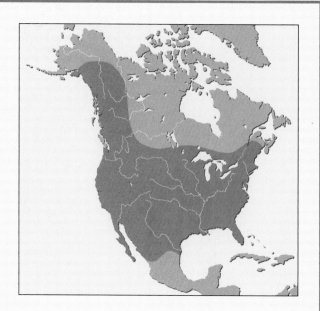

Falcon, American peregrine
Falco peregrinus anatum

Description and biology

Peregrine (pronounced PER–a–grin) comes from the Latin word *peregrinus*, meaning "foreigner" or "traveler." One of nature's most beautiful birds of prey, the peregrine falcon is noted for its speed, grace, and aerial (flying) skills. There are three subspecies of the peregrine falcon in North America: American, Arctic, and Peale's.

The American peregrine falcon is a medium–sized bird with long, pointed wings. It measures 15 to 21 inches (38 to 53 centimeters) long, with a wingspan of about 44 inches (118 centimeters). The plumage (covering of feathers) on its wings is slate blue–gray in color. Its bluish back is marked with black bars, and its underside is pale. Its white face has a black stripe on each cheek. It has large, dark eyes. Younger peregrine falcons are darker underneath and browner overall.

Peregrine falcons feed on smaller birds such as songbirds, shorebirds, and ducks. In urban areas, they eat starlings and pigeons. Falcons usually hunt their prey while in flight. Flying high above their intended prey, they "stoop" or dive at speeds of more than 200 miles (320 kilometers) per hour. In mid–air, they strike and kill prey with a blow from their sharp talons.

Peregrine falcons first breed when they are two or three years old. After selecting a nesting site on a high cliff (or on a bridge or ledge of a skyscraper in a city), a male peregrine begins a series of aerial acrobatic displays to attract a female. After rising to a great height, the male folds his wings and streaks down like a missile, pulling up at the last moment

An American peregrine falcon grasping its prey with its talons.

and soaring into a series of loops. Once the male and female mate, the female lays 3 to 5 eggs, which hatch after 32 to 34 days. The nestlings or young leave the nest when they are 35 to 40 days old. Pairs will usually use the same nesting site for many years.

Habitat and current distribution

American peregrine falcons live mostly along mountain ranges, river valleys, and coastlines from Alaska and the Arctic tundra south into Mexico. Historically, they were most common in the Rocky Mountains, the upper Mississippi River Valley, and in parts of the Appalachian Mountains and nearby valleys from New England south to Georgia.

Biologists (people who study living organisms) estimate that more than 1,200 breeding pairs of American peregrine falcons exist in the contiguous United States (the connected 48 states) and Alaska, with additional birds in Canada and Mexico.

History and conservation measures

Peregrine falcons have never been very abundant. In the 1930s and 1940s, it was estimated that about 500 breeding pairs of peregrine falcons existed in the eastern United States and about 1,000 pairs in the West and Mexico. Then, beginning in the late 1940s, peregrine falcons suffered a rapid decline.

The reason behind the falcon's devastating drop was the rampant spraying of the powerful pesticide dichlorodiphenyl-trichloroethane (DDT), especially after World War II (1939–45). Farmers, foresters, and others used DDT to kill weeds, insects, rodents, and other pests that harmed agricultural crops. It was sprayed heavily along coastal areas and wetlands to control mosquitoes and other insects.

DDT does not dissolve in water and does not break down chemically in the environment. Animals that ate insects and plant materials in these sprayed areas ingested DDT. Once inside the body, the chemical never leaves; it stays in the fatty tissues. At each step higher in the food chain, the DDT residue becomes more concentrated in the fatty tissues of the contaminated animals. As predators, peregrine falcons are at the top of the food chain. When they eat a contaminated animal, they ingest a concentrated form of the pesticide.

DDT reduces the amount of calcium in the eggshells of female peregrines (and other birds of prey). Thus, peregrines began laying thin–shelled eggs that cracked before they were able to hatch. Fewer and fewer nestlings were born, and the falcon population plummeted. By the mid–1960s, no breeding pairs of falcons remained in the eastern United States.

The U.S. Fish and Wildlife Service (USFWS) placed the American peregrine falcon on the Endangered Species List in 1970. Two years later, DDT was banned for most uses in the United States. Cooperating together, the USFWS, state wildlife agencies, and the Peregrine Fund (at Cornell University) began releasing captive–bred young falcons into the wild in 1974.

The American peregrine falcon's recovery has been successful. Reintroduction of peregrines in the eastern United States ended in 1991; only a few small reintroductions are still taking place in certain areas of the west. In all, more than 4,000 peregrines have been released to their former habitat as part of this recovery plan.

In May 1998, the U.S. secretary of the interior proposed that the American peregrine falcon be one of 29 species either downgraded or removed from the Endangered Species List. On August 25, 1999, it was delisted as a recovered species (with a required five–year monitoring program), and is considered one of the success stories of U.S. conservation.

FINCH, LAYSAN
Telespiza cantans

PHYLUM: Chordata
CLASS: Aves
ORDER: Passeriformes
FAMILY: Drepanididae
STATUS: Vulnerable, IUCN
Endangered, ESA
RANGE: USA (Hawaii)

Finch, Laysan
Telespiza cantans

Description and biology

The Laysan finch is a songbird that averages 6 inches (15 centimeters) long. The plumage (covering of feathers) differs between females and males of the species. In females, the upper plumage is brown, marked by black streaks tinged with yellow–green. The breast is light yellow, and the abdomen and tail are dull white. All underparts have brown streaks. In males, the head, throat, and breast are bright yellow during breeding season. The upper back is yellow–green with broad black streaks. The lower back is gray. The black wings and brown tail are edged with yellow–green. Both sexes have a heavy, gray bill.

Laysan finches have a varied diet. They eat seeds, shoots, flowers, fruits, seabird eggs, and insects and their larvae.

Breeding season for Laysan finches extends from April to June. The birds build their nests in clumps of bunchgrass 4 to 17 inches (10 to 43 centimeters) off the ground. After laying 3 eggs, the female incubates (sits on or broods) them for about

A female Laysan finch. The plumage of males and females differs in color, although both have a gray bill.

16 days. The young chicks fledge (develop flying feathers) in just over a month.

Habitat and current distribution

The Laysan finch is native to Laysan Island, an islet (very small island) of the Hawaiian Islands, located about 750 miles (1,200 kilometers) northwest of Niihau Island. It has also been introduced to nearby Pearl Island and Hermes Reef, as well as other small islands in the area. Biologists (people who study living organisms) estimate the Laysan Island population to be at least 10,000. Between 500 and 1,000 Laysan finches exist on the other islands.

On Laysan Island, the finches inhabit sand dunes around the coastline and a brackish (mixture of freshwater and salt water) lagoon in the center of the island.

History and conservation measures

Early explorers to the region believed the Laysan finch's pleasing song made it an attractive cage bird. At the beginning of the twentieth century, as many as 4,000 of the birds may have inhabited Laysan Island.

In 1903, rabbits were introduced to the island. They quickly ate most of the natural vegetation, destroying the habitat and food supply of the island's native birds. In 1909, U.S. president Theodore Roosevelt designated Laysan Island and other islands in the Hawaiian chain as part of the Hawaiian Islands Bird Reservation. However, this move did little to stop the decline of the Laysan finch population. In 1922, when the last rabbits were finally removed from the island, only about 100 of the finches remained.

Despite its growing numbers, the Laysan finch is still considered vulnerable. Introduced predator species, such as rats, could still easily wipe out the birds. Diseases carried by introduced birds could also destroy the finch population.

Laysan Island is now part of the Hawaiian Islands National Wildlife Refuge. This limits the number of humans allowed to visit the island, providing further protection for the Laysan finch.

FLAMINGO, ANDEAN
Phoenicoparrus andinus

PHYLUM: Chordata
CLASS: Aves
ORDER: Ciconiiformes
FAMILY: Phoenicopteridae
STATUS: Vulnerable, IUCN
RANGE: Argentina, Bolivia, Chile, Peru

Flamingo, Andean
Phoenicoparrus andinus

Description and biology

Flamingos are tall wading birds. They have long legs, a long curved neck, and distinctive pink plumage (covering of feathers). The birds move gracefully, whether walking or flying. The Andean flamingo stands 40 to 43.5 inches (102 to 110.5 centimeters) tall and weighs 4.4 to 5.3 pounds (2 to 2.4 kilograms).

The flamingo has a stocky bill that curves downward. Thin, flat membranes or gills line the rim of the bill. As the flamingo wades through marshes and lagoons, it scoops up muddy water with its bill and these membranes strain out food such as minute algae.

The flamingo's breeding season extends from December to February. Before mating, male and females undergo an elaborate courtship ritual, which they perform in unison. The fe-

Two captive Andean flamingos. In the 1980s, captive–breeding programs were begun in an attempt to restore the dwindling flamingo population.

male lays a single egg in a nest built out of mud into a cone 12 to 24 inches (30 to 61 centimeters) high and 12 inches (30 centimeters) wide. Both parents incubate (sit on or brood) the egg for 27 to 30 days. The chick often leaves the nest just 12 days after hatching. Sometimes, it is carried under one of its parent's wings.

Habitat and current distribution

As the names indicates, Andean flamingos are found in the Andes Mountains in the South American countries of Argentina, Bolivia, Chile, and Peru. They usually occupy areas above 11,500 feet (3,505 meters). Biologists (people who study living organisms) believe the only major breeding site for Andean flamingos is in northern Chile. It is estimated that 26,000 Andean flamingos currently exist.

Andean flamingos prefer to inhabit salt lakes and to breed on small islands within those lakes.

History and conservation measures

The Andean flamingo once existed in great numbers. Now, this elegant bird is considered in jeopardy. As humans move deeper into its environment, the flamingo is threatened on many fronts. Human collectors steal its eggs. The body fat of the bird has historically been used as a rub to treat rheumatism, a disease of the joints. Mining operations pollute and destroy its habitat. Introduced wildlife species compete with it for food. Some, like the fox, prey directly on the bird. A long–term drought (lack of rain) in northern Chiles that began in 1987 has taken a huge toll on the population of the species.

With this in mind, efforts were started in the 1980s to protect the known breeding grounds of the Andean flamingo.

GOOSE, HAWAIIAN
Branta sandvicensis

PHYLUM: Chordata
CLASS: Aves
ORDER: Anseriformes
FAMILY: Anatidae
STATUS: Vulnerable, IUCN
Endangered, ESA
RANGE: USA (Hawaii)

Goose, Hawaiian

Branta sandvicensis

Description and biology

The Hawaiian goose or nene (pronounced NAY–nay) is uniquely colored. Its gray–brown feathers have white tips that form widely spaced bars on the bird's back. On its underside, the bars are closer together. The sides of the nene's neck are reddish–brown with black and white markings. The bill, face, cap, and back of the neck are all black.

An average nene measures 22 to 30 inches (56 to 76 centimeters) long and weighs between 4 and 5 pounds (1.8 and 2.8 kilograms). The bird has excellent senses of hearing and sight. It also has strong legs and wings. It feeds mainly on vegetation, including grasses, leaves, herbs, and berries.

The breeding season for Hawaiian geese begins in October or November and extends through February. Male–female pairs (a male is known as a gander, a female as a goose) build nests on the ground, usually in a patch of vegetation. The female lays 3 to 5 eggs. Both the gander and

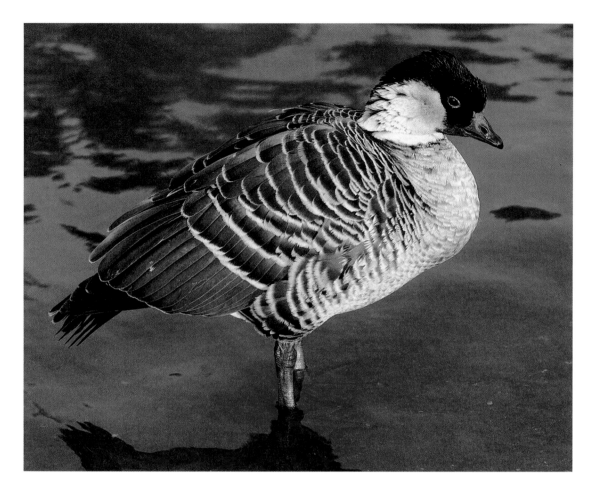

goose incubate (sit on or brood) the eggs for about 30 days until they hatch. The goslings fledge (develop flying feathers) in 10 to 12 weeks.

Before 1800, the Hawaiian goose population was estimated at 25,000. By 1952, however, a population of only 30 birds remained.

Habitat and current distribution

Hawaiian geese are found on the island of Hawaii. A small population of the birds has been reintroduced to the island of Maui. Two more populations have recently established themselves on the island of Kauai. In 1997, biologists (people who study living organisms) estimated that 890 nenes existed in the wild: 375 on Hawaii, 250 on Maui, and 265 on Kauai.

Nenes breed at elevations between 5,000 and 8,000 feet (1,524 and 2,438 meters). Water is not often plentiful at those heights, but the birds can survive for long periods of time by feeding on plants that contain a high amount of water.

History and conservation measures

Before 1800, the Hawaiian goose was common throughout the islands of Hawaii and Maui. Its population at that time has been estimated at 25,000. Although native inhabitants of the islands had hunted the bird for centuries, its population remained stable. That soon changed in the nineteenth century with the arrival of European settlers. They hunted the bird mercilessly and also introduced predators of the nene. These cats, dogs, rats, and mongooses preyed on the bird's eggs and on the young goslings. By 1900, the nene existed only at high altitudes in remote areas on Hawaii. It was extinct on Maui.

As more people began inhabiting Hawaii in the twentieth century, the nene's habitat and food sources were reduced. By 1952, only 30 birds survived.

In 1949, scientists started a captive–breeding program for the Hawaiian goose. The birds bred and raised in captivity were eventually reintroduced on Maui and Hawaii. In 1982, a hurricane destroyed cages containing captive nenes in Kauai. They escaped to the wild and fared quite well on the island. The reintroduced birds have survived well in all the locations in Hawaai, but have not bred in the wild as well as scientists had hoped. Because of this, scientists have had to keep adding captive–bred nenes to the wild population.

GREBE, PUNA
Podiceps taczanowskii

PHYLUM: Chordata

CLASS: Aves

ORDER: Podicipediformes

FAMILY: Podicipedidae

STATUS: Critically endangered, IUCN

RANGE: Peru

Grebe, Puna

Podiceps taczanowskii

Description and biology

Grebes are swimming birds that inhabit quiet waters around the world. They resemble both the loon (to which they are related) and the duck (to which they are not related). The Puna or Junín grebe has a grayish–brown plumage (covering of feathers) on the top portion of its body. Its underparts and neck are white. An average Puna grebe measures 13 to 15 inches (33 to 38 centimeters) in length. It has a long neck and a fairly long, pointed bill. Its diet consists primarily of fish.

Puna grebes spend most of the year in close flocks numbering less than 12 birds. A male–female pair breeds in patches of tall vegetation in deep water. After breeding, they build a nest in a colony with other mating pairs on semi–floating vegetation beds. A colony consists of 8 to 20 nests, which are generally situated 3 to 13 feet apart.

Puna grebes spend most of the year in close flocks numbering fewer than 12 birds.

A female Puna grebe lays one to three eggs between November and March. Biologists (people who study living organisms) are unsure how long it takes the eggs to hatch. After hatching, the young are carried by the male. This leaves the female free to dive to obtain food for herself and her young.

Habitat and current distribution

This species of grebe is found only on Lake Junín (Lago de Junín) in the highlands of west–central Peru. Located at an altitude of 13,000 feet (3,962 meters), Lake Junín is a large, shallow lake bordered by extensive reed beds. During breeding season, the grebes forage along the coast of the lake in open water. During the dry season, the birds move into the deeper central parts of the lake.

In the 1980s, scientists estimated the Puna grebe population to be between 200 and 300. In the early 1990s, that population had slumped to about 50, but after a good breeding season in 1998, the population was estimated to be back up to around 200, and rose to 300 the following year.

History and conservation measures

At one time, several thousand of the birds inhabited Lake Junín. By the 1970s, the Puna grebe population was less than 400. It continued to drop steadily to a low of less than 50 birds in the early 1990s, but has since rebounded to about 300 individuals. It remains in very risky circumstances.

The number of Puna grebes declined primarily because Lake Junín has become polluted by the runoff of poisons from nearby copper mines. In addition, these mines receive their water supply from the lake. As the demand for water to the mines has increased, the lake's water level, which is regulated by a hydro–electric power plant, has decreased. In 1992, open water was left only in the center of the lake. Little suitable nesting habitat remained for the Puna grebes. In 1998, when the population grew, it was due to better water levels in the lake.

Wildlife researchers tried to relocate four adult grebes to nearby Lake Chacacancha in 1985, but the birds disappeared in just two years. Local fishermen believe the birds had been caught in fishing nets intended to snare trout. A suitable relocation site for the surviving grebes has yet to be found.

There has been no long–term study of the Puna grebe. In recent years, the plight of the species has been taken up by a conservation group in Peru called PeruVerdes.

**GROUND–DOVE,
PURPLE–WINGED**
Claravis godefrida

PHYLUM: Chordata
CLASS: Aves
ORDER: Columbiformes
FAMILY: Columbidae
STATUS: Endangered, IUCN
RANGE: Argentina, Brazil,
Paraguay

Ground-dove, purple-winged
Claravis godefrida

Description and biology

The purple–winged ground–dove derives its common name from the three wide purple bars on its wings. The male has dark bluish–gray plumage (covering of feathers) with lighter underparts. Its tail is gray in the center and has white edges. The female is reddish–brown in color with lighter underparts. It has a brown tail with black and pale yellow edges.

An average purple–winged ground–dove measures 9 inches (23 centimeters) in length. Bamboo seeds make up the bulk of the bird's diet. It also feeds on fruit, grass seeds, and sedges (grassy plants growing in wet areas).

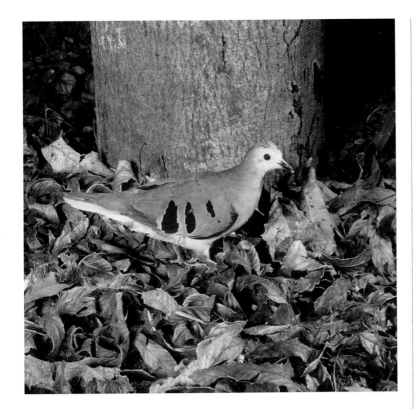

The purple–winged ground–dove is quite rare. When seen, it is usually in a small flock. Not much is known about the bird's breeding habits other than the fact that its breeding season begins in November or December when bamboo plants begin to flower.

Habitat and current distribution

This species is found only in the Atlantic forest region of southeastern South America. Biologists (people who study living organisms) do not know how many purple–winged ground–doves currently exist. Although there are occasional sightings at various locations throughout its range, the bird is considered very rare or possibly extinct.

Purple–winged ground–doves prefer to inhabit dense forests and forest borders with nearby bamboo plants. They tend to build their nests in thick, bushy trees.

History and conservation measures

Because the purple–winged ground–dove is such a specialized eater (mainly bamboo seeds), it requires a large range in which to find the proper amount of food. Even moderate deforestation greatly reduces the bird's habitat and its food source.

The purple–winged ground–dove is legally protected throughout its range. A complete ban on its capture in the wild has been recommended. It is thought to exist in small numbers in some parks and reserves along the Serra do Mar mountain range in southern Brazil and at the Iguazú National Park in Argentina. Unfortunately, since little is known about the purple–winged ground–dove's particular needs, no special measures have been taken on its behalf in those parks.

GULL, AUDOUIN'S
Larus audouinii

PHYLUM: Chordata

CLASS: Aves

ORDER: Charadriiformes

FAMILY: Laridae

STATUS: Lower risk: near threatened, IUCN Endangered, ESA

RANGE: Algeria, Cyprus, France, Gabon, Gibraltar, Greece, Italy, Libya, Mauritania, Morocco, Senegal, Spain, Tunisia, Turkey, Western Sahara

Gull, Audouin's

Larus audouinii

Description and biology

Gulls are aquatic birds found near all oceans and many inland waters around the world. The Audouin's gull is a moderately large gull. Its plumage (covering of feathers) is pale gray and white. It has black wing tips and a black and red bill. The bird feeds primarily on fish it plucks from the sea while in flight.

The breeding season for Audouin's gulls lasts from April until June. The female lays 2 to 3 eggs in a depression she has scraped out in the ground. Both parents incubate (sit on or brood) the eggs for about 28 days until they hatch. The young gulls are fed and raised by both parents. They fledge (develop flying feathers) after about 35 to 40 days and become completely independent after 3 or 4 months.

Habitat and current distribution

Audouin's gulls breed primarily in the western Mediterranean, on rocky islets (small islands) far from human

337

Audouin's gulls are in jeopardy due to the polluting of their feeding areas and the disruption of their breeding grounds.

civilization. Biologists (people who study living organisms) have estimated the total population of the species as it has changed over the years, from about 800 to 900 male–female pairs in 1965 to 9,000 to 9,500 pairs in 1989, to 15,000 pairs in 1995 to 19,200 pairs in 2000 The vast majority of these birds currently inhabit Spain.

These gulls usually feed over water not far from land. They nest on small, low–lying islands covered with grass or low bushes.

History and conservation measures

The significant increase in the population of Audouin's gulls is largely due to an increase in the fish it eats in the western Mediterranean. Despite its remarkable rise in numbers, the species remains vulnerable. The primary threat facing Audouin's gulls is having their breeding areas disturbed by people, especially fishermen, tourists, and shepherds. Since these areas are unprotected, many people regularly collect the birds' eggs. The gulls are also threatened by pollution, which is destroying their feeding areas.

HAWK, GALÁPAGOS
Buteo galapagoensis

PHYLUM: Chordata
CLASS: Aves
ORDER: Falconiformes
FAMILY: Accipitridae
STATUS: Vulnerable, IUCN
Endangered, ESA
RANGE: Ecuador (Galápagos
Islands)

Hawk, Galápagos
Buteo galapagoensis

Description and biology

Hawks are members of the family that includes eagles, kites, and Old World vultures—all birds of prey. The Galápagos hawk is deep dark brown with lighter markings on its sides and belly. It has a gray tail with dark bars and a yellow, dark–tipped bill. An average adult measures 21 to 23 inches (53 to 58 centimeters) long.

While young sea iguanas form the bulk of its diet, this bird will also eat a variety of birds, rats, and lizards. It also feeds on carrion (decaying flesh of dead animals). While flying, the hawk soars to great heights, then swoops down on prey in a zig–zag pattern.

Galápagos hawks generally form groups that stake out or claim territory within their habitat. These groups consist of

Galápagos hawks are now considered extinct on the Galápagos islands of Baltra, Daphne, Floreana, San Cristóbal, and Seymour.

up to four males and one female. Some other Galápagos hawks form more standard male–female pairs. Breeding takes place all year, with peak activity occurring between May and July. Females usually lay one to three eggs. After hatching, the young, or nestlings, are cared for by the males.

Habitat and current distribution

The Galápagos hawk is found only on the Galápagos Islands of Española, Fernandina, Isabela, Marcena, Pinta, Santa Cruz, Santa Fé, and Santiago. A province of Ecuador, the Galápagos Islands lie about 600 miles (965 kilometers) off the west coast of the country. Biologists (people who study living organisms) are unsure of the total number of Galápagos hawks in existence, although they believe about 250 of the birds reside on Santiago Island.

The hawks prefer to nest in low trees or on rocky outcrops. Much of their range lies within the Galápagos National Park, which covers all areas of the islands that are uninhabited by humans.

History and conservation measures

Until the 1930s, the Galápagos hawk was found on almost all of the Galápagos Islands. It existed in such great numbers that it was considered a threat to domestic chickens. Eventually, though, the number of Galápagos hawks began to decline. This was the direct result of hunting by humans and the destruction of its habitat.

The hawk is now considered extinct on the Galápagos islands of Baltra, Daphne, Floreana, San Cristóbal, and Seymour. To date, biologists have no plans to reintroduce the Galápagos hawk to any of its former island habitats.

HAWK, HAWAIIAN
Buteo solitarius

PHYLUM: Chordata
CLASS: Aves
ORDER: Falconiformes
FAMILY: Accipitridae
STATUS: Lower risk: near threatened, IUCN Endangered, ESA
RANGE: USA (Hawaii)

Hawk, Hawaiian
Buteo solitarius

Description and biology

The Hawaiian hawk, also called the io, is the only hawk native to the Hawaiian Islands. The color of its plumage (covering of feathers) varies from dark brown to tawny brown to almost white. Dark spots mark its chest, belly, and the undersides of its wings. An average adult Hawaiian hawk measures 16 to 18 inches (41 to 46 centimeters) long. Females are slightly larger than males.

The Hawaiian hawk is an agile flier, performing acrobatic movements at great heights. It often flies on thermal, or warm, air currents above volcanoes. To hunt, the bird generally perches in a tree before swooping down on its prey. Large insects and birds originally made up its diet. It now feeds on rodents that human settlers have introduced to its habitat.

A male–female pair builds a nest fairly low in a tree and then reuses it each year, adding sticks and branches. The nest can become quite large, up to 40 inches (102 centimeters) wide and 30 inches (76 centimeters) deep. Nesting begins in March,

Conservation efforts to save the Hawaiian hawk have proved successful.

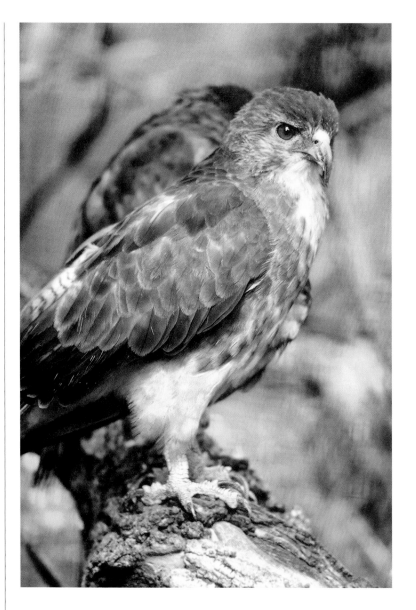

with the female laying a single egg in April or May. While she incubates (sits on or broods) the egg for 38 days, the male hunts and gathers food. The young hawk fledges (develops flying feathers) after eight or nine weeks, but remains dependent on its parents for several months.

Habitat and current distribution

The Hawaiian hawk breeds only on the island of Hawaii, but ranges as far as the islands of Maui and Oahu. It is found from sea level to 8,500 feet (2,590 meters), but generally prefers elevations from 2,000 to 5,000 feet (610 to 1,524 meters). The bird adapts to various habitats, including light woodland, forests, and farmland or other cultivated areas bordered by trees.

Biologists (people who study living organisms) estimate the Hawaiian hawk population to be about 2,000.

History and conservation measures

The greatest threat to the Hawaiian hawk has been the movement of humans into its habitat. Lowland areas of its habitat have been developed for businesses, homes, or farms. Higher areas have been cleared by logging and then turned into farms. To a lesser degree, the Hawaiian hawk population has been reduced by illegal hunting.

In the mid–1970s, biologists estimated that only a few hundred Hawaiian hawks existed. Since then, a number of protected areas for the hawks and other endangered forest birds have been set aside. Their recovery has been substantial. In 1993 the U.S. Fish and Wildlife Service proposed to reclassify the Hawaiian hawk from endangered to threatened. Again, in May 1998, U.S. Interior Secretary Bruce Babbitt included the Hawaiian hawk on a list of 29 species whose status on the Endangered Species List would be changed. The matter remained pending well into the twenty–first century.

HONEYCREEPER, CRESTED
Palmeria dolei

PHYLUM: Chordata
CLASS: Aves
ORDER: Passeriformes
FAMILY: Drepanididae
STATUS: Vulnerable, IUCN
Endangered, ESA
RANGE: USA (Hawaii)

Honeycreeper, crested
Palmeria dolei

Description and biology

The crested honeycreeper, called the 'akohekohe in Hawaiian, is a small songbird. An adult of the species has an average length of 7 inches (18 centimeters). Its black plumage (covering of feathers) is speckled with gray and orange. It has orange bars on its wings and an orange band on the back of its neck. The bird's bill is straight and pointed, and it has a grayish–white tuft on its forehead.

The crested honeycreeper feeds on nectar from the ohia (lehua) tree (tree in the myrtle family with bright red flowers and hard wood). It also feeds on nectar from a number of other flowering plants. In addition, the bird eats insects and fruits.

Biologists (people who study living organisms) know little about the crested honeycreeper's reproductive habits. They believe the bird begins to build a nest in February or March. A female crested honeycreeper will generally lay two to four

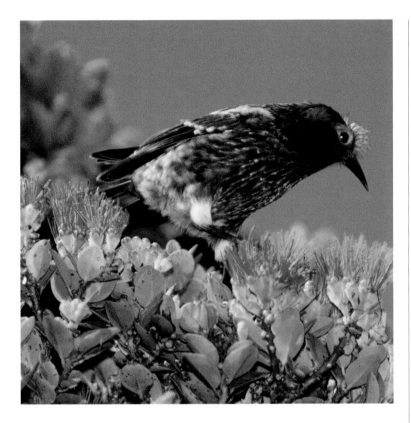

The crested honeycreepers' population, which lives in Hawaii, declined because humans brought into the birds' habitat plants and animals that were not native to the area, completely changing the environment.

eggs shortly afterward, but it is not known how long it takes them to hatch.

Habitat and current distribution

The crested honeycreeper inhabits rain forests on the eastern side of the island of Maui in the Hawaiian Islands. It is most often found at elevations of 4,000 to 7,000 feet (1,220 to 2,135 meters). Biologists estimate the bird's total population to be 3,800.

History and conservation measures

The crested honeycreeper was once common on the Hawaiian islands of Molokai and Maui. It has been extinct on Molokai since 1907. On Maui, it is confined to a narrow area of upland rain forest.

The crested honeycreepers' population declined because humans brought into the birds' habitat plants and animals that were not native to the area, completely changing the environment. These non–native or alien plants outgrew and took over the plants on which the bird normally fed. Also, introduced animals such as pigs, goats, and deer grazed on the bird's food sources, further limiting what it had to eat. Perhaps most damaging to the bird were diseases carried by introduced animals or insects. Many crested honeycreepers fell victim to the diseases known as avian malaria and bird pox that are transmitted by a particular type of mosquito.

The bird has also suffered because large areas of its forest habitat have been cleared to create farms and other human settlements.

Current conservation efforts to stop the decline of the crested honeycreeper include the control of introduced animals and plants. This is of particular importance in such protected areas as the Hanawi Natural Area Reserve, the Haleakala National Park, and the Waikamoi Preserve.

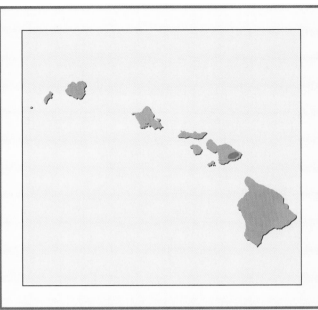

HONEYCREEPER, PO'OULI
Melamprosops phaeosoma

PHYLUM: Chordata
CLASS: Aves
ORDER: Passeriformes
FAMILY: Drepanidinae
STATUS: Critically endangered,
IUCN
Endangered, ESA
RANGE: USA (Hawaii)

Honeycreeper, po'ouli
Melamprosops phaeosoma

Description and biology

The po'ouli (poe–OO–lee) is the most endangered bird in the world today, with only three known individual birds remaining. The name *po'ouli* means "black face" in Hawaiian. The po'ouli's face is black, but the throat is white, the belly is cream–colored, the top of the head is gray, the back is brown, and the posterior is a light brown. It measures about 5.5 inches (14 centimeters) long and weighs about one ounce (25 grams). It has a short black bill and long dark brown legs.

The po'ouli spends its life hidden in the forests, searching for food in the understory—the leaves and bark of trees underneath a forest's canopy, or top. Its diet consists of snails, insects, and spiders. It builds its nest in the tree branches, constructing it out of twigs and branches. It generally lives alone in its home range area within the forest. The po'ouli's call is seldom heard, but has been described as a sharp repetition of "chick, chick" or "whit, whit." Not much is known about the mating behavior of the species, but po'ouli nests

The po'ouli is the most endangered bird in the world today, with only three known individual birds remaining.

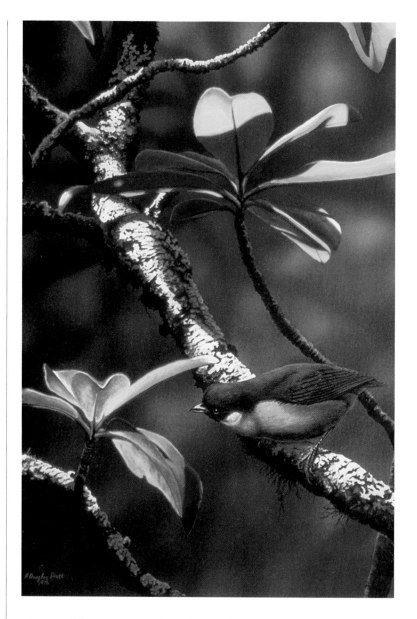

observed between April and June have contained one or two baby birds.

Habitat and current distribution

The world's three remaining po'oulis, one male and two females, all live in the Hanawi Natural Area Reserve on Maui (an island of Hawaii). They live in the rain forest on the steep northeastern slopes of Haleakala (an east Maui volcano) at an altitude of about 4,600 to 6,700 feet (1,400 to 2,040 meters). The area receives about 350 inches (900 centimeters) of rain each year. Its vegetation is very dense. The trees in this forest are primarily the native Hawaiian 'ohi'a tree and the 'olapa tree. Fossils indicate that po'oulis were once abundant in the dry forests of Maui. It is likely that the species lived in a much larger range in the past.

Although the 20–acre (8–hectare) home ranges of the three remaining po'oulis are all within 1.5 miles (2.4 kilometers) of one another, they do not overlap. Because of the lack of overlap of home ranges, there is little likelihood that, on their own, the birds would ever meet in the wild. The last known breeding between po'oulis was in 1995.

History and conservation measures

In 1973, several University of Hawaii students first discovered the po'ouli on the slopes of Haleakala. At that time the total population of the species was an estimated 200 birds. Although the population rose to 280 in 1980, the decline since then has been drastic. There have been several causes for the population decline, but no one knows for sure why it has been so severe. The habitat has been damaged by feral pigs (pigs that escaped from domestication and became wild) that root around in the forests, destroying the understory. The rooting of the pigs also creates a breeding ground for mosquitoes, which transmit deadly diseases to birds. Rats and feral cats also present a threat to the species. Birds not native to the forests have been introduced and have brought disease and competed for the po'ouli's food.

Whatever the cause of the decline in population, the situation has become very urgent. With only three birds left, and each of them more than seven years old, biologists (people who study living organisms) and avian conservationists (people who work to manage and protect the natural bird world)

DID YOU KNOW?

In 1961, a section of the Hawaii National Park on the upper slopes of the Haleakala Crater on the eastern side of the island of Maui was designated by the U.S. government as Haleakala National Park. Haleakala, the tallest mountain on Maui at 10,023 feet (3,055 meters), is a dormant volcano with a 3,000–foot (914–meter) deep crater. At 7.5 miles (12.1 kilometers) long and 2.5 miles (4 kilometers) wide it is big enough to fit the entire island of Manhattan within it. Haleakala is known for its great beauty and for its variety of habitats and biodiversity. Within the park are coral reefs, grasslands, shrublands, dry forests, bogs, alpine cinder deserts, and an intact rainforest. It has an abundance of plant and animal species, 90 percent of which are endemic (unique) to the Hawaiian Islands. The only mammals native to the island are a bat and a seal. Plants and other animals in what is now the park flourished for millions of years without natural predators, more than 2,000 miles away from any continent. Because the Hawaiian species evolved without predators or disease, when alien species were introduced to their ecosystem by human beings, the native species had little or no defense against them. Today, there are 91 threatened, endangered, or proposed endangered species on the island of Maui. Haleakala National Park is the record–holder for having the most threatened and endangered species of any national park in the United States. This is largely due to the introduction of alien species to the island.

felt they had to make a move to bring about breeding before it was too late. The first attempt was in 2001, when wildlife biologists captured one of the female po'oulis and moved her into the male's home range. Within hours, the female went back to her home range without breeding. In 2003, experts believe the only possibility for saving the species is to take the three birds into captivity in the hope that they will breed within the confines of the Maui Bird Conservation Center.

IBIS, NORTHERN BALD
Geronticus eremita

PHYLUM: Chordata

CLASS: Aves

ORDER: Ciconiiformes

FAMILY: Threskiornithidae

STATUS: Critically endangered, IUCN
Endangered, ESA

RANGE: Algeria, Egypt, Ethiopia, Morocco, Saudi Arabia, Senegal, Syria, Turkey, Yemen

Ibis, northern bald

Geronticus eremita

Description and biology

The northern bald ibis, also known as the waldrapp, grows to an average length of 27.5 to 31.5 inches (70 to 80 centimeters). The birds' naked red head and fringe of dark feathers around its neck give it the appearance of a vulture. Its feathers, chiefly black in color, have an iridescent bronze–green gloss. A patch on its forewing or "shoulder" is a shade of shiny bronze–purple. The bald ibis has a long tapering bill that curves downward. It uses its bill to probe for and feed on insects, such as beetles and grasshoppers, and fish and other aquatic animals.

The northern bald ibis nests in small colonies, usually on rocky cliffs or ledges in semi–arid (partly or mostly dry) areas near water. Breeding season begins in February. In late March or early April, after making a nest of straw, grasses, and twigs,

353

Hunting and the use of
pesticides have been the major
factors contributing to the
northern bald ibis's decreasing
numbers.

a female northern bald ibis lays a clutch (eggs produced at one time) of 3 to 4 eggs. In about 60 days, the nestlings will have hatched and fledged (developed flying feathers). By the end of June, they will leave the nesting grounds with their parents.

Main predators of the bald ibis include ravens (which sometimes prey on nestlings or eggs) and falcons (which have been seen attacking nesting ibises).

Habitat and current distribution

Although the range of the northern bald ibis seems to have increased in recent years, the bird is considered critically endangered. The majority of birds inhabit northwest Africa, mainly Morocco. Although the bird was thought to be extinct in the Middle East, in the spring of 2002 a colony of the species was found in central Syria, consisting of three male–female pairs that were at the time incubating eggs and a seventh individual. Biologists (people who study living organisms) believe the bird's total population now numbers around 315.

The northern bald ibis prefers to inhabit rocky, semi–arid regions, often with running water nearby. Feeding habitat includes sea coasts, edges of streams, river beds, sand banks, marshes, and other damp ground with sparse vegetation.

History and conservation measures

The northern bald ibis once ranged throughout southern Europe, the Middle East, and northern Africa, including the coast along the Red Sea. At the end of the seventeenth century, the bald ibis could still be found in European countries such as Austria, Italy, Germany, Switzerland, Hungary, and portions of the Balkan Peninsula.

Over a period of several centuries, the northern bald ibis slowly disappeared from its historic range. Widespread hunting and capture, both for food and zoo collections, contributed to the bird's decline. In the twentieth century, the use of pesticides on farmland, especially in Turkey, poisoned many bald ibises. With the population already very low, it was disastrous to the species when, in May 1996, a total of 21 adults were found dead and another 17 disappeared from their Moroccan colonies. The exact cause of this major loss is still not known.

Conservation programs on behalf of the bald ibis have begun in Morocco. Massa National Park, a 40–mile (64–kilometer) belt along the Atlantic coast between the cities of Agadir and Tiznet, was recently established. This wetland site is home to almost half of the breeding ibis population remaining in Morocco. It is also a major wintering area. The number of northern bald ibises has increased from a low of 220 birds in the mid–1990s to about 315 in the early 2000s.

This bird breeds well in captivity. Stocks of captive northern bald ibises are maintained in Birecik, Turkey, and at Tel Aviv University in Israel. Biologists hope to reintroduce these captive–bred bald ibises to undisturbed areas in their former range.

KAKAPO
Strigops habroptilus

PHYLUM: Chordata
CLASS: Aves
ORDER: Psittaciformes
FAMILY: Psittacidae
STATUS: Critically endangered,
IUCN
Endangered, ESA
RANGE: New Zealand

Kakapo

Strigops habroptilus

Description and biology

The kakapo is a nocturnal (active at night), flightless member of the parrot family. Because the stiff feathers around its eyes give it an owl–like appearance, it is also called the owl–parrot. The kakapo is the largest and heaviest of all parrots. It has an average length of 25 inches (63.5 centimeters). Males of the species can weigh as much as 7.75 pounds (3.5 kilograms). Females are much lighter, weighing up to 3.3 pounds (1.5 kilograms).

The color of the kakapo's plumage (covering of feathers) is a mixture of yellow and light green. Its tail is darker. The bird feeds on many different kinds of plants and flowers, chewing the food with its heavy, serrated bill.

The breeding habits of the kakapo are complex and mysterious. The male creates a series of trails between odd bowl–shaped depressions in the ground. Every few years in

January or February, the male emits a booming sound from these depressions that can be heard up to 0.5 mile (0.8 kilometer) away. These sounds continue throughout the night, for months at a time. Meanwhile, the female tries to discover the location of the male emitting the sound. Often, she cannot. If she does and mating takes place, the female lays two to four eggs in a nest built out of vegetation. It is not known how long it takes the eggs to hatch, but once they do, the female cares for the nestlings alone.

The kakapo, considered extinct in the wild in the early 1990s, has made a comeback.

Habitat and current distribution

The kakapo was once widespread on the North, South, and Stewart Islands in New Zealand. It then only existed in smaller numbers on the islands of Stewart, Little Barrier, and Codfish. The species, considered extinct in the wild in the early 1990s, has a total population of 84 individuals in 2002.

The kakapo prefers to nest in dense scrub–forests and to feed in nearby grasslands.

History and conservation measures

The kakapo once existed in an environment where it had no natural predators and no food competitors. That situation changed when humans brought predators (such as cats and rats) and competitors (such as opossums and deer) into the bird's habitat. By the 1970s, the kakapo's population was so low it was considered extinct.

In 1976, a small breeding population was discovered on Stewart Island, but introduced cats quickly killed most of the birds. The remaining 61 birds were taken to Maud and Codfish Islands off New Zealand's South Island and to Little Barrier Island in the Hauraki Gulf. For three decades there was little success with breeding among these relocated birds, and biologists (people who study living organisms) classified the species as extinct in the wild. In 2001, however, the protection measures had clearly paid off. There were, again, a total of 61 birds. By 2002, the number had risen to 84. By 1999, the kakapo had advanced enough in population that it no longer met the criteria for critically endangered status on the International Union for Conservation of Nature and Natural Resources (IUCN) Red List. The IUCN status will remain, though, for several more years in case of further declines in population.

KESTREL, MAURITIUS
Falco punctatus

PHYLUM: Chordata
CLASS: Aves
ORDER: Falconiformes
FAMILY: Falconidae
STATUS: Vulnerable, IUCN
Endangered, ESA
RANGE: Mauritius

Kestrel, Mauritius

Falco punctatus

Description and biology

The Mauritius kestrel is a small member of the falcon family. Its plumage (covering of feathers) is mostly reddish–brown in color. The feathers on its breast are white, punctuated by dark heart–shaped markings. The bird has short, rounded wings that allow it to maneuver easily in the air, darting after prey. This kestrel feeds primarily on geckos (small tropical lizards). It also eats insects (dragonflies, cicadas, cockroaches, crickets) and small birds (gray white–eyes, common waxbills, Indian house shrews).

Mauritius kestrels have an estimated home range of 370 to 740 acres (150 to 300 hectares). Their breeding season begins in September or October. Females then lay 3 eggs in a scraped–out hollow on a cliff, which take 30 to 32 days to

An immature Mauritius kestrel after a rainstorm. Young kestrels may stay with their parents for almost a year before venturing out on their own.

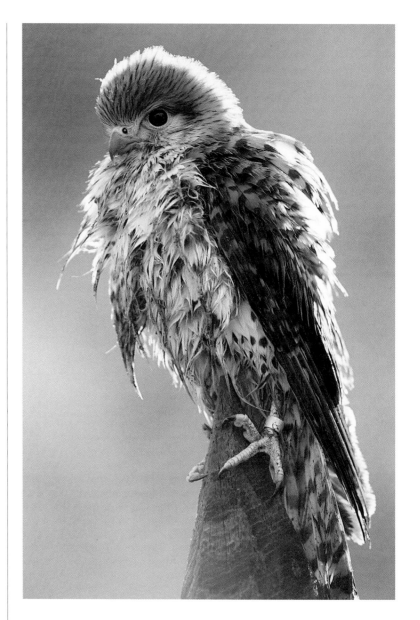

hatch. After hatching, the young kestrels may stay with their parents until the beginning of the next breeding season.

Habitat and current distribution

The Mauritius kestrel is confined to remote areas in the southwestern part of Mauritius Island, which lies in the Indian Ocean about 450 miles (724 kilometers) east of the island of Madagascar. The bird prefers to inhabit cool evergreen forests where the trees form a canopy about 50 feet (15 meters) above the ground.

Biologists (people who study living organisms) estimate the bird's population at 650 kestrels, including about 100 breeding pairs.

History and conservation measures

When Mauritius was covered in vast forests, the kestrel was found throughout the island. Heavy logging and clearing of the forests in the twentieth century quickly destroyed the Mauritius kestrel's habitat and food sources. By the 1950s, the bird was found only in the remote forests of the southwestern plateau. Twenty years later, biologists believed less than 10 birds remained alive.

Conservation efforts have focused on preserving the habitat of the Mauritius kestrel. In 1974, the 8,880–acre (3,552–hectare) Macabé–Bel Ombre Nature Reserve was created. In 1993, a national park linking this and other areas was declared, providing a greater protected region.

A captive–breeding program for the kestrel was initiated in the 1970s. Through this program, researchers have reintroduced Mauritius kestrels into their native habitat and also onto the neighboring island of Réunion. The program has been so successful that the kestrel has been removed from endangered status on the Red List of the International Union for Conservation of Nature and Natural Resources and is now classified as vulnerable.

LOVEBIRD, BLACK–CHEEKED
Agapornis nigrigenis

PHYLUM: Chordata
CLASS: Aves
ORDER: Psittaciformes
FAMILY: Psittacidae
STATUS: Vulnerable, IUCN
RANGE: Botswana, Namibia,
Zambia, Zimbabwe

Lovebird, black-cheeked
Agapornis nigrigenis

Description and biology

Lovebirds are small African parrots. The black–cheeked lovebird is perhaps the most threatened of all lovebird species in the wild. This bird is primarily green, with a black face and cheeks and a white eye–ring. Its forehead is dusky–red. It feeds mainly on seeds, grass seeds, and leaves. Breeding takes place in November and December.

Habitat and current distribution

The black–cheeked lovebird is confined mainly to the extreme southwestern part of Zambia. Outside of Zambia, it is found along the Zambezi River in northern Zimbabwe, at the very northernmost tip of Botswana, and at the eastern tip of the Caprivi Strip in Namibia. The total number of these lovebirds currently in existence is unknown, though it has been estimated that there are less than 10,000 in the wild.

The bird prefers to inhabit medium–altitude forests dominated by deciduous (shedding) trees. The total habitat range is about 2,300 square miles (5,960 square kilometers).

History and conservation measures

In the twentieth century, black–cheeked lovebirds have been trapped and sold around the world as caged pets. During a four–week period in 1929, as many as 16,000 of the birds were captured. The species has never recovered from this assault.

Despite legal protection in Zambia, this lovebird is still trapped illegally. It remains a common cage bird. Another

Although legally protected from being trapped, black–cheeked lovebirds are often illegally caged as pets. It is this illegal trapping that remains one of the biggest threats to the birds' existence.

threat to the black–cheeked lovebird is the draining of water sources in its habitat to supply agricultural needs. The destruction of its habitat to create farmland also remains a potential threat.

Black–cheeked lovebirds have become better established in captivity. Although the captive–bred population is still relatively small, it has grown steadily over the last twenty years.

MACAW, LEAR'S
Anodorhynchus leari

PHYLUM: Chordata
CLASS: Aves
ORDER: Psittaciformes
FAMILY: Psittacidae
STATUS: Critically endangered,
IUCN
Endangered, ESA
RANGE: Brazil

Macaw, Lear's
Anodorhynchus leari

Description and biology

Macaws are members of the parrot family. The Lear's macaw is also known as the indigo macaw because the color of its plumage (covering of feathers) is a beautiful indigo or dark purplish–blue. It has grayish–green accents on its head and breast. A yellow patch appears at the base of the bird's black bill. Its legs are dark gray. An average Lear's macaw measures 30 inches (76 centimeters) long.

This bird uses its bill as well as its feet for climbing. It prefers to eat the small nut that grows on the licuri palm tree. Each day before sunrise, the flock of Lear's macaws is awakened by the loud cawing of individual "scout" macaws. The flock then leaves its nesting area for feeding grounds.

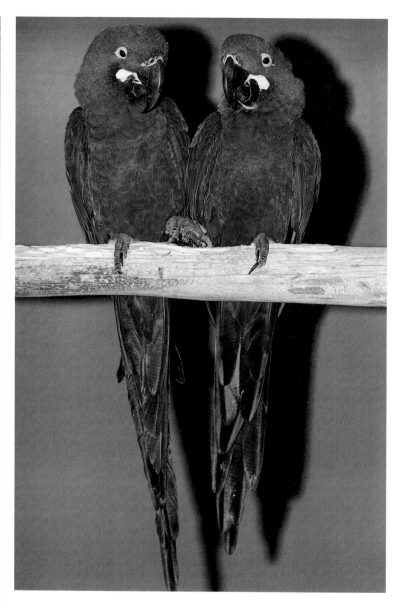

Habitat and current distribution

Little is known about the Lear's macaw mating habits. However, it is known to nest only in the Rasa de Catarina region in the northeastern Brazilian state of Bahia. Biologists (people who study living organisms) estimate the bird's current total population to be 246.

The Lear's macaw prefers to inhabit deep canyons and dry, desertlike plateaus. It nests in burrowed tunnels in the sandstone cliffs of the region. The bird sometimes roosts (rests or sleeps) on cliff faces or ledges.

History and conservation measures

The Lear's macaw is probably one of the rarest parrots in the world. Only captive–bred birds were known until 1979, when biologists discovered a wild population in a remote area of Brazil. In the early 1990s, the population in the wild was only about 65 birds.

Habitat destruction has posed the major threat to the Lear's macaw. Cattle from nearby farms in the bird's habitat feed upon the nut of the licuri palm, limiting the bird's primary food source. The Lear's macaw has also always been hunted by local people for food. An additional threat comes from trappers, who capture the bird for the illegal pet trade. At the end of the 1990s, it was estimated that nearly a quarter of all of the species' nest were raided annually, despite laws protecting the birds.

A number of all–out efforts by several different conservation groups has brought the population up to about 250 birds in 2001 and rising. Current conservation efforts to save the Lear's macaw from extinction include transplanting licuri palms into its habitat and halting illegal smuggling activities.

MAGPIE–ROBIN, SEYCHELLES
Copsychus sechellarum

PHYLUM:	Chordata
CLASS:	Aves
ORDER:	Passeriformes
FAMILY:	Muscicapidae
STATUS:	Critically endangered, IUCN
	Endangered, ESA
RANGE:	Seychelles

Magpie-robin, Seychelles

Copsychus sechellarum

Description and biology

The Seychelles magpie–robin is a thrushlike bird with fairly long legs. The color of its plumage (covering of feathers) is glossy black. Large white patches appear on each wing. The bird's diet includes small lizards and a small amount of fruit.

A female Seychelles magpie–robin lays a single egg, which she incubates (sits on or broods) for 16 to 20 days. After the nestling hatches, it remains in the nest for about 3 weeks. It becomes independent after another 3 to 5 weeks.

Habitat and current distribution

This bird species now survives only on Fregate Island in the Seychelles, a republic consisting of a group of islands in

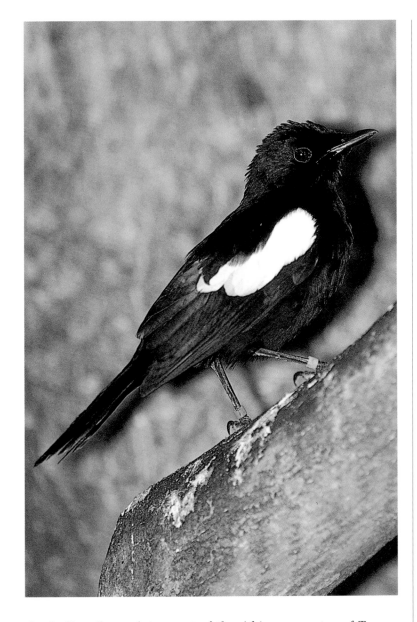

A perched Seychelles magpie–robin. Once very common, the magpie–robin had a close brush with extinction from the 1960s to the 1990s.

the Indian Ocean lying east of the African country of Tanzania. In 2000, biologists (people who study living organisms) estimated that 90 birds existed in the wild.

Historically, the Seychelles magpie–robin inhabited coastal woodland. However, that habitat has been cleared to create farmland. Very few native plants survive on Fregate Island. In response, the bird has adapted to living on plantations that grow cashews, citrus trees, coconut trees, or coffee. It can also be found in vegetable gardens. The bird normally nests in tree holes.

History and conservation measures

Now one of the rarest birds in the world, the magpie–robin was once a very common bird in the Seychelles Islands group. It disappeared quite early in the twentieth century from the islands of Félicité, La Digue, and Praslin. The bird was present on the islands of Marianne and Aride until the 1930s and on Alphonse until the late 1950s. By 1959, only ten pairs were known to survive on Fregate Island.

Although this bird has been able to adapt to the loss of its habitat, it has not fared well against predators brought to the islands by humans. A tame, ground–feeding bird, it has been an easy prey for feral (once domesticated, now wild) cats. In the 1960s, efforts were made to control the feral cat population. By 1982, most had been eliminated. The bird now faces competition for nesting sites and food sources from the Indian myna, a bird that has been introduced recently to Fregate Island. Seychelles magpie–robins eat cockroaches, dead or alive. When people used household pesticides to kill cockroaches, the poisons were also harming the birds.

In 1978, a few Seychelles magpie–robins were transferred to the island of Aride (a cat–free nature preserve) in hopes they would survive and multiply. They did not. In 1980, the total population of the species was 27. In 1990, with the species population down to 23 birds, Birdlife International initiated the Seychelles Magpie–Robin Recovery Program. The conservationists built nest boxes for the birds and provided them with food every day. They replanted native trees in their habitat and banned the use of household pesticides. They began to control the mynah population. They also educated the people of Fregate about the birds. Within a few years the Seychelles magpie–robin population had doubled, and it has continued to rise since then. Although the species is by no means out of danger, it has made remarkable progress.

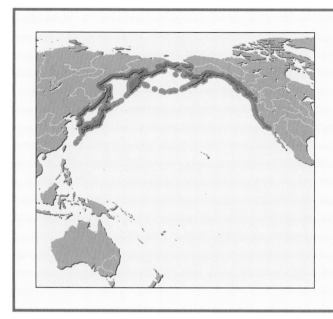

MURRELET, MARBLED
Brachyramphus marmoratus marmoratus

PHYLUM: Chordata

CLASS: Aves

ORDER: Charadriiformes

FAMILY: Alcidae

STATUS: Vulnerable, IUCN Threatened, ESA

RANGE: Canada, USA (Alaska, California, Oregon, Washington)

Murrelet, marbled
Brachyramphus marmoratus marmoratus

Description and biology

The marbled murrelet belongs to the family of diving seabirds known as auks (or alcids), which includes species such as puffins, murres, auklets, and guillemoots. The marbled murrelet is small and chunky, with a wingspan of 9.5 to 10 inches (24 to 25 centimeters). It weighs about 10.5 ounces (300 grams). It has webbed feet, a sharp black bill, and pointed wings. Like many other birds, the murrelet grows two sets of feathers each year. In summer, its plumage (covering of feathers) is marbled in shades of dark brown and whitish–gray. In winter, its upperparts are black while its underparts are white.

Murrelets generally feed within 2 miles (3 kilometers) of shore. They prey on small fish such as sandlance, capelin, herring, and smelt. They pursue their prey underwater, diving well below the surface. Steering with their webbed feet, they use their wings like flippers to propel themselves forward. Often, a dive will last no more than 30 seconds. Predators of

Since marbled murrelets feed close to shore, oil spills and water pollution have become great threats to the birds.

the murrelet include peregrine falcons and bald eagles.

Marbled murrelets nest primarily in old–growth forests where the trees range from 175 to 600 years old. While most nesting sites are located within 12 miles (19 kilometers) of shore, some have been found up to 50 miles (80 kilometers) away from the ocean. They build their nests on natural platforms underneath an overhanging branch, often at a height more than 100 feet (30 meters) above the ground.

Breeding season lasts from mid–April to the end of August. After a male and female marbled murrelet mate, the female lays one large, spotted, yellowish egg. Both the male and the female incubate (sit on or brood) the egg for about 30 days. After hatching, the nestling or young murrelet stays in the nest for about another 28 days before it fledges (develops flying feathers).

Habitat and current distribution

Marbled murrelets are found near coastal waters, bays, and mountains from Alaska's Aleutian Islands and Kenai Peninsula south along the coast of North America to Santa Barbara County in south–central California. In winter, they leave the northernmost parts of their range and travel as far south as San Diego County, California.

In the mid–1990s, biologists (people who study living organisms) estimated the total North American marbled murrelet population to be 360,000. They also estimated that approximately 85 percent of that population bred along the coast of Alaska.

History and conservation measures

Because marbled murrelets face few natural threats in their environment, they can live as long as 25 years. However, human activities can have a serious effect on the birds. Oil pollution, fishing nets, and habitat loss have all combined to threaten the existence of this bird. It is considered critically endangered in California and Oregon, and threatened in Oregon, Washington, and British Columbia. The species remains abundant in Alaska.

The greatest threat to the marbled murrelet is the loss of its habitat due to the clear–cut logging of old–growth forests. In the past century, more than 95 percent of the old–growth forests along the Pacific coast have been cleared. Very little of the existing old–growth forests is currently protected.

Concern has been raised recently about the number of murrelets killed in gill nets, which are fishing nets designed to catch fish by their gills and drown them; however, the nets end up catching many different aquatic creatures, including murrelets. Studies have reported that 600 to 800 or more marbled murrelets are killed annually in gill nets in Prince William Sound, Alaska, alone.

Since the murrelet feeds close to shore, it is highly vulnerable to oil spills and other types of water pollution. The development of the petroleum industry along the Pacific coast has increased the threat of oil pollution in the murrelet's range.

Conservation efforts on behalf of the marbled murrelet include the Headwaters Murrelet Project, a scientific investigation of the bird in northern California. The project is studying the effect of transferring about 7,500 acres (3,000 hectares) of old–growth forest to public ownership and how that might help the continued survival of the marbled murrelet.

OWL, CACTUS FERRUGINOUS PYGMY

Glaucidium brasilianum cactorum

PHYLUM: Chordata
CLASS: Aves
ORDER: Strigiformes
FAMILY: Strigidae
STATUS: Endangered, ESA
RANGE: Mexico, USA (Arizona, Texas)

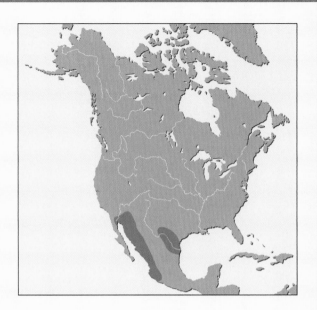

Owl, cactus ferruginous pygmy

Glaucidium brasilianum cactorum

Description and biology

The cactus ferruginous pygmy owl, the most endangered species of owl in the world, is one of three subspecies of the ferruginous pygmy owl. As its name suggests, it is one of the smallest of the owl family, usually measuring less than 7 inches (17 centimeters) long. Males weigh about 2.2 ounces (62 grams), while females weigh more, at about 2.6 ounces (75 grams). The pygmy owl's feathers, or plumage, are usually a reddish–brown color, with a streaked beige belly and crown. The owl has no ear tufts, and on the back of its head there are two black spots outlined in white that look like eyes. The bird has yellow eyes and an unusually long tail for an owl.

The cactus ferruginous pygmy owl flies short distances directly from one perch to another. It will then sit in its perch

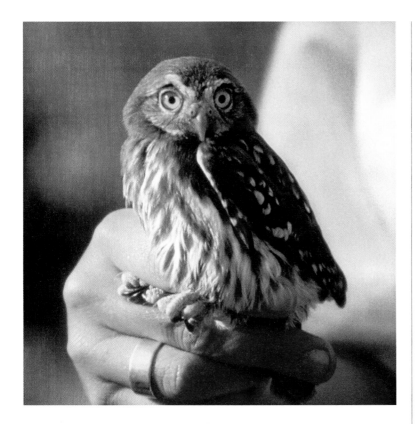

The cactus ferruginous pygmy owl is one of the smallest of the owl family, measuring less than 7 inches, and is the most endangered species of owl in the world.

in a tree branch for hours. It is diurnal, or active during the day, and an avid hunter. Its diet is comprised of birds, lizards, insects, small mammals, frogs, and earthworms. It roosts at night in holes in trees or large cacti in dense desert scrub thickets. Its call is made up of a series of short, shrill notes. The small owl is nonmigratory—it does not travel seasonally to other habitats.

The cactus ferruginous pygmy owl begins its nesting activities in early spring. It usually nests in holes in trees or in cacti—most often in the large saguaro cactus in holes dug out by woodpeckers. The female lays between three and six eggs at a time. Incubation (sitting on the eggs to keep them warm until they hatch) lasts for about 28 days. Within another 28 days, the owlets will begin to fly.

Habitat and current distribution

The cactus ferruginous pygmy owl's range is from central Arizona south through western Mexico to the states of Colima and Michoacan, and from southern Texas south through the Mexican states of Tamaulipas and Nuevo Leon. The species is most likely to be found in desert oases or washes where there is moisture—along the banks of streams or other waterways—and where they can find a good variety of the animals they eat. They generally live at elevations below 4,000 feet (1,200 meters).

In 2002 a total of 18 cactus ferruginous pygmy owls were found in Arizona. Some of the pygmy owl's habitat is found in the fastest–growing areas of Tucson, where a few adult owls remain. There have also been a few sightings of these owls in Texas. The reported sightings in western Mexico are not complete enough to form population estimates, but the species is more common there.

History and conservation measures

At one time cactus ferruginous pygmy owls in Arizona ranged from an area north of Phoenix to the Mexican border. Due to habitat loss, however, the few remaining owls in the state are found only between Tucson and the Mexican border. The decline in population is due to the destruction of the pygmy owl's preferred environments: both riparian (on the banks of natural waterways) and desert habitats. The plight of the Arizona owls is dire. Housing developments, clearing for farming and logging, water diversion, livestock overgrazing, and many other symptoms of the ever–growing human population in the area have severely reduced the habitat of the species.

The U.S. Fish and Wildlife Service listed the Arizona population of pygmy owl as an endangered species in March 1997, designating 731,000 acres of protected critical habitat. Since that time there has been a battle between conservationists (people who work to protect and preserve the natural world) and the developers of urban sprawl—the people responsible for building housing, shopping malls, and related industry farther out into the desert, who stand to lose money if the land cannot be developed. In 1998, conservationists sued to stop a school from being built on the critical habitat of the pygmy owl. The courts ruled against them, allowing the school construction to continue. The National Association of Home Builders sued to have the cactus ferruginous pygmy owl removed from endangered status. The Southern Arizona Home Builders Association then fought to have the critical habitat designation removed from the area selected for the pygmy owl. In September 2001, a federal judge complied with their wishes, removing the critical habitat protection from the land until further studies could be accomplished. In 2003, a new proposal for critical habitat for the pygmy owl was issued. If enacted, it will encompass 1,208,001 acres (489,070 hectares), but there is very little time left for the cactus ferruginous pygmy owl. The species appears to be on the brink of extinction.

OWL, NORTHERN SPOTTED
Strix occidentalis caurina

PHYLUM: Chordata

CLASS: Aves

ORDER: Strigiformes

FAMILY: Strigidae

STATUS: Lower risk: near threatened, IUCN Threatened, ESA

RANGE: Canada (British Columbia), USA (California, Oregon, Washington)

Owl, northern spotted

Strix occidentalis caurina

Description and biology

The northern spotted owl is one of three subspecies of spotted owl. This owl has chocolate brown plumage (covering of feathers) that is speckled with white or light brown spots. It has a round face and dark eyes surrounded by light facial disks. An average northern spotted owl measures 16 to 19 inches (41 to 48 centimeters) long and has a wingspan of about 42 inches (107 centimeters). Females are slightly larger than males.

Northern spotted owls have very keen hearing and vision. Although sometimes active during the day, they are mainly nocturnal (active at night). They perch on trees and then swoop down to catch their prey. Mammals—especially the northern flying squirrel—make up 90 percent of the owl's diet. Birds and insects make up the other 10 percent. Predators of the northern spotted owl include the great horned owl, the northern goshawk, and the red–tailed hawk.

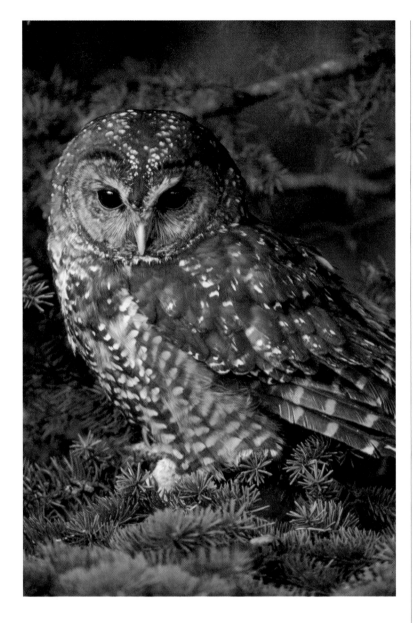

The northern spotted owl population is in decline because of increased logging by the lumber industry. This logging eliminates the trees in which the owls live.

The northern spotted owl's home range can vary widely. Depending on the amount of food available in the area, the type of habitat, and the geographic location, this range can extend from 2,000 to 14,000 acres (800 to 5,600 hectares). Biologists (people who study living organisms) believe male and female northern spotted owls mate for life. The female lays a clutch (eggs produced at one time) of 2 to 4 eggs in a naturally occurring nest such as a broken–top tree or a cavity in an older tree. She alone incubates (sits on or broods) the eggs. During incubation, the male hunts for food. After the nestlings hatch, they are cared for by both parents until they leave the nest three to five weeks after birth.

Habitat and current distribution

The northern spotted owl is found from southern British Columbia, Canada, south to Marin County, California (the other subspecies inhabit California, the U.S. Southwest, and Mexico). In the northern part of this area, the owl's range extends from sea level up to elevations of 5,000 feet (1,524 meters). In the southern part, its range extends to elevations of 7,500 feet (2,286 meters). Although not quite sure, biologists believe between 3,000 and 5,000 pairs of northern spotted owls currently exist in the wild.

This owl lives almost exclusively in old–growth forests dominated by Douglas fir, western hemlock, and redwood trees. "Old growth" refers to forests made up of trees that are at least 200 years old and that haven't been cut or altered in any way by man. Additionally, the physical structure of an old–growth forest is very complex. It has multiple layers in its canopy, trees of varying sizes, and many standing dead trees and dead logs that provide cavities for nesting sites.

History and conservation measures

The northern spotted owl has been at the center of a battle between lumber companies and environmentalists. Timber from old–growth forests is highly valued by loggers because of its fibrous, grainy nature. The Pacific Northwest region has some of the last remaining old–growth forests in America, and roughly 80 percent of that has already been cleared. Of the forest that remains, 90 percent is on federally owned land. Once the northern spotted owl was placed on the Endangered Species List in 1990, logging of the remaining old–growth forests was curtailed, and the debate over the fate of old–growth forests and the northern spotted owl became a federal issue.

Lumber companies have argued that preserving old–growth forests will simply cost jobs—as many as 12,000 people would be put out of work. Environmentalists counter that the lumber companies are simply delaying what is destined to happen: at the rate lumber companies are cutting trees, the old–growth forests will soon disappear, and just as many people will become unemployed. In addition, old–growth forests are necessary for the survival of many species, such as the northern spotted owl, the marbled murrelet, and the red–cockaded woodpecker.

In 1995, the U.S. Fish and Wildlife Service and the Weyerhaeuser Company (a lumber company) agreed to a recovery plan. The plan designated areas of forest as protected owl habitat. In between those areas, Weyerhaeuser was allowed to cut down enough timber to maintain its yearly production levels. The federal government and the lumber company hoped this was tthe beginning of a solution to save both jobs and the northern spotted owl. In 2000, after five years under this plan, it was reported that the decline in the owl population had slowed from 4.5 percent a year to 3.9 percent a year. The drop was far less than conservationists had hoped.

PARAKEET, GOLDEN
Aratinga guarouba (also guarouba guarouba)

PHYLUM: Chordata
CLASS: Aves
ORDER: Psittaciformes
FAMILY: Psittacidae
STATUS: Endangered, IUCN
Endangered, ESA
RANGE: Brazil

Parakeet, golden

Aratinga guarouba (also Guarouba guarouba)

Description and biology

Parakeets belong to the parrot family: they are, in fact, small parrots. The golden parakeet, also known as the golden conure, has a distinctive yellow–and–green plumage (covering of feathers). Because these colors are the same as those making up the national flag of Brazil, some Brazilians believe the golden parakeet should be adopted as the national bird.

This parakeet forages in the treetops for fruits, berries, seeds, and nuts. It also feeds on some farm crops, especially corn. Depending upon its environment, the bird faces different predators. Toucans prey on the golden parakeet's eggs and young in clearings. In the forest, monkeys and snakes are its main predators.

The golden parakeet is a very social creature. It roosts (rests or sleeps) with up to 9 fellow parakeets in a single tree hole.

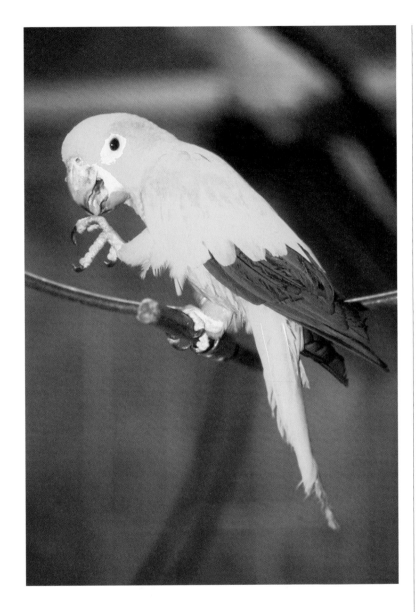

A perched golden parakeet. The bird is highly prized as a pet, and collectors have been known to pay more than $15,000 to own one.

When moving between roosting and feeding areas, the birds move in flocks of up to 30. Breeding season lasts between December and April. Females in a group all lay their eggs—2 to 3 apiece—in a single nest located in the cavity of an isolated tree 50 to 100 feet (15 to 30 meters) tall. The cavity is usually in the highest part of the trunk or in a high, thick branch. Both males and females incubate (sit on or brood) the eggs for about 30 days. They also share in raising the young after the nestlings have hatched.

Habitat and current distribution

The range of the golden parakeet in northern Brazil extends from the northwestern part of the state of Maranhao west through the state of Pará. Scientists have recently discovered a small population in the western Brazilian state of Rondônia. This has led them to believe that the bird may have expanded its historic range. No estimates of the golden parakeet's total population size currently exist.

The golden parakeet prefers to inhabit tropical rain forests. During breeding season, it seeks out cleared areas with isolated trees near forests.

History and conservation measures

Scientists have long considered the golden parakeet rare. Where good forest remains, the bird may still be seen regularly. Nonetheless, the overall number of golden parakeets has declined sharply.

Habitat destruction is the primary threat to the golden parakeet. Wanton (merciless) clearing of the tropical forest to build roads and settlements has destroyed much of the bird's habitat in Maranhao. Major development projects such as railroad construction, lumbering, cattle ranching, and gold mining have also contributed to the decline of its habitat.

Another serious threat to the golden parakeet is illegal capture. It is among the most highly prized birds in the world, selling to collectors for more than $15,000. Despite legal protection, the golden parakeet is still smuggled within Brazil and around the world. In addition to live capture, the bird is hunted for food or sport and is killed because it eats corn crops.

The only nature reserve currently in the golden parakeet's western range is the Tapajós (Amazonia) National Park in Pará. Further areas in its range must be protected and managed so the golden parakeet can survive and breed.

PARROT, IMPERIAL
Amazona imperialis

PHYLUM: Chordata
CLASS: Aves
ORDER: Psittaciformes
FAMILY: Psittacidae
STATUS: Endangered, IUCN
Endangered, ESA
RANGE: Dominica

Parrot, imperial

Amazona imperialis

Description and biology

The imperial parrot, known as sisserou in the Caribbean republic of Dominica, is a large parrot. An average adult measures 18 to 20 inches (46 to 51 centimeters) in length and weighs about 2 pounds (0.9 kilograms). It has a wingspan of about 30 inches (76 centimeters). The color of the bird's plumage (covering of feathers) on its upper parts and back is green. Its head is greenish–blue, and it has a red streak on its wingtips. The bird feeds primarily on seeds, fruit, young shoots, vines, and shrubs.

Parrots mate for life. The imperial parrot's breeding season lasts from February to June, with peak breeding taking place between March and May. Male and female pairs rarely leave their nesting territory throughout the year. On average,

The imperial parrot is unique to the island of Dominica. It is Dominica's national bird, and its image appears at the center of the republic's flag.

a female imperial parrot lays two eggs every other year in a nest high in the trunk of a tree. It is unknown how long it takes the eggs to hatch. After they do hatch, usually only one of the nestlings is raised to adulthood.

Habitat and current distribution

The imperial parrot is unique to the island of Dominica, which lies in the center of the Lesser Antilles between Guadeloupe and Martinique. It is Dominica's national bird, and its image appears at the center of the republic's flag.

The parrot seems to be confined to rain forests on the east, north, and west slopes on the upper reaches of Morne Diablotin, a mountain peak in the northern part of the island. It is found chiefly at elevations between 1,500 and 3,300 feet (457 and 1,006 meters). In the early 1990s, biologists (people who study living organisms) estimated that 80 to 120 imperial parrots existed in the wild. Since then, the population has increased somewhat, but it is still under 250 birds.

History and conservation measures

In the past, the imperial parrot was probably found throughout the mountainous island of Dominica, although the center of its range has most likely always been Morne Diablotin.

Early threats to the parrot included hunting for food, for sport, and for the pet trade. In the 1880s, a road was built through the bird's forest habitat, allowing hunters easy access. They continued to plague the imperial parrot into the 1970s. Predators brought into the bird's range—including opossums, rats, boas, and hawks—may have also played a part in the decline of the species.

Because of its remote range, habitat destruction was not considered a threat to the parrot until recently. Beginning in the 1980s, prime forest land bordering the imperial parrot's habitat has been cleared and converted into farmland. There have been reports that aerial spraying of nearby banana crops with pesticides has led to the deaths of many parrots.

Following Hurricane David, which stuck Dominica in 1979 and destroyed millions of trees, officials imposed a ban on the hunting of all wildlife. Forest patrols have since kept most hunters at bay. Conservationists (people protecting the natural world) are currently trying to raise funds to purchase privately owned parrot habitat before it can be cleared. A plan has also been established to designate one of the most important imperial parrot habitat areas at Morne Diablotin as a national park. The efforts have had good effect, and the population of the Imperial parrot has risen, although slowly, in the early years of the twenty–first century.

DID YOU KNOW?

Aviculture (pronounced A–vi–kul–chur) is the keeping and raising of birds—especially wild birds—in captivity. Humans have kept songbirds and other caged birds for thousands of years. Until about the mid–twentieth century, the hobby of aviculture centered on birds such as canaries and fancy pigeons. Since then, however, bird keepers have learned to successfully breed parrots and other exotic wild birds in captivity. As a result, the demand for parrots as caged birds increased, and large numbers were captured in the wild to meet the new demand. Not surprisingly, many parrot species were put at risk. International conservation organizations soon opposed the capture of wild parrots, and concerned nations enacted laws against the capture and trade of wild birds.

PARROT, THICK-BILLED
Rhynchopsitta pachyrhyncha

PHYLUM: Chordata
CLASS: Aves
ORDER: Psittaciformes
FAMILY: Psittacidae
STATUS: Endangered, IUCN
Endangered, ESA
RANGE: Mexico

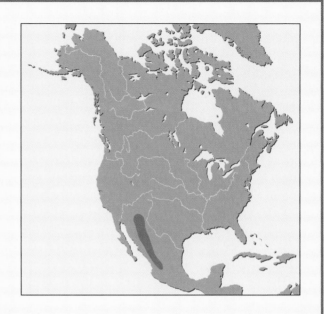

Parrot, thick-billed

Rhynchopsitta pachyrhyncha

Description and biology

The thick-billed parrot is about 15 inches (38 centimeters) long from head to tail. It is a bright green bird with a red forehead and red patches at the crook of the wing and thigh. Its eyes are marked with a small brownish spot and it has yellow sections under its wings and gray feathers on its lower surfaces. It has gray legs and feet and its thick bill is black.

Thick-billed parrots feed mainly on the seeds of pine trees, shredding the pinecones of a variety of conifers (evergreen trees and shrubs) in order to extract the seeds. They also eat acorns, juniper berries, flower nectar, insects, and tree bark. They hunt during the day and sleep in their roosting places high in the pine trees at night. Thick-billed parrots live in flocks, which may be as small as seven or eight members or they may be comprised of a thousand or more birds. They are strong flyers, often forming a V or other formation when they

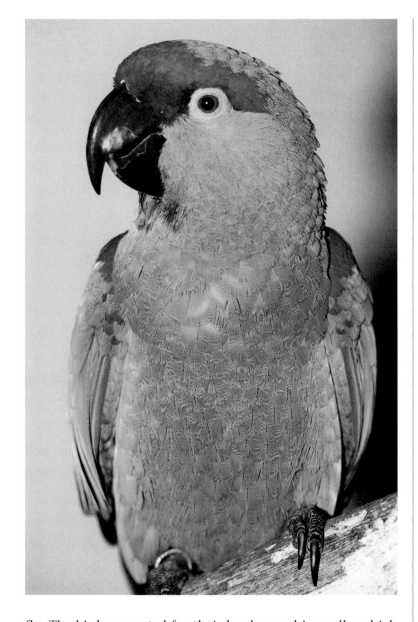

Thick-billed parrots are noted for their loud screeching calls, which can be heard from great distances.

fly. The birds are noted for their loud screeching calls, which can be heard from great distances.

Thick-billed parrots breed from July through September, nesting in cavities of trees at high elevations. The female lays from two to four eggs, with spaces of one or two days between each egg. While she incubates the eggs (sits on them to keep them warm), the male goes off during the day to get food and bring it back to her. About 26 to 28 days later the eggs hatch, one at a time, as they were laid. The chicks will have their full plumage (feathers) within 56 days of their birth and they will fly shortly thereafter. The parents remain with them up to about seven months, continuing to feed them as they instruct them how to extract seeds from pinecones for themselves.

Thick-billed parrots live under constant threat from predators. When they feed, they often have one bird in the flock standing watch for predators, ready to signal to the other birds the moment an enemy is spotted. Their main enemies are raptors (birds of prey), such as red-tailed hawks, Apache goshawks, and peregrine falcons. When they are roosting in the trees they are also preyed upon by ring-tailed cats.

Habitat and current distribution

Thick-billed parrots spend the nesting season in the conifer forests of the northern Sierra Madre Occidental Mountains, mainly in the states of Durango and Chihuahua in northern Mexico. After the breeding season, the birds form flocks and migrate south. They prefer to nest and roost at high elevations, above 6,500 feet (1,981 meters).

An estimated population of 500 to 2,000 pairs (male and female partners) survives today.

History and conservation measures

Thick-billed parrots once ranged from their primary habitat in northern and central Mexico as far north as southeastern Arizona and southwestern New Mexico. Early settlers in the southwest United States hunted the birds for food, virtually wiping out the entire U.S. population by the 1920s. (Some birds, though, were reintroduced to the wild in the Southwest in the 1980s.) The species continued to live in its main habitat in Mexico, but during the last decades of the twentieth century, the extensive logging in the Sierra Madre Occidental Mountains greatly reduced the population in Mexico. Thick-billed parrots are also captured for trade as pets.

Numerous studies are underway in an attempt to determine how to save the thick-billed parrot as its habitat continues to diminish. The World Parrot Trust provides funding to groups that attempt to determine the species' habitat requirements and study the effects of moving the birds to a new habitat. The Instituto Tecnologico de Estudios Superiores de Monterrey, in Nuevo Leon, Mexico, in collaboration with the

U.S. Fish and Wildlife Service, has provided funds to protect the breeding range of the thick-billed parrot in Nuevo Leon, Mexico, through the development of management plans and training. Because of the dangers posed by trade in the pet market, the Convention on International Trade in Endangered Species of Wild Fauna and Flora (CITES) listed the thick-billed parrot on its Apendix 1, which includes species threatened with extinction. This listing makes trade of the species subject to particularly strict trade regulations, authorized only under "exceptional circumstances."

PARTRIDGE, SICHUAN HILL
Arborophila rufipectus

PHYLUM: Chordata
CLASS: Aves
ORDER: Galliformes
FAMILY: Phasianidae
STATUS: Endangered, IUCN
RANGE: China

Partridge, Sichuan hill
Arborophila rufipectus

Description and biology

The Sichuan hill partridge, or Sichuan partridge, is very rare and shy of humans. Little was known about the species until studies were initiated in the 1990s. This partridge is about 11 inches (28 centimeters) long. It is grayish–brown in color, with white markings on its forehead, a brown crown, distinctive markings around its eyes, and a black–streaked white throat. Males and females are similar in appearance except that the female coloring is not as bright.

When searching for food, the Sichuan hill partridge generally forages in the growth and litter (dead leaves and twigs) of a forest floor. The species is territorial. Sichuan hill partridge male–female pairs will often send out territorial calls together. These are loud, repetitious whistles. Wildlife biologists (people who study living organisms) have begun to study the behavior of the species, but little information is currently available about breeding or other social behavior.

The Sichuan hill partridge is found in warm forest environments in which some of the trees have leaves rather than needles at elevations of 3,600 to 7,300 feet.

Habitat and current distribution

The Sichuan hill partridge is found in subtropical broadleaf forests (warm forest environments in which some of the trees have leaves rather than needles) at elevations of 3,600 to 7,300 feet (1,100 to 2,250 meters). The species is endemic to (is native to and occurs only in) China. In 1997, Sichuan hill partridge populations were found in six forest areas in Ebian, Leibo and Mabian counties within the Daliang Shan mountains of south central Sichuan province, and in Pingshan, Suijiang and Yongshan counties within the Wumeng Shan mountains of northeastern Yunnan. The total population of the species has been estimated to be between 860 and 1,722 birds.

History and conservation measures

The primary threat to the Sichuan hill partridge is logging, which has severely reduced its habitat. The broadleaf forests in China it requires for survival have been rapidly disappearing for years. By the early 1990s, all of the remaining broadleaf forests inhabited by the species were scheduled to be logged. If not for the intervention of conservationists (people who work to protect and preserve the natural world), the habitat would have been wiped out entirely. There were other threats to the partridge as well. Humans were gathering bamboo shoots, and livestock was grazing in the remaining forest areas, greatly disturbing the birds' normal behavior patterns. Since little was known about the species' habitat requirements, many predicted that the partridge would be extinct by 2030.

Fortunately, in the mid–1990s, several major projects were undertaken by a variety of Chinese and international conservation groups in an effort to understand and protect the Sichuan hill partridge. The studies brought in vital information about the species' distribution, population density, and habitat requirements. They revealed that altering forestry practices could benefit the partridge, especially if strips of primary forest were left along ridge tops and broadleaf trees were replanted where they had been cleared. Extensive work is continuing, because scientists have determined that the Sichuan hill partridge serves as an excellent indicator of the ecological health of the whole region. If the species is declining, it is a clear signal of major problems throughout the ecosystem (the ecological community, including plants, animals, and microorganisms, considered together with their environment).

As it became apparent that the Sichuan hill partridge population was very low and fragmented, conservation groups put pressure on the Chinese government to alter its logging and forest management practices. Soon the Sichuan hill partridge became a protected species within China. Other circumstances caused the Chinese government to rethink its logging practices. In 1998, catastrophic (very destructive) flooding of the Yangtze River was linked to the logging of the slopes around it. At the same time, there were concerns about the effects that deforestation (removing all trees) was having on the Three Gorges Dam, a huge new dam on the river. In August 1998, the Chinese government enacted a ban on logging in the area, which happened to be part of the partridge's range. Since that time, local people who used to be loggers in the area have been put to work replanting the forests.

In 2001, the Sichuan Forestry Department created the first protected area for the Sichuan hill partridge at Laojunshan. There, conservationists are putting new forest management practices in effect, trying to find methods that will conserve the area for the benefit of the Sichuan hill partridge as well as for other species, including humans.

PELICAN, DALMATION
Pelecanus crispus

PHYLUM: Chordata
CLASS: Aves
ORDER: Pelecaniformes
FAMILY: Pelecanidae
STATUS: Lower risk, conservation dependent, IUCN
RANGE: Afghanistan, Albania, Armenia, Azerbaijan, Bangladesh, Bulgaria, China, Egypt, Greece, India, Iran, Iraq, Kazakhstan, Lebanon, Mongolia, Pakistan, Romania, Russia, Serbia and Montenegro, Syria, Turkey, Turkmenistan, Ukraine, Uzbekistan

Pelican, Dalmation
Pelecanus crispus

Description and biology

The Dalmation pelican is the largest member of the pelican family. An average adult measures 5.2 to 5.9 feet (1.6 to 1.8 meters) and weighs between 22 and 29 pounds (10 and 13 kilograms). Males are slightly larger than females. The bird has a wingspan of almost 11 feet (3.3 meters), and its long, straight bill measures between 14 and 17.5 inches (35.5 and 44.5 centimeters) in length.

This pelican has long, curly feathers on the nape of its neck. Its overall plumage (covering of feathers) is white–gray in color. Dark fingerlike tips mark the edges of its wings. Its legs and feet are gray–black. Its pouch, which is attached to the lower part of its bill, is yellow in color most of the year. During breeding season, it turns orange–red.

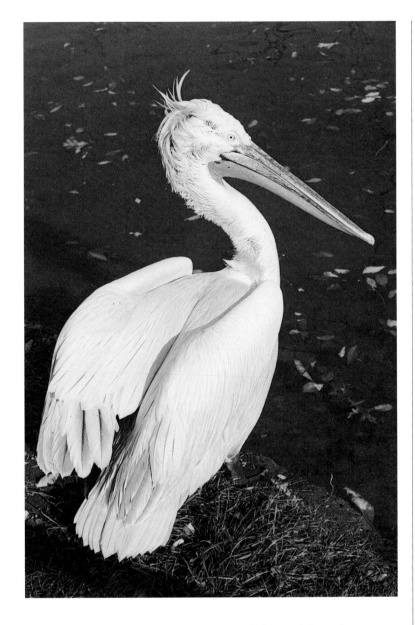

Although awkward walkers, Dalmation pelicans are good fliers and strong swimmers.

The Dalmation pelican is a good flier, although it must make a heavy running start in order to take off. Once in the air, however, the bird is fast and soars easily. On land, the pelican waddles and moves awkwardly because of its large, webbed feet. In water, these feet make the bird a strong swimmer. Hunting mainly by plunging its head under water, the Dalmation pelican feeds on a variety of fish.

Breeding season for the pelican takes place between February and April. The female, assisted by the male, builds a nest out of reed stalks, grass, and branches. She then lays a clutch (eggs produced at one time) of 1 to 4 eggs, and both male and female incubate (sit on or brood) them for 32 days. The nestlings fledge (develop flying feathers) about 80 days after they hatch, but remain dependent on their parents for 3 more weeks. Crows, magpies, and gulls prey on the pelican's eggs.

Habitat and current distribution

The Dalmation pelican breeds from Yugoslavia (Montenegro) to Mongolia and winters from Albania to China. Biologists (people who study living organisms) estimate that the bird's total world population is between 4,000 and 5,000 breeding pairs.

This species of pelican prefers to inhabit estuaries, lagoons, rivers, deltas, lakes, and coastal waters. Its nests are found in overgrown reeds and along seasides, lakes, deltas, and the lower reaches of rivers.

History and conservation measures

The Dalmation pelican was once found throughout Asia and Europe, numbering in the millions. In fact, in 1873 there were apparently millions of pelicans in the country of Romania alone. During the twentieth century, the bird's population drastically declined.

Great numbers of Dalmation pelicans have been killed by fishermen, who view the birds as competitors for fish. They have also been hunted for food and for the skin of their pouches. Much of their habitat has been lost, as wetlands have been cleared to create farmland. Electric power lines, installed to service a growing human population throughout the bird's range, have killed many flying pelicans.

Reserves and national parks in a number of areas protect colonies of Dalmation pelicans—particularly the largest Dalmation pelican colony at Lake Mikri Prespa in Greece—and the population has begun to recover. The International Union for Conservation of Nature and Natural Resources (IUCN) upgraded the bird's status from vulnerable to lower risk in 2000. But without the conservations and special protections that have been responsible for its new growth, the Dalmatian pelican would quickly become threatened again, so it is listed as conservation dependent.

PENGUIN, YELLOW-EYED
Megadyptes antipodes

PHYLUM: Chordata
CLASS: Aves
ORDER: Sphenisciformes
FAMILY: Spheniscidae
STATUS: Endangered, IUCN
RANGE: New Zealand

Penguin, yellow-eyed
Megadyptes antipodes

Description and biology

Penguins are flightless sea birds. Like other penguins, the yellow–eyed penguin is mainly gray and white in color. What separates this penguin from others are its striking crown of yellow feathers and its bright, yellow eyes. Its cheeks are pale yellow, and its bill and feet are beige.

An average adult yellow–eyed penguin can measure 30 inches (76 centimeters) long and weigh 11 pounds (5 kilograms). Its torpedo–shaped body allows the bird to travel swiftly in water, where it catches squid, crustaceans (such as crabs and shrimp), and small fish. On land, the penguin shuffles along on well–used paths from the sea to grassy cliffs and inland forests. It often walks more than 0.5 mile (0.8 kilometer) a day.

Penguins are normally very social, but the yellow–eyed penguin is sometimes only mildly so. It may live in colonies

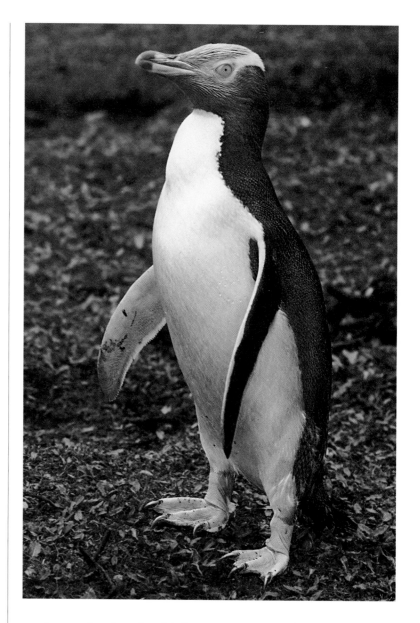

Its crown of yellow feathers and bright, yellow eyes are what differentiate a yellow–eyed penguin from other types of penguins.

made up of only a few birds or as many as 50 pairs. Penguins tend to mate for life. The breeding season for yellow–eyed penguins lasts only from late September to mid–October. Their nests, made of sticks and coarse grass, are located in holes in the ground, among rocks, or within stunted trees or shrubs.

A female yellow–eyed penguin lays 2 eggs, the second of which is laid 4 days after the first. Both parents incubate (sit on or brood) the eggs for about 42 days. Upon birth, the chicks are covered in fine, short, dark brown feathers. As they grow older, their distinctive yellow crown begins to emerge. When they are about six weeks old, the chicks are left alone in the nest, and they may venture out to sea shortly thereafter.

Habitat and current distribution

The yellow–eyed penguin is found in New Zealand on South, Stewart, Codfish, Campbell, and Auckland Islands. Biologists (people who study living organisms) estimate that between 5,000 and 6,000 of these penguins currently exist.

The birds prefer to inhabit coastal waters. They feed in inshore waters and roost (rest or sleep) on sandy beaches.

History and conservation measures

The primary threat to the yellow–eyed penguin has been the disturbance or destruction of its nesting habitat. Much of its habitat has been converted into farmland. Other areas have been degraded or worn down by grazing livestock from nearby farms. Predators that have been brought into the area by humans (such as dogs, cats, and pigs), have taken their toll on the bird's population.

Yellow–eyed penguins have also suffered at the hands of fishermen. The birds often become tangled in fishing nets, and many have died as a result. Pesticides and other forms of pollution have also killed many yellow–eyed penguins by contaminating their food sources.

Wildlife organizations in New Zealand have purchased nesting sites to preserve what remains of the yellow–eyed penguin's habitat. Within these sites, they have removed introduced predators and have begun to replant trees and other types of vegetation.

PHEASANT, CHEER
Catreus wallichii

PHYLUM: Chordata
CLASS: Aves
ORDER: Galliformes
FAMILY: Phasianidae
STATUS: Vulnerable, IUCN
Endangered, ESA
RANGE: India, Nepal, Pakistan

Pheasant, cheer

Catreus wallichii

Description and biology

The male cheer pheasant has a striking appearance. The color of the plumage (covering of feathers) on its neck and upper back is silvery–gray. The feathers on its lower back are reddish. Its tail, measuring 18 to 24 (46 to 61 centimeters) inches long, is marked with heavy, dark bars. The male has an overall length of 35 to 47 inches (89 to 119 centimeters). Females are not so dramatically colored and are smaller, measuring 24 to 30 inches (61 to 76 centimeters) in length. This pheasant is mainly vegetarian (plant-eating). It digs for roots and seeds with its stout feet and beak. It also plucks at leaves, shoots, and berries on the ground or in shrubs.

Breeding takes place in the spring. A male–female pair and one of their young male offspring defend a territory of 38 to 100 acres (15 to 40 hectares). This territory is often called the "crowing area" because of the sound the males make at dawn

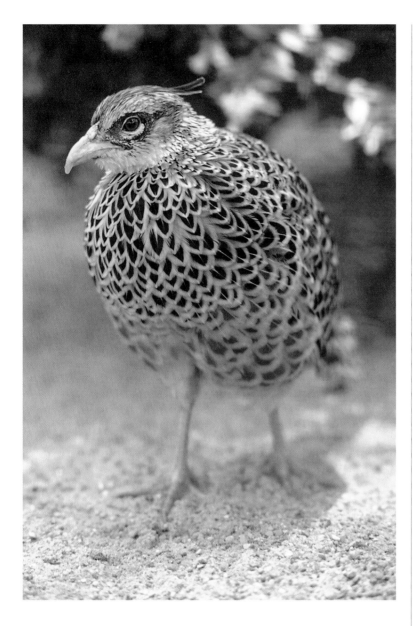

The cheer pheasant inhabits grassy hillsides with scattered patches of oak and pine and is often found grazing close to hill villages.

and dusk as a sign of defense. After building a shallow nest on the ground among boulders or stunted shrubs, a female cheer pheasant lays a clutch (eggs produced at one time) of 8 to 10 eggs. She then incubates (sits on or broods) the eggs for 26 to 28 days. After hatching, the chicks stay with their parents until the following spring. When not breeding, cheer pheasant families many come together to form flocks of 15 or more birds.

Habitat and current distribution

The cheer pheasant's range extends southeast from the northern Indian state of Himachal Pradesh to the Kali–Gandaki Valley in central Nepal. A small population has recently been discovered in Pakistan. The exact number of pheasants in this range is currently unknown.

The pheasant inhabits grassy hillsides with scattered patches of oak and pine at elevations between 3,280 and 10,665 feet (1,000 and 3,250 meters). It is often found grazing close to hill villages.

History and conservation measures

Because cheer pheasants are found in groups that stay in one place, they are easily hunted. Despite having legal protection throughout their range, the birds are widely shot and trapped. Cheer pheasants have also suffered because cattle graze on their habitat and farmers often burn their grassy hillsides to create cleared land for farming.

Cheer pheasants are protected in the Margalla Hills National Park in Pakistan. However, park officials have allowed dense thorn shrubs to grow, overtaking the extensive grasslands inhabited by the cheer pheasants there. Because of this, a program to reintroduce captive–born pheasants into the park has not been successful.

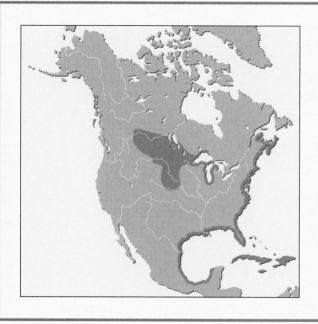

PLOVER, PIPING
Charadrius melodus

PHYLUM: Chordata
CLASS: Aves
ORDER: Charadriiformes
FAMILY: Charadriidae
STATUS: Vulnerable, IUCN
Threatened, ESA
Endangered, ESA (Great Lakes)
RANGE: Bahamas, Barbados,
Bermuda, Canada, Cuba,
Dominican Republic, Haiti,
Jamaica, Mexico, Puerto Rico,
USA, Virgin Islands (British),
Virgin Islands (US)

Plover, piping
Charadrius melodus

Description and biology

The piping plover is so–named because of its distinctive call, a two–note piping or peeping sound. The color of this shore bird's plumage (covering of feathers) is sandy–beige above and white below. It has a short black bill and yellow legs. During breeding season, the piping plover develops black markings on its forehead and throat. Its bill turns orange, except at the tip, which remains black. Its legs also turn bright orange.

This bird's diet includes insects and small marine animals such as crawfish, snails, and clams. It locates its food by following the backwash of waves, which deposit or uncover these animals on beaches. The bird's predators include racoons, foxes, opossums, gulls, skunks, rats, and feral (once domesticated, now wild) cats and dogs.

Breeding season takes place between March and August. The male piping plover courts the female with both aerial (flying) and ground displays or movements. After having mated, the female lays a clutch (eggs produced at one time) of 4 eggs in a shallow hollow in the ground lined with pebbles or plant debris. Both the male and female incubate (sit on or brood) the eggs for about 30 days. The chicks fledge (develop flying feathers) approximately 30 days after they hatch.

Habitat and current distribution

The piping plover is found on open beaches and sand and mud flats in North America. It breeds primarily in three regions: the Atlantic coast from southern Canada to North Carolina, along rivers and wetlands in the Great Plains from southern Canada to Nebraska, and the western Great Lakes. In winter, the bird migrates to coastal areas and sand flats from the Carolinas south to Yucatán, Mexico. It also migrates to the Bahamas and other islands of the West Indies.

In the early 1990s, biologists (people who study living organisms) estimated that only 2,500 piping plover pairs existed. The majority, over 1,350, were found on the Great Plains. Only about 16 pairs inhabited the Great Lakes, a region where the piping plover is labeled endangered.

History and conservation measures

The piping plover was almost certainly more plentiful at the beginning of the twentieth century than it is today. The earliest cause of the bird's decline was excessive hunting. Now that hunting of the plover is outlawed, habitat disturbance and destruction are its main threats.

Because the piping plover nests on open coastal beaches, it is easily disturbed by humans and their pets. In addition, the bird has lost much of its nesting area as beaches and other waterfronts have been converted into recreational and living areas for humans. This has been especially true in the Great Lakes region.

Many conservation efforts to protect the piping plover's nesting areas are currently being undertaken. These include restricting the use of off–road vehicles on beaches and building barriers around nests to prevent contact by humans and predators.

QUETZAL, RESPLENDENT
Pharomachrus mocinno

PHYLUM: Chordata

CLASS: Aves

ORDER: Trogoniformes

FAMILY: Trogonidae

STATUS: Lower risk, near threatened, IUCN Endangered, ESA

RANGE: Costa Rica, El Salvador, Guatemala, Honduras, Mexico, Nicaragua, Panama

Quetzal, resplendent
Pharomachrus mocinno

Description and biology

The resplendent quetzal (pronounced ket–SAL) is a stunning forest bird, considered to be among the most beautiful in the Western Hemisphere. Although both males and females have crested feathers on their heads and brilliant green upperparts, the color of the plumage (covering of feathers) on the rest of the body differs. Females have brown breasts and bellies and fairly short, black–and–white tails. Males have orange–red breasts and bellies. Their magnificent, three–foot–long (one–meter–long) tail is the same shimmering green color as their upper body. An average adult quetzal measures 13.75 to 15 inches (35 to 38 centimeters) in length.

The quetzal feeds mainly on fruit. It usually stays in the canopy of the cloud forest (humid tropical mountain forest)

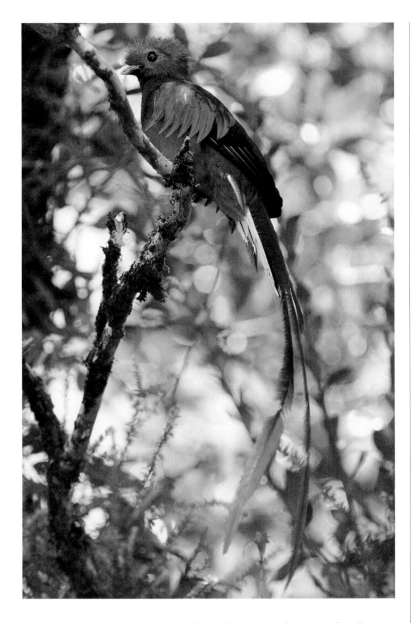

A male resplendent quetzal in a tree in the Santa Elena Cloud Forest Reserve. Biologists are hoping that protected reserves will help to stabilize the quetzals' population.

that makes up its habitat. Like other members in the Trogonidae family, the quetzal has large eyes that adapt easily to the dim light of its forest home. The bird is quite territorial, and the male patrols his home range of 15 to 25 acres (6 to 10 hectares) each morning and evening.

To court a female for breeding, a male flutters his long tail in various displays. After mating, the pair build a nest in a natural cavity in a tree stump. Sometime between March and

June, the female lays 2 blue eggs. Both the female and male take turns incubating (sitting on or brooding) the eggs for 17 to 19 days until they hatch.

Habitat and current distribution

The resplendent quetzal is found in Central America, from southern Mexico to Panama. Biologists (people who study living organisms) are unaware of the total number of quetzals currently in existence.

The bird prefers to inhabit cloud forests, usually from 4,000 to 10,000 feet (1,220 to 3,050 meters) in elevation. Occasionally, it will wander into partially cleared areas or pastures next to its forest habitat.

History and conservation measures

The resplendent quetzal has long been revered by people throughout its range for its beauty and religious significance. The Maya and Aztec—powerful ancient South American civilizations—both worshipped the bird as the god of the air and used its tail in religious ceremonies. It was also associated with (and its tail used in the image of) the Aztec god Quetzalcóatl (pronounced ket–sel–coe–OT–el).

In modern times, the bird has been threatened by the clearing of cloud forests in its range. However, the quetzal has been designated as Guatemala's national bird. Cloud forests are now protected in various areas in Mexico, Guatemala, and Costa Rica. With these safe habitats, biologists believe the resplendent quetzals' population will eventually stabilize.

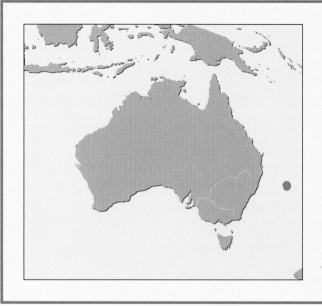

RAIL, LORD HOWE WOOD
Gallirallus sylvestris

PHYLUM: Chordata
CLASS: Aves
ORDER: Gruiformes
FAMILY: Rallidae
STATUS: Endangered, IUCN
Endangered, ESA
RANGE: Australia

Rail, Lord Howe wood
Gallirallus sylvestris

Description and biology

The Lord Howe wood rail, also called the Lord Howe wood hen, is a flightless marsh bird that averages 14 inches (36 centimeters) in length. The color of its plumage (covering of feathers) is brown. Dark brown and black stripes mark its wings. The bird has a strong, curved bill and red eyes. As it ages, the feathers around its neck and on the sides of its head turn gray.

The wood rail feeds on worms, grubs, and insects. Its home territory averages 7.5 acres (3 hectares) in size. Owls and feral (once domesticated, now wild) pigs are its main predators.

Lord Howe wood rails mate for life, and a male–female pair often remain apart from other wood rails. They breed primarily in late spring and summer. After building a nest on the ground, a female wood rail lays a clutch (eggs produced at one time) of 1 to 4 eggs. Biologists (people who study living organisms) estimate that it takes 19 to 20 days for the eggs to hatch. Upon hatching, the chicks are black in color.

A captive–breeding program, begun in 1980, has successfully increased the Lord Howe wood rail population.

Habitat and current distribution

The Lord Howe wood rail is found on the island from which it takes its name, Lord Howe Island, a volcanic island lying about 300 miles east off the coast of the southeastern Australian state of New South Wales.

The bird inhabits both lowland palm forests and higher elevation mountain forests. In a 1990 survey, biologists estimated that the wood rail's population was between 170 and 200. Its population is believed to have stabilized in the early 2000s.

History and conservation measures

When English explorers first set foot on Lord Howe Island in 1788, the Lord Howe wood rail was found throughout the island. Not long after, English whaling ships began stopping at the island. Since the flightless wood rail could be easily captured, it became an abundant food source for sailors. By the 1850s, the English had established permanent settlements on the island. In time, some of the goats and pigs the English had brought with them to the island escaped from farms and became feral. They quickly killed off many of the remaining wood rails. By the beginning of the twentieth century, the birds existed in low numbers only on the island's mountaintops.

By the mid–1970s, biologists believed the Lord Howe wood rail population numbered fewer than 30 birds. Conservationists (people protecting the natural world) then began taking steps to eliminate introduced predators such as the wild pig. In 1980, a captive–breeding program was initiated using three of the remaining wood rail pairs. The birds reproduced rapidly, and over the next four years, 85 birds bred in captivity were released into the wild. By 1990, the wild wood rail population had increased to about 50 breeding pairs and almost 200 total birds.

Even with the success of captive breeding, feral pigs, cats, and dogs remain a threat to the wood rail. Another major threat is the masked owl, introduced to the island in the 1920s to contain the rat population. Current conservation efforts to save the Lord Howe wood rail are focused on controlling all these predators.

ROBIN, CHATHAM ISLANDS
Petroica traversi

PHYLUM: Chordata
CLASS: Aves
ORDER: Passeriformes
FAMILY: Muscicapidae
STATUS: Endangered, IUCN
Endangered, ESA
RANGE: New Zealand

Robin, Chatham Islands

Petroica traversi

Description and biology

The Chatham Islands robin (also known as the black robin) is a species of the New Zealand robin. It has coal black feathers, legs, feet, and bill. The adult robin is about 6 inches (15 centimeters) tall and weighs just under an ounce (23.4 grams). It is similar in size to a sparrow but has longer legs. Females are smaller than males. The Chatham Islands robin has dark brown eyes that provide excellent vision for hunting in the dark. It hunts for food both day and night, foraging through the litter (layers of dead leaves and twigs) on the forest floor for worms, grubs, cockroaches, and particularly for an insect related to the grasshopper called the weta. Chatham Islands robins are noted for their song, which fills the forests around them during breeding season. They fly only short distances, from branch to branch, and stay in the lower branches of the forests in order to avoid the strong winds that blow over the islands. They are territorial animals, par-

The Chatham Islands robin, which lives in New Zealand, has virtually come back from extinction and is one of the most tremendous success stories in conservation.

ticularly during breeding season, and will protect their home areas from other birds of their species. They can live to be about 13 years old.

Chatham Islands robins are usually monogamous—they stay with the same breeding partner throughout their lives. When it is breeding time, the female makes a nest in a hollow tree or tree stump and usually lays two eggs at a time. She incubates the eggs (sits on them to keep them warm) and the male brings her food. The eggs hatch in about 18 days and the chicks begin to fly and leave the nest after 3 weeks. The parents continue to feed the chicks for a couple of months after they hatch, long after they leave the nest.

Habitat and current distribution

Chatham Islands robins live in the lower branches of a scrub–forest habitat. There are currently only two populations of this species, one on South East Island and the other on Mangere Island of the Chatham Island Group of New Zealand. There is a total population of about 250 birds.

History and conservation measures

The Chatham Islands robin has virtually come back from extinction and is one of the most tremendous success stories in conservation (protecting nature). However, there is much to be done before the species is out of trouble.

The range of the robin once encompassed most of the Chatham Islands. When Europeans arrived in New Zealand in the mid–nineteenth century, they began clearing the forests and destroying the habitats vital to the species. They also introduced rats and cats, predators to the robin. By 1880, the range of the Chatham Islands robin was severely reduced, and the species existed only on Little Mangere Island.

By the late 1970s, there were only seven birds left to represent the entire species. Because the habitat on Little Mangere had been badly damaged, scientists very carefully moved these last seven robins to Mangere Island. The birds were given a home in a forest that had been newly replanted, where the habitat was protected. For several years no mating took place and, by 1981, two of the seven birds had died. Only one female Chatham Islands robin remained in the world. Her name was "Old Blue" (named after the color of the band that scientists had placed on her leg in order to track her.) The future of the species seemed doomed.

Then, a group of scientists with the New Zealand Wildlife Service (now the Department of Conservation) set up a black robin recovery project on the islands. When Old Blue mated with one of the remaining males, "Old Yellow," her eggs were placed in the nests of Chatham Islands tit females, which became foster parents to the robin chicks. This project produced many new young, and soon a portion of the new Chatham Islands robin population was moved to Southeast Island. By 1999, the two locations, Mangere and Southeast Island, were home to about 259 Chatham Island robins, and plans were underway to open more critical habitat for the species. In these areas, there are no predators and the habitat is restored.

The spectacular recovery, from 5 birds to 259 birds in about 15 years, is still overshadowed by the fact that all of the new population stems from a single breeding pair, Old Blue and Old Yellow. Because of this, the gene base (the number of biological units that pass on hereditary traits) of the species is very low. So far, this has not been a problem for the new and growing populations, but because all the birds in the species will have similar weaknesses, a newly introduced predator or disease could drastically reduce the populations again.

STARLING, ROTHCHILD'S
Leucopsar rothschildi

PHYLUM: Chordata
CLASS: Aves
ORDER: Passeriformes
FAMILY: Sturnidae
STATUS: Critically endangered, IUCN
Endangered, ESA
RANGE: Indonesia

Starling, Rothchild's
Leucopsar rothschildi

Description and biology

The Rothchild's starling is also known as the Bali starling or the Bali mynah (mynah or myna is the common name for any of various Asian starlings). The color of this starling's plumage (covering of feathers) is mostly white. The bird has blue markings running through its eyes and black tips on its wings and tail. It also has a crest of feathers on the top of its head that it is able to raise and lower. An average Rothchild's starling measures 8.7 inches (22.1 centimeters) in length. It feeds mainly on insects, fruits, and small reptiles.

The starling usually breeds in colonies and makes its nest in a tree cavity. A female Rothchild's starling lays 2 to 7 eggs, then incubates (sits on or broods) them for 11 to 18 days. After hatching, the chicks leave their nest within a month.

Biologists estimate that fewer than fifty Rothchild's starlings exist in the wild.

Habitat and current distribution

The Rothchild's starling is unique to the Indonesian island of Bali, which lies off the eastern end of the larger Indonesian island of Java. It is restricted to the remaining
savanna woodland in the northwestern coastal area of the island, which is situated within the Bali–Barat National Park.
Biologists (people who study living organisms) estimate that
fewer than 50 starlings remain in the wild.

History and conservation measures

A number of factors have played a part in the decline of the Rothchild's starling. The bird's habitat has been reduced by the clearing of forests to create farmland and other types of human settlements. A beautiful bird, the starling has always been popular with collectors. Over the years, trapping has greatly reduced the bird's numbers.

The starling is legally protected in Indonesia, and several conservation programs are in place to ensure its recovery. However, the bird is still threatened by trapping, forest clearing, and widening human settlements. One of the strongest threats in 2000 was illegal poaching for the cage–bird trade. Because of these factors, the population of the species continues to decline.

The Rothchild's starling breeds well in captivity. Despite the fact that recently begun captive–breeding programs have provided birds for reintroduction into the wild, the Rothchild's starling remains critically endangered.

STORK, ORIENTAL WHITE
Ciconia boyciana

PHYLUM: Chordata
CLASS: Aves
ORDER: Ciconiiformes
FAMILY: Ciconiidae
STATUS: Endangered, IUCN
Endangered, ESA
RANGE: Bangladesh, China,
Hong Kong, India, Japan, Korea,
Democratic People's Republic of
Korea, Republic of Mongolia,
Myanmar, Philippines, Russian
Federation, Taiwan

Stork, Oriental white

Ciconia boyciana

Description and biology

The Oriental white stork is also known as the Japanese white stork and the Far Eastern white stork. With a body length of 43 to 45 inches (110 to 115 centimeters) and a wingspan of about 46 inches (118 centimeters), it is bigger than its cousin, the European white stork. It has a distinctive black bill and long white wings with black tips. Male Oriental white storks, weighing about 11 pounds (5 kilograms) are larger than females, which weigh about 10 pounds (4.7 kilograms).

The Oriental white stork's diet is made up of insects, fish, frogs, snails, small reptiles, and small mammals, such as rodents. The stork is a migratory bird, traveling very long distances to relocate seasonally. It tends to be quite aggressive with other members of its species.

Breeding male and female Oriental white storks make their nests in sections of the forest as far away from human communities as possible. The nests are made from branches and

The Oriental white stork lives only in the wilderness. It currently breeds in the Amur and Ussuri regions of southeast Siberia in Russia and in northeast China.

straw and are about 6.5 feet (2 meters) in diameter. The female stork usually lays about four or five eggs. Then the male and the female take turns incubating, or sitting on the eggs to keep them warm. When the chicks are born, both parents feed them by regurgitating (vomiting) undigested food into their mouths. The young leave the nest after about 65 days and begin to find their own food. In captivity an Oriental white stork lives about 48 years.

Habitat and current distribution

The Oriental white stork lives only in the wilderness. It currently breeds in the Amur and Ussuri regions of southeast Siberia in Russia and in northeast China. These storks migrate each winter. Most travel a distance of about 1,860 miles (3,000 kilometers) to spend the winter in the Yangtze River valley in

China. Some storks winter in Hong Kong, Taiwan, Japan, and North and South Korea. The total population of Oriental white storks in the world is estimated to be between 2,000 and 2,500 individual birds.

History and conservation measures

The Oriental white stork once had a large range in Asia. It became extinct as a breeding species in Japan in 1959, and in North and South Korea in 1971. In the past, Oriental white storks spent winters in India, Myanmar, and Bangladesh, but the species is no longer to be seen in those countries.

The reasons for the decline in the Oriental white stork population are human–related. The trees that the storks nest in have been cleared and the wetlands (areas where there is a lot of water in the soil, such as swamps or tidal flats) where they find their food have been drained. In Japan and the Koreas, people hunted the birds until the population had totally vanished from those countries. Pollution has probably further reduced the populations. In China, the building of the Three Gorges Dam on the Yangtze River and other hydro–electric (creating electricity from water power) projects are expected to have a heavy impact on the Oriental white stork's habitat. In Russia, development of the wetlands for farming has crowded the birds into increasingly smaller regions.

Russia, China, South Korea, and Japan have enacted strictly enforced laws protecting the Oriental white stork. After the species became extinct within the country, Japan created special reserves for the stork, notably the Hyogo Prefecture in Toyooka City, established on the site where storks once nested in Japan. There, Oriental white storks have been bred in captivity; about 200 now exist in the reserve. The reserve has a special section where storks are trained to hunt and fly before being released into the wild. It also has facilities for research into the species. Russia and South Korea have also established reserves for the Oriental white stork.

Conservationists (people who work to protect nature and natural resources) are studying ways to create a better habitat for the storks by planting elm trees near their feeding areas. One of the great difficulties in conservation with this species is its migratory (relocating) habits: its welfare depends on the abilities of several countries to work in concert with one another to protect it.

PHYLUM: Chordata
CLASS: Aves
ORDER: Anseriformes
FAMILY: Anatidae
STATUS: Endangered, IUCN
RANGE: Madagascar

Teal, Madagascar
Anas bernieri

Description and biology

The Madagascar teal is a small duck of about 16 inches (40 centimeters) in length, weighing about 1 pound (450 grams). The plumage (covering of feathers) is brownish gray, and there is a black–and–white band on each wing. The feathers under the wing are gray with white edges. The Madagascar teal has a long neck, large eyes, and a light red bill.

The Madagascar teal is found in either fresh or salt water where there is abundant plant life and rich mud. Like all teals, it is a "dabbler" (rather than a diver); it feeds while wading in shallow waters less than 4 inches (10 centimeters) deep by sifting through the water and mud for invertebrate (lacking spinal column) animals and some water plant seeds. The teal sifts for food throughout the day and night, but prefers the

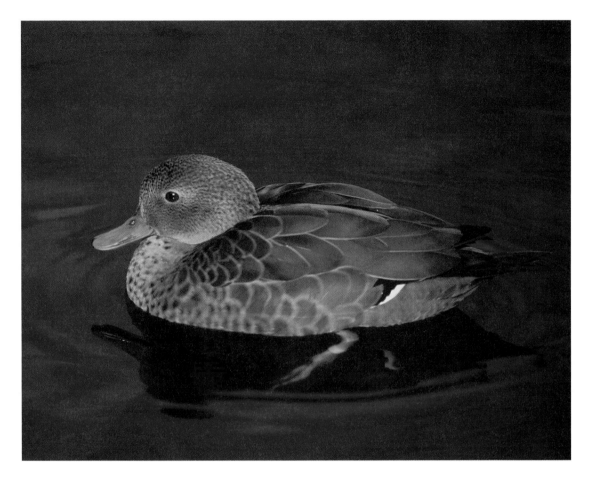

morning and evening hours. It walks well on land and has wings large enough to fly very slowly.

Madagascar teals are monogamous: once a male and female mate, they stay together for life. Breeding takes place from December to March, the rainy season in Madagascar. The male and female build a nest, usually in a hole in a mangrove tree trunk. They are territorial and will defend their territory against other teals. The female produces about six eggs and incubates them (sits on them to keep them warm) for about a month. The male watches over the female carefully while she is tending the eggs. The ducklings are well developed when they hatch, covered in soft down and able to move about and eat by themselves. Within about six weeks from hatching they will be able to fly. When not breeding, groups of teals form small flocks. The female Madagascar teal makes a quacking call; the male makes a whistling sound.

The Madagascar teal lives in the coastal wetlands of western Madagascar, an island nation off the southeast coast of Africa. The total population is estimated to be between 500 and 1,000 birds and is declining.

Habitat and current distribution

The Madagascar teal lives in very limited areas of the coastal wetlands of western Madagascar, an island nation off the southeast coast of Africa. The total population is estimated to be between 500 and 1,000 birds and is declining.

History and conservation measures

Before humans arrived on Madagascar 2,000 years ago, there is evidence that the Madagascar teal had a much greater range throughout the island. The species was first discovered in 1860 (when it became known as Bernier's teal), but none were observed for nearly a century and the species was virtually forgotten. Then, in 1969, the species was "discovered" again. Still, little was known about this teal. In 1992, the Durrell Wildlife Conservation Trust began extensive research on the species, finding that the population had dipped drastically.

A growing population of humans in Madagascar throughout the breeding range of the teal has caused extensive habitat loss. In particular, most of the shallow muddy waters that these ducks require for feeding have been converted into rice fields. The mangrove trees in which the teals build their nests have been cleared for timber and agricultural uses.

The Durrell Wildlife Conservation Trust moved quickly in the 1990s to initiate a breeding–in–captivity program, which has been highly successful. The organization has also been responsible for shedding light on the habits and habitat requirements of this previously little–known species and for educating local people living within the teal's habitat areas about the plight of the Madagascar teal.

THRASHER, WHITE–BREASTED
Ramphocinclus brachyurus

PHYLUM: Chordata
CLASS: Aves
ORDER: Passeriformes
FAMILY: Mimidae
STATUS: Endangered, IUCN
Endangered, ESA
RANGE: Martinique, Saint Lucia

Thrasher, white-breasted

Ramphocinclus brachyurus

Description and biology

An average white–breasted thrasher measures 9 to 9.5 inches (23 to 24 centimeters) long. The color of the plumage (covering of feathers) on the majority of the bird's body is dark brown. The side of its head is black, and its underparts are strikingly white.

This thrasher often gathers in single pairs or in small flocks of four or five pairs. It feeds by foraging on the ground for insects, seeds, and berries. The white–breasted thrasher is very territorial: when threatened, it will cock its tail and chatter like a wren. (Thrashers tend to sing in short, musical sounds. Birds like wrens often make scolding, chattering sounds.)

Breeding season appears to take place between April and July. The female white–breasted thrasher lays a clutch (eggs

Although this white–breasted thrasher is perched in a tree, thrashers are often easy prey for animals like mongooses and rats because the birds spend much of their time on the ground looking for food.

produced at one time) of 2 greenish–blue eggs in a bulky nest made of twigs and leaves. Based on related species, biologists (people who study living organisms) estimate that it probably takes 12 to 13 days for the eggs to hatch. The nest is often found 7 to 20 feet (2 to 6 meters) above ground in young trees.

The white–breasted thrasher species is divided biologically into two subspecies: *Ramphocinclus brachyurus brachyurus* and *Ramphocinclus brachyurus santaeluciae*. The main physical difference between the two is color. The birds of the subspecies *brachyurus* are lighter than those of the subspecies *santaeluciae*.

Habitat and current distribution

The white–breasted thrasher is unique to the Caribbean islands of Martinique and Saint Lucia. Martinique is home to the thrasher subspecies *brachyurus*. Biologists estimate that be-

428 | Endangered Species, 2nd Edition

tween 15 and 40 pairs of these birds currently exist. On Saint Lucia, home to the thrasher subspecies *santaeluciae*, fewer than 50 pairs of birds exist.

White–breasted thrashers prefer to inhabit dense thickets in semi–arid (partly or mostly dry) woodland. Those thrashers on Martinique have also been found to inhabit deep woods and areas bordering streams. On Saint Lucia, some thrashers have been observed inhabiting deciduous (shedding) trees ranging in height from 10 to 70 feet (3 to 21 meters).

History and conservation measures

The white–breasted thrasher is one of the rarest birds of the West Indies. Although considered quite common on Martinique in the nineteenth century, the bird was considered extinct there by 1950. That same year, it was rediscovered on the Presqu'île de la Caravelle, a peninsula that juts 5 miles (8 kilometers) out from the island into the Atlantic Ocean.

On Saint Lucia, the thrasher was also considered common and widespread during the nineteenth century. By the 1930s, however, it was extinct in some areas and rare in others on the island.

Habitat destruction on both Martinique and Saint Lucia has been, and continues to be, one of the major threats to the white–breasted thrasher. The bird is also threatened by introduced predators such as mongooses and rats. The white–breasted thrasher is easy prey for these animals because it spends much time feeding on the ground and it is not a strong flier.

On Martinique, the white–breasted thrasher's range lies within the Caravell Natural Reserve. On Saint Lucia, part of it lies within the Castries Forest Reserve.

VIREO, BLACK–CAPPED
Vireo atricapillus

PHYLUM: Chordata
CLASS: Aves
ORDER: Passeriformes
FAMILY: Vireonidae
STATUS: Vulnerable, IUCN
Endangered, ESA
RANGE: Mexico, USA
(Oklahoma and Texas)

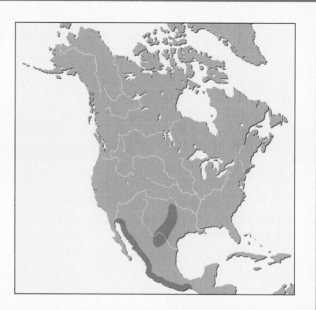

Vireo, black-capped
Vireo atricapillus

Description and biology

The black–capped vireo (pronounced VEER–ee–o), also called the black–capped greenlet, is a small songbird that averages about 4.7 inches (12 centimeters) in length. The color of the male's plumage (covering of feathers) is dull yellowish–green above and whitish below. The female is slightly darker above with yellowish underparts. The head is black in the male and gray in the female. Both have white eye markings. The bird forages in leaves and branches for insects, spiders, fruit, and seeds.

A female black–capped vireo lays a clutch (eggs produced at one time) of 3 to 5 eggs in a rounded nest made of vegetation. Both the male and female take turns incubating (sitting on or brooding) the eggs for 14 to 17 days until they hatch. Snakes and scrub jays sometimes prey on the eggs or the young nestlings.

A black–capped vireo feeding her nestlings. Young vireos are often in danger from South American fire ants who invade the vireos' nests and devour the nestlings.

Habitat and current distribution

The black–capped vireo currently breeds only in west–central Oklahoma, Texas, and the northeastern Mexican state of Coahuila. It is believed the bird winters in central and western Mexico, but biologists (people who study living organisms) are unsure. Approximately 300 vireos exist in Oklahoma and 3,000 in Texas. Results of population surveys in Mexico have been questionable: some list fewer than 30 birds, but others list over 9,000.

The black–capped vireo requires a very special nesting habitat. It nests in shrubs on rocky slopes or eroded banks in areas between forests and grasslands.

History and conservation measures

The black–capped vireo once bred throughout the south–central United States. Over the years, much of the bird's habitat was converted into farms and urban areas. Other portions of its habitat were destroyed by the overgrazing of cattle and other livestock.

The changing of natural habitat by humans has affected the black–capped vireo in another serious way. The brown–headed cowbird normally inhabits grasslands and prairies. As its habitat has been taken over by humans, it has had to expand its range into that of the black–capped vireo. The cowbird likes to lay its eggs in the nests of smaller birds, such as vireos and sparrows. Once the cowbird nestlings hatch, they compete with the other nestlings for food from the new parents. Many times, the smaller nestlings die from starvation. In some areas, this type of behavior, called parasitism (pronounced pair–a–si–TIZ–um), occurred in over 90 percent of black–capped vireo nests.

Recently, scientists have discovered that South American fire ants, accidentally brought into the black–capped vireo's range, are preying on the bird's nestlings. The ants attack the nest and devour the nestlings within the course of a single night.

Current conservation measures on behalf of the vireo include controlling the cowbird population and protecting the vireo's habitat. A National Wildlife Refuge is being established outside of Austin, Texas, to maintain a habitat specifically for the black–capped vireo.

VULTURE, CAPE
Gyps coprotheres

PHYLUM: Chordata
CLASS: Aves
ORDER: Falconiformes
FAMILY: Accipitridae
STATUS: Vulnerable, IUCN
RANGE: Botswana, Lesotho, Mozambique, Namibia, South Africa, Swaziland, Zimbabwe

Vulture, Cape
Gyps coprotheres

Description and biology

The Cape vulture, also called the Cape griffon, is an Old World vulture that belongs to the same family as hawks and eagles. It has a long, bare neck and a specially shaped tongue that allows it to feed inside the carcasses (dead bodies) of sheep, cattle, pigs, goats, and horses. The bird roosts (rests or sleeps) with other vultures in colonies on cliffs. Unlike most birds of prey, the Cape vulture does not use thermals (rising warm air currents) to fly. Instead, it uses the swift air currents that exist around its roosting sites. The vulture used to eat the carcasses of large migratory mammals. Now, it must depend on dead livestock for food.

Cape vultures begin to build their nests in early March. The nests are made of grass with a rim of feathers and sticks.

433

Cape vultures feast on their prey.

They are usually built on south–facing cliffs that have ledges. Once constructed, the nests are often used for several years.

A female Cape vulture lays a clutch (eggs produced at one time) of only one egg between April and July. Once the chick hatches, it is fed the meat and, sometimes, bones from animal carcasses. Both eggs and newborn chicks face several natural threats. Clouds that settle on south–facing cliffs can often cause them to freeze to death. They also are preyed upon by black eagles and white–necked ravens.

Habitat and current distribution

The Cape vulture is found only in the southern African countries of South Africa, Lesotho, Swaziland, Botswana, Namibia, Zimbabwe, and Mozambique. It breeds primarily in two areas. An estimated 2,300 breeding pairs are found in

Transvaal (northeastern province in South Africa) and in eastern Botswana. Another group of about 950 breeding pairs are located in the Transkei (self–governing republic in South Africa), Natal (eastern province in South Africa) and Lesotho.

Because Cape vultures generally live and forage for food away from their breeding areas, their range extends almost over all of southern Africa. Biologists (people who study living organisms) have estimated that about 12,000 Cape vultures currently exist. The birds prefer to inhabit open spaces. They forage over grassland, desert, and other areas with sparse vegetation.

History and conservation measures

In the nineteenth century, the Cape vulture was seen in high numbers in southern Africa. It began to decline in the early twentieth century, though, when a disease wiped out many cattle in the region, robbing the bird of its food source. A drop in the number of cattle due to disease and other factors between the years 1950 and 1971 again hurt the Cape vulture population.

Today, the main threat facing the Cape vulture is not food quantity but food quality. Cape vulture chicks require calcium in their diets to prevent osteodystrophy (pronounced os–tee–o–DIS–trow–fee), a disease that causes their bones to become weak and deformed. When large mammals kill and feed upon animals, they often crush their bones in the process. Vultures then feed on the remaining carcass, and the chicks are fed meat that has bone flakes (calcium) mixed in it. Since the number of large mammals in southern Africa has declined, however, vulture chicks have suffered because they have not been able to eat enough meat mixed with bone flakes.

Cape vultures are also threatened by humans who disturb their breeding grounds and who poison them. Many farmers and ranchers in the bird's range believe it attacks sheep and then transmits to other animals any disease the sheep might carry. To prevent this, these farmers and ranchers often put out poisoned carcasses for the vultures to feed on, and the birds die as a result.

The belief that Cape vultures normally attack sheep and spread disease is a mistaken one. Conservation groups in southern Africa have tried to stop farmers and ranchers from leaving poisoned carcasses for the birds. Conservationists (people protecting the natural world) have also set up areas where carcasses with crushed bones have been put out for the vultures. This practice has helped reduce the number of vulture chicks suffering from osteodystrophy. The Cape vulture has full legal protection throughout its range.

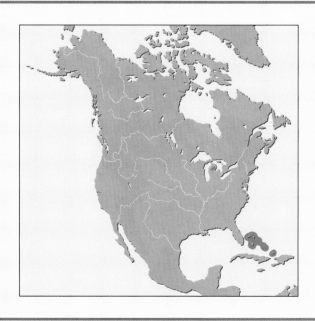

WARBLER, KIRTLAND'S
Dendroica kirtlandii

PHYLUM: Chordata
CLASS: Aves
ORDER: Passeriformes
FAMILY: Parulidae
STATUS: Vulnerable, IUCN
Endangered, ESA
RANGE: Bahamas, Canada, Turks
and Caicos Islands, USA

Warbler, Kirtland's
Dendroica kirtlandii

Description and biology

The Kirtland's warbler is a songbird that grows to an average length of 6 inches (15 centimeters). It has a blue–gray head and upper body with black streaks on its back. Its underside is pale yellow speckled with darker streaks. Males have a black spot on their cheeks while females have a gray one. Both sexes have incomplete white rings around their eyes. The Kirtland's warbler has a habit of bobbing its tail as it moves along the ground. The bird has been seen feeding on moths, caterpillars, ants, and numerous other insects.

The Kirtland's warbler nests and breeds in a very specific habitat. It rejects areas that have dense underbrush or forests that are dominated by deciduous (shedding) trees. It chooses only areas at least 80 acres (32 hectares) in size with large stands of young jack pine on relatively level ground. These areas develop naturally only as a result of intense forest fires. The warbler moves into the area 9 to 13 years after a fire has

A female Kirtland's warbler guarding her nest. Warblers are very particular about where they nest and breed.

swept through and the new jack pines are about 5 feet (1.5 meters) tall. After 6 to 12 years, when the pines have reached 12 to 18 feet (3.6 to 5.5 meters) in height, the warbler abandons the area for a new one.

The warbler builds a nest of grass, bark, and fibers on the ground beneath a jack pine. A female Kirtland's warbler lays 3 to 5 brown–speckled white eggs between mid–May and mid–July. She then incubates (sits on or broods) them for 10 to 14 days until they hatch.

Habitat and current distribution

The Kirtland's warbler breeds only in a few counties in the area of north–central Michigan's lower peninsula where extensive stands of young jack pine are found. Beginning in late September, the bird migrates to the Bahamas and the Turks and Caicos Islands located at the southeast end of the Bahamas. Its winter habitat consists mainly of pine woods. The warbler returns to its summer habitat in early May.

During the summer, a few Kirtland's warblers may range to Wisconsin, Minnesota, and even Ontario or Quebec, Canada. However, they do not nest in these areas. Biologists (people who study living organisms) estimate that over 1,400 Kirtland's warblers currently exist in the world.

History and conservation measures

The Kirtland's warbler was first discovered in the Bahamas in 1841, but its nesting grounds in Michigan were not discovered until 1903. These were found near the Au Sable River at the border of Oscoda and Crawford Counties. Roughly 90 percent of the warbler's current nesting grounds are found within a three–county vicinity of these original grounds.

Because of its finicky nesting habits, the Kirtland's warbler probably never existed in great numbers. At the beginning of the twentieth century, extensive logging in Michigan reduced the bird's already meager habitat. Then, officials who oversaw the way forests were managed in the state limited the number of forest fires. As a result, forests grew and developed beyond the specific needs of the warbler. In the 1950s and 1960s, 15,000 acres (6,000 hectares) of suitable warbler nesting habitat existed. Today, only 30 percent, or 4,500 acres (1,800 hectares), exists.

The Kirtland's warbler has also been threatened by the brown–headed cowbird. This bird normally inhabits farmland and meadowland. As forests have been cleared in Michigan, it has expanded its range into that of the Kirtland's warbler. The brown–headed cowbird likes to lay its eggs in the nests of other birds, including the warbler. This behavior is called parasitism (pronounced pair–a–si–TIZ–um). When the cowbird nestlings hatch, they are raised by the new parents. The parents' own nestlings often cannot compete with the cowbird nestlings for food, and they starve to death. From the 1930s to the 1970s, as many as 60 percent of warbler nests were believed to be parasitized by the cowbird.

The Kirtland's warbler made a comeback in the 1990s. Conservationists and public land managers have worked to maintain and develop suitable nesting habitat for the bird in Michigan. They have also tried to control the brown–headed cowbird population within the range of the Kirtland's warbler.

WOODPECKER, IVORY–BILLED
Campephilus principalis

PHYLUM: Chordata
CLASS: Aves
ORDER: Piciformes
FAMILY: Picidae
STATUS: Critically endangered, IUCN
Endangered, ESA
RANGE: Cuba, USA

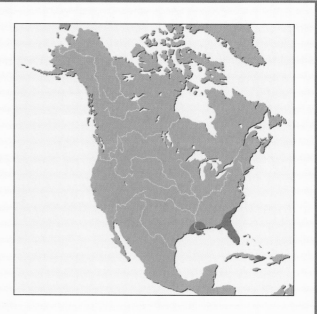

Woodpecker, ivory-billed

Campephilus principalis

Description and biology

The ivory–billed woodpecker is the largest North American woodpecker. It measures from 18 to 20 inches (46 to 51 centimeters) long. The color of the plumage (covering of feathers) on its body is a shiny blue–black. Broad white markings appear on its wings and neck. Its strong, straight, heavy bill is pure white. Males of the species have a bright red crest (projecting tuft on top of its head); females have a black one. The bird has short legs and feet that end in large, curved claws.

The ivory–billed woodpecker uses its bill to strip bark from dead or dying trees in search of wood–boring beetle larvae and other insects. Male–female pairs occupy a large territory of up to 4,000 acres (1,600 hectares).

Breeding season lasts from March to June. The woodpecker creates a nest by boring out a hole high up in a tree. The female ivory–billed woodpecker then lays a clutch (eggs pro-

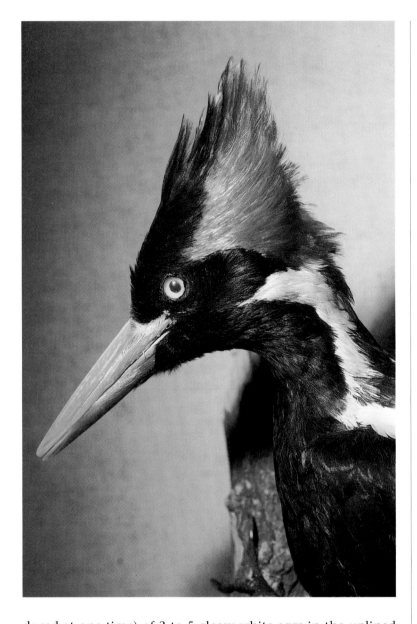

A model of the ivory–billed woodpecker. In the early 1990s, biologists believed that the woodpeckers were extinct in the wild, but after some sightings there is hope that a few have survived.

duced at one time) of 3 to 5 glossy white eggs in the unlined hole. Both parents incubate (sit on or brood) the eggs for about 20 days. The nestlings fledge (develop flying feathers) about 35 days after hatching.

Habitat and current distribution

Many biologists (people who study living organisms) consider the ivory–billed woodpecker to be extinct, or almost extinct. Up until the early 1990s, they believed that a few of the woodpeckers still survived in eastern Cuba. There had been unconfirmed sightings of the bird along the Gulf Coast of North America from the 1950s through the 1970s. These "sightings" led biologists to believe at the time that the bird might still survive in remote forests in Louisiana, South Carolina, Mississippi, Georgia, or Florida. In the 1990s, biologists had lost hope that the bird existed anywhere, but in April 1999, a student saw what many believe was a couple of ivory–billed woodpeckers on the Pearl River in Louisiana. There were other credible, but unconfirmed, sightings after that.

In the United States, the woodpecker inhabits hardwood swamp forests and, on occasion, pine forests. In Cuba, it occupies mixed pine and hardwood forests.

History and conservation measures

The ivory–billed woodpecker was always considered rare throughout its range in the United States. At the end of the nineteenth century, the logging and clearing of virgin swamp forests in the southern United States decimated the remaining population of these woodpeckers. Hunters and trappers also quickened the bird's decline. By 1941, the ivory–billed woodpecker population was estimated at 24 birds in five scattered areas. Just seven years later, the last identified population disappeared. Over the next 30 years, reports were made that the bird had been sighted. However, none of these were ever confirmed. No reports had been made in the 20 years leading up to 1999.

In Cuba, the ivory–billed woodpecker was thought to have existed over much of the island. By 1956, due to the clearing of its natural habitat, the bird's Cuban population numbered only about 12. These birds disappeared shortly afterward, and the woodpecker was believed to have become extinct on the island. In 1986, however, Cuban biologists working in eastern Cuba found three woodpeckers in a hilly pine forest called Ojito de Agua. Hopes were raised that the birds could make a comeback, but expeditions to find these birds in 1991 and 1993 proved futile.

In 1996, the ivory–billed woodpecker was declared extinct by the International Union for the Conservation of Nature and Natural Resources (IUCN). In 1999, with several new sightings of the bird in southeastern Louisiana, a flurry of research and then extensive searches were conducted in the Pearl River area in 2000 and 2001. In 2002, Cornell University's Lab of Ornithology (study of birds) in cooperation with Zeiss Sports Optics and the Louisiana Department of Wildlife and Fisheries used high–tech recording equipment to record the sounds at twelve different positions within the remote forest area for a period of three months. The project turned up no indication of the ivory–billed woodpecker's presence. The IUCN changed the bird's status to critically endangered, in the hope that there are a few remaining birds in the wild.

PHYLUM: Chordata
CLASS: Aves
ORDER: Piciformes
FAMILY: Picidae
STATUS: Vulnerable, IUCN
Endangered, ESA
RANGE: USA

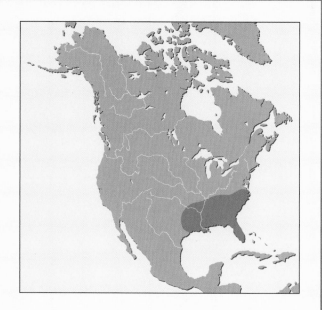

Woodpecker, red-cockaded

Picoides borealis

Description and biology

The red–cockaded woodpecker is so–named because the male of the species has tiny red patches or "cockades" on the sides of his head (a cockade is an ornament worn on a hat as a badge). Female red–cockaded woodpeckers lack these patches. An average red–cockaded woodpecker measures 7 inches (18 centimeters) long and has a wingspan of 15 inches (38 centimeters). The plumage (covering of feathers) on the bird's upperparts is black with white stripes. Its chest and belly are white with black–flecked sides. The bird has a black crown and prominent black bands that start at its bill and run down both sides of its neck. On each cheek, between the band and the bird's crown, is a large white patch.

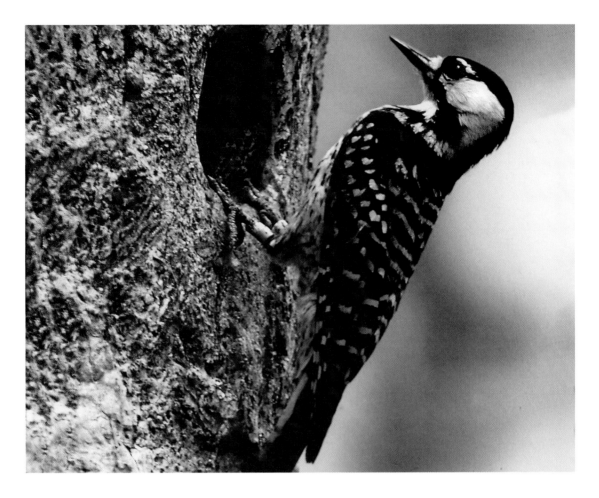

The red–cockaded woodpecker feeds on insects (ants, beetles, caterpillars, roaches, and spiders) both on and below tree bark. It also eats fruits, berries, and seeds. The bird nests in groups called clans. These clans consist of a male–female pair, their fledglings (young that have just developed flying feathers), and their young male offspring from previous years called "helpers." Clans forage or feed over territories of approximately 200 acres (40 to 80 hectares).

This bird is the only woodpecker that bores out a nesting hole with its sharp, chisellike bill in live, mature pine trees (other woodpeckers create holes in dead or dying trees). A female red–cockaded woodpecker lays a clutch of two to five white eggs in the nesting hole in April or May. The helpers assist their parents in incubating (sitting on or

The red–cockaded woodpecker is the only woodpecker species that creates holes in living trees. Most woodpeckers make nesting holes in dead trees.

brooding) the eggs for about ten days. They then assist in raising the nestlings.

Habitat and current distribution

The red–cockaded woodpecker is found in the southeastern United States from Texas and from Oklahoma east to the southern Atlantic Coast. The largest concentrations of birds are located in Florida and South Carolina. Biologists (people who study living organisms) estimate the total red–cockaded woodpecker population to be between 10,000 and 14,000 birds.

These woodpeckers prefer to inhabit old–growth pine forests, mainly those with long–needled pines averaging 80 to 120 years old. These types of forests usually have very little underbrush.

History and conservation measures

The red–cockaded woodpecker was once abundant throughout a range that stretched as far north as Missouri, Kentucky, and Virginia. At the beginning of the twentieth century, however, the bird's population began to decline and its range began to shrink.

The main reason was habitat loss. Mature pine forests were rapidly cleared to create farmland or cut down to supply the increased demand for timber. If new trees were planted in these areas, they were not the long–needled pines favored by the red–cockaded woodpecker, but faster–growing hardwood trees. Over the last 100 years, 90 percent of the bird's habitat in the southeast has been cleared.

Most of the remaining forested pine areas suitable for the woodpeckers are on federal lands and are, therefore, protected. In other areas, foresters and wildlife specialists are trying to increase the amount of red–cockaded woodpecker habitat by burning underbrush and small trees, leaving only old pines standing.

In 1993, the Georgia–Pacific Company (a timber company) signed an agreement with the U.S. Fish and Wildlife Service to help protect the woodpecker on thousands of acres of company land. Two more timber companies, Hancock Timber Resource Group and Champion International Corporation, have since signed similar agreements to protect the red–cockaded woodpecker on their lands.

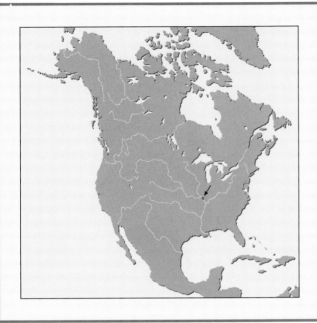

AMPHIPOD, ILLINOIS CAVE
Gammarus acherondytes

PHYLUM: Arthropoda
CLASS: Crustacea
ORDER: Amphipoda
FAMILY: Gammaridae
STATUS: Endangered, IUCN
Endangered, ESA
RANGE: USA (Illinois)

Amphipod, Illinois cave

Gammarus acherondytes

Description and biology

The Illinois cave amphipod is a small freshwater crustacean. It is light blue–gray in color, with small eyes and one long and one shorter antenna. A male Illinois cave amphipod is usually about .8 inch (20 millimeters) long and a female about .5 to .6 inches (12 to 16 millimeters) long. Illinois cave amphipods live in utter darkness in cave streams. They need very cold water and avoid light. They cannot leave their caves, so they will eat any kind of food matter they can find by means of their keen sense of touch, including dead animals, plants, and bacteria.

Illinois cave amphipods are extremely sensitive to pollutants that are introduced into their water supply. The species is an excellent indicator of the quality of the water in the cave systems it inhabits and the groundwater from the surrounding area.

The Illinois cave amphipod is a small freshwater crustacean that lives in utter darkness in cave streams.

The Illinois cave amphipod is a small freshwater crustacean that lives in utter darkness in cave streams.

Because they live underground and away from humans, little is known about the behavior of this species.

Habitat and current distribution

The Illinois cave amphipod lives in karst regions (areas composed of limestone that feature sinkholes, underground streams, and caverns). It is known to occur only in Monroe and St. Clair counties in southwestern Illinois.

History and conservation measures

The Illinois cave amphipod is endemic (native to and occurring only in a particular region) to several cave systems in Monroe and St. Clair counties in southern Illinois. The species was once known to occur in six cave systems, all within a 10–mile radius of Waterloo, Illinois. In 1995, the species was found in only three of these systems, all in Monroe County. This reduction in its range signals a decline in the population of the species.

Groundwater contamination, usually from pesticides used by farmers, is the principal threat to the species. Contamination from human and animal wastes from sewers and septic systems and livestock feedlots in the area also pose a grave danger. The poor water quality, if not corrected, will probably cause the extinction of the species. Sinkholes in the karst region inhabited by the amphipods are sometimes used to dump trash and other pollutants. Because there is no natural filter in a sinkhole to stop the pollutants from reaching the underground waters, the risk of contamination is very high. When amphipods are damaged or killed by the contamination of the streams and groundwater, there is good reason to believe that humans who use the same water sources will be affected as well.

The small range of the Illinois cave amphipod is very close to St. Louis, Missouri, and so the habitat may face further harm from the urban (city; densely populated) environment. The Illinois Department of Natural Resources owns the entrances to two of the three caves known to be Illinois cave amphipod habitats. The entrances to the third cave are privately owned, but have been designated as nature reserves. There are several recovery plans in progress, which include pursuing a better scientific understanding of the species and its habitat needs. The Illinois cave amphipod is currently protected by the Illinois State Endangered Species Protection Act, which prohibits harming or killing it.

CRAYFISH, HELL CREEK CAVE
Cambarus zophonastes

PHYLUM: Arthropoda
CLASS: Crustacea
ORDER: Decapoda
FAMILY: Cambaridae
STATUS: Critically endangered, IUCN
Endangered, ESA
RANGE: USA (Arkansas)

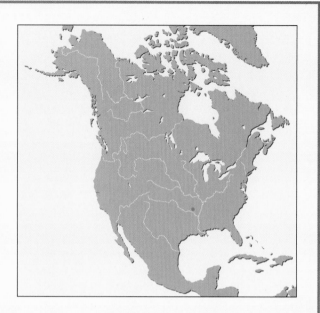

Crayfish, Hell Creek Cave

Cambarus zophonastes

Description and biology

The Hell Creek Cave crayfish is colorless. It has small eyes that lack any pigment (color) and a spined rostrum (snout). An average adult measures 2.6 inches (6.6 centimeters) long. Like other crayfish, it feeds on both plants and animals, including algae, snails, insects, worms, and mussels.

Although appearing similar to lobsters (their salt water cousins), crayfish have a different life cycle. They do not pass through any larval stages, but go directly from an egg to a miniature adult form. Hell Creek Cave crayfish reproduce very slowly. Biologists (people specializing in the study of living organisms) believe they lay eggs once every five years, on average. As in other crayfish species, the female Hell Creek Cave crayfish shelters her fertilized eggs by carrying them attached to her abdomen. After the eggs hatch, the young crayfish cling to that spot on the mother's body for several weeks before letting go.

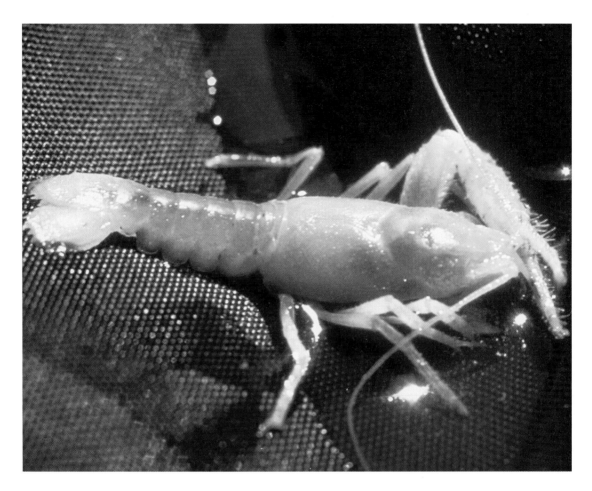

Crayfish are preyed on by bass, sunfish, raccoons, otters, herons, and kingfishers.

Habitat and current distribution

The Hell Creek Cave crayfish is found only in a deep pool in Hell Creek Cave, which is located in the Ozark Mountains in Stone County, Arkansas. Surveys conducted in the mid–1980s recorded less than 50 crayfish at this site and the population has remained near that figure into the 2000s.

Hell Creek Cave is mostly wet and muddy throughout the year. Many of its passages are flooded during the rainy seasons and after storms. A narrow, shallow stream leads to the pool inhabited by the crayfish. The pool is approximately 150 feet (46 meters) away from the cave entrance.

The Hell Creek Cave crayfish is found only in a deep pool in Hell Creek Cave, which is located in the Ozark Mountains in Arkansas.

History and conservation measures

There are about 330 known species of crayfish, which are also known as crawfish or crawdads. Although nearly half of those species are endangered or imperiled, only four species have been placed on the U.S. Endangered Species List. The Hell Creek Cave crayfish is one of those four.

This species of crayfish faces a number of threats. A surface stream supplies water to the cave's pool. This stream can easily become polluted with wastes from nearly industries. Once polluted, the stream will in turn contaminate the pool, destroying the crayfishs' fragile habitat.

Biologists believe the Hell Creek Cave crayfish reproduces so slowly because it does not get enough nourishment. The cave has a shortage of organic matter for the crayfish to use as energy. In the past, most of this organic matter came from the guano (feces) of gray bats (*Myotis grisescens*). However, the gray bat is now an endangered species. It has disappeared from Hell Creek Cave as well as from many other caves.

Finally, the Hell Creek Cave crayfish is threatened by human collectors who venture into the cave to capture specimens. The removal of any adult crayfish, especially reproducing females, can have a dramatic effect on the future population of the species.

A tract of land that includes the entrance to Hell Creek Cave has recently been placed under protection. This act should limit the number of humans entering the cave and disturbing its ecosystem (an ecological system including all of its living things and their environment). Conservationists (people protecting the natural world) hope it will also allow gray bats to return to the cave, which will greatly benefit the Hell Creek Cave crayfish.

CRAYFISH, NASHVILLE
Orconectes shoupi

PHYLUM: Arthropoda
CLASS: Crustacea
ORDER: Decapoda
FAMILY: Cambaridae
STATUS: Critically endangered, IUCN
Endangered, ESA
RANGE: USA (Tennessee)

Crayfish, Nashville

Orconectes shoupi

Description and biology

The Nashville crayfish, also called the Shoup's crayfish, measures about 2 inches (5 centimeters) long. It has thickened ridges on its rostrum (snout), four pair of walking legs, and two long–fingered chelae (pronounced KEY–lee; claws or pincers). It consumes plants and animals, including algae, insects, worms, fish eggs, snails, and mussels. Raccoons, fish, and reptiles are among the main predators of this crayfish.

Biologists (people who study living organisms) know very little about the reproductive habits of the Nashville crayfish. Mating can take place from late summer to early spring. Egg laying seems to occur in early spring. Like females of other crayfish species, the female Nashville crayfish shelters her fertilized eggs by carrying them attached to her abdomen. Upon hatching, the young crayfish are fully formed, miniature versions of the adults. They cling to the mother's abdomen for several weeks after hatching before venturing out on their own.

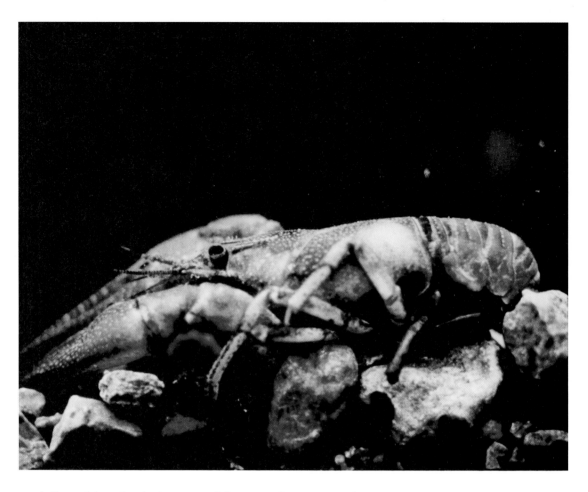

Nashville crayfish are found only in Mill and Sevenmile Creeks, tributaries of the Cumberland River near Nashville, Tennessee.

Habitat and current distribution

This crayfish is found only in Mill and Sevenmile Creeks, tributaries of the Cumberland River near Nashville, Tennessee. In its streambed habitat, the Nashville crayfish requires adequate cover. Those crayfish in Mill Creek have been found typically in pool areas under flat slabs of limestone and other rocks.

Biologists do not know how many Nashville crayfish currently exist, although they believe the number is quite low.

History and conservation measures

Biologists have classified about 330 species of crayfish, which are also called crawfish or crawdads. Tennessee alone has more than 70 distinct species. Of the total number of crayfish species known, almost half are endangered or imperiled.

Only four crayfish species in the country have been granted federal protection by being placed on the U.S. Endangered Species List. The Nashville crayfish is one of those four listed.

In the past, the Nashville crayfish was found in three additional areas in Tennessee: Big Creek in Giles County, South Harpeth River in Davidson County, and Richland Creek in Davidson County. Biologists are unsure exactly why the crayfish disappeared from these locations, but they do know it cannot tolerate pollution and increased silt (mineral particles).

This is the threat currently facing the Nashville crayfish in its Mill Creek habitat. A constant barrage of pollutants has been flowing into the creek. Industries have built warehouses right up to the edge of the creek's banks. Nearby roads and parking lots drain into the creek. Upstream from the crayfish's habitat, pesticides and fertilizers sprayed on farmland run off into the creek.

To ensure the survival of the Nashville crayfish, conservation efforts must focus on protecting Mill Creek from further contamination.

DID YOU KNOW?

Crayfish are found on all continents on Earth except Africa and Antarctica. They are an essential part of the food chain. They feed on algae, insects, mussels, and snails, while in turn being fed on by fish, herons, otters, and other larger animals. This feeding balance has been maintained for hundreds of thousands of years. However, pollution and introduced species are currently threatening this delicate balance. The Nature Conservancy, an international nonprofit environmental organization, states in its *1997 Species Report Card: The State of U.S. Plants and Animals* that crayfish and mussels are currently in the worst condition of all endangered species.

ISOPOD, MADISON CAVE
Antrolana lira

PHYLUM: Arthropoda
CLASS: Crustacea
ORDER: Isopoda
FAMILY: Cirolanidae
STATUS: Vulnerable, IUCN
Threatened, ESA
RANGE: USA (Virginia)

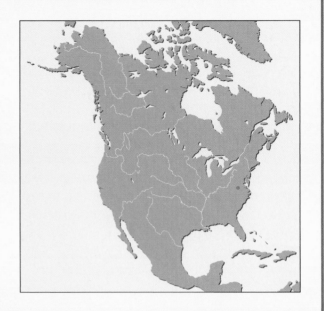

Isopod, Madison Cave

Antrolana lira

Description and biology

Isopods are tiny, shrimplike crustaceans that have flattened bodies and no carapace (pronounced KAR–a–pace) or shell. The Madison Cave isopod measures 0.47 inch (1.19 centimeters) long and 0.16 inch (0.41 centimeter) wide. It has no eyes and is colorless. Its diet consists of decaying organic matter such as leaf litter, small twigs, wood particles, and insect remains.

Biologists (people who study living organisms) have been unable to observe the reproductive habits of this isopod.

Habitat and current distribution

The Madison Cave isopod is found only in caves and fissures (long narrow cracks or openings) in the Shenandoah Valley in northwestern Virginia. It inhabits two deep subterranean (underground) pools in Madison Cave and one in nearby Stegers Fissure. The pools seep into the South River,

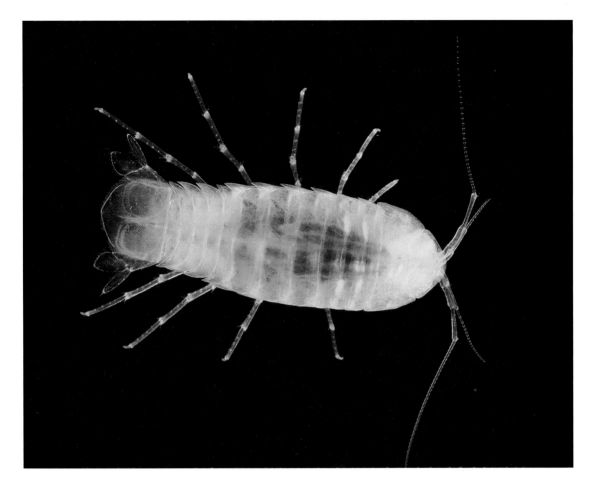

a tributary of the South Fork Shenandoah River. Biologists recently discovered new populations at four nearby locations, thereby extending the isopod's range.

Madison Cave isopods prefer to inhabit freshwater pools that have clay banks.

History and conservation measures

Madison Cave has a significant place in American history. Thomas Jefferson mapped the cave, the first instance of cave–mapping in the United States. George Washington's signature also appears on one of the walls in the cave.

The first Madison Cave isopod specimen was not collected until 1958; biologists did not name the species until 1964. It is the only species of its kind found in North America north of Texas.

In order to preserve the Madison Cave isopods' habitat, only scientists and students are now allowed in Madison Cave, the only place where the isopod is found.

The Madison Cave isopod currently faces many threats. Because a single groundwater system feeds the caves and connects them to South River, the cave pools can become quickly contaminated with pollution. Mercury has been discovered in South River. Conservationists (people protecting the natural world) worry that herbicides and pesticides, which run off into the river from nearby farms, could easily reach toxic (poisonous) levels.

Madison Cave has also been damaged by humans. Many people like to explore caves (an activity called spelunking) for recreation. Others have entered the cave to collect bat guano or feces, which is used to produce saltpeter (potassium nitrate), a component of gunpowder. As people have walked along the banks, they have knocked clay into the pools, destroying the isopod's habitat by increasing the amount of silt (mineral particles) in the water. Garbage has also accumulated in the cave as more and more humans have come and gone.

In 1981, a gate was put up over the entrance to Madison Cave. Only scientists and educators seeking to study the Madison Cave isopod and other species in its habitat are now allowed access to the cave.

SHRIMP, CALIFORNIA FRESHWATER
Syncaris pacifica

PHYLUM: Arthropoda

CLASS: Crustacea

ORDER: Decapoda

FAMILY: Atyidae

STATUS: Endangered, IUCN
Endangered, ESA

RANGE: USA (California)

Shrimp, California freshwater

Syncaris pacifica

Description and biology

The California freshwater shrimp is similar in appearance to the common marine (ocean) shrimp. It has a greenish–gray body with light blue tail fins. When seen in the water, it looks transparent. An average adult can measure up to 2.5 inches (6.4 centimeters) long.

After mating, a female California freshwater shrimp carries her eggs on her body throughout the winter. The eggs, which number between 50 and 120, grow very slowly over a nine–month period. Only about half of the eggs hatch.

Habitat and current distribution

This species of shrimp is found in three counties in California. In Napa County, it inhabits the Napa River near

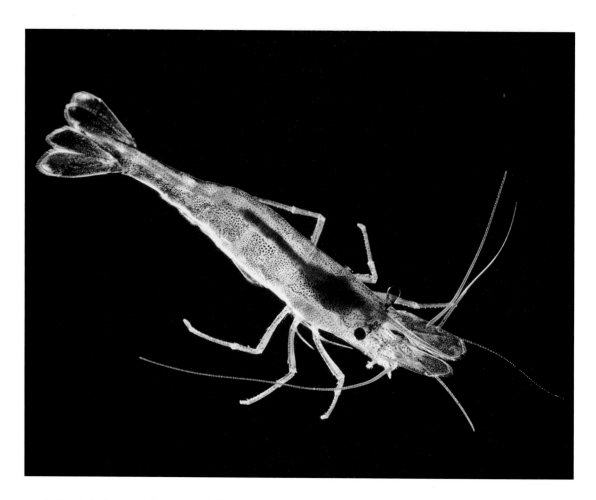

California freshwater shrimps look transparent when seen in the water.

Calistoga. In Marin and Sonoma Counties, it inhabits Big Austin, East Austin, Blucher, Green Valley, Huichica, Jonive, Lagunitas, Salmon, Walker, and Yulupa Creeks. Biologists (people who study living organisms) do not know the total number of these shrimp currently in existence.

The California freshwater shrimp prefers to inhabit quiet, clear freshwater streams. These streams are usually tree–lined and have underwater vegetation and exposed tree roots. Water in the streams is fairly slow–moving.

History and conservation measures

The range of the California freshwater shrimp has not changed, but areas within that range where the shrimp is found have decreased. The shrimp has disappeared completely from streams that it formerly inhabited.

The primary threat to this shrimp is the loss or destruction of its habitat. Many streams in its range have been diverted or dammed to help irrigate farms. In some areas, the water quality of the streams has decreased. Runoff from farms has introduced pesticides and other agricultural chemicals into the water system. The amount of silt (mineral particles) in the water has also increased because of construction along the banks of many streams.

Some dams have been removed in an attempt to restore the California freshwater shrimp's habitat. To further save this species, the effects of future damming and construction projects will have to be examined.

SHRIMP, KENTUCKY CAVE
Palaemonias ganteri

PHYLUM: Arthropoda
CLASS: Crustacea
ORDER: Decapoda
FAMILY: Atyidae
STATUS: Endangered, IUCN
Endangered, ESA
RANGE: USA (Kentucky)

Shrimp, Kentucky cave

Palaemonias ganteri

Description and biology

The Kentucky cave shrimp is a small freshwater shrimp that grows only to a maximum length of 1.2 inches (3 centimeters). It lacks pigmentation (coloring) and is almost transparent. Because it lives in dark underground streams, it is blind. This shrimp feeds on organic matter such as decaying plants, bat feces, algae, fungi, and insect remains.

Biologists (people who study living organisms) have very little information regarding the reproductive habits of this species.

Habitat and current distribution

The Kentucky cave shrimp is found in the Mammoth Cave National Park region in south–central Kentucky. In this area, it inhabits freshwater streams and pools located deep in caves. In the early 1980s, biologists estimated the shrimp's

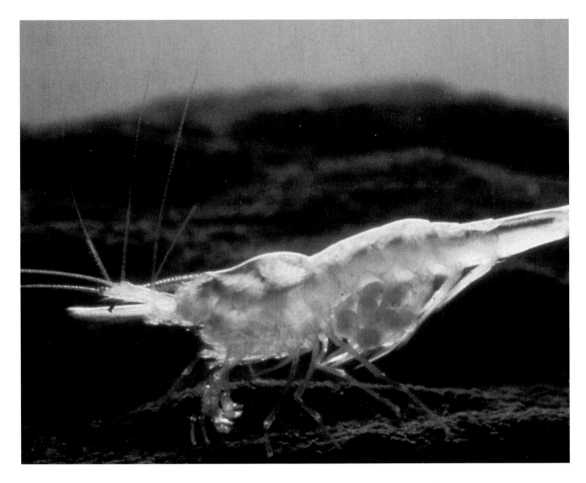

total population to be about 500. Since then, small populations have been discovered at additional sites in the area. Currently, Kentucky cave shrimp populations are found at five locations in the Mammoth Cave system.

The Kentucky cave shrimp inhabits freshwater streams and pools located deep in caves of the Mammoth Cave National Park region in south–central Kentucky.

History and conservation measures

Pollution is the main threat to the Kentucky cave shrimp. The food supply on which it depends is washed into the caves by a complex system of sinkholes and streams. Fertilizers, pesticides, and herbicides are used on the surface near the caves. These chemicals run off into the waterways supplying the caves. Once this water becomes contaminated, so does the shrimp's food and habitat. So far, biologists do not believe outside chemicals have polluted the water inside the caves, but the amount of silt (mineral particles) contained in that water has recently increased.

The small number of Kentucky cave shrimp in existence makes the species vulnerable. If a clean water supply to the caves is not maintained, the shrimp could face extinction.

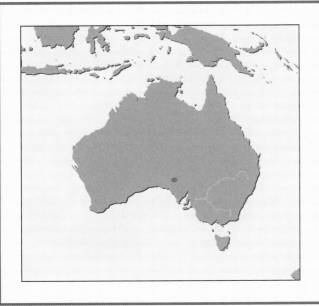

ANT, AUSTRALIAN
Nothomyrmecia macrops

PHYLUM: Arthropoda

CLASS: Insecta

ORDER: Hymenoptera

FAMILY: Formicidae

STATUS: Critically endangered, IUCN

RANGE: Australia

Ant, Australian

Nothomyrmecia macrops

Description and biology

Biologists (people who study living organisms) have identified about 9,500 species of ants (the actual number of ant species on Earth may be two or three times that many). The Australian ant, also known as the dinosaur ant, is considered one of the most primitive ants alive. Workers measure approximately 0.4 inch (1 centimeter) long and are golden yellow. They have long jaws and a single waist node (narrow area where the abdomen attaches to the thorax or chest). Their stings are very strong and effective. The ants have a sound–producing organ on their abdomens that they use to create a barely audible chirp. In related ant species, this organ is located on the back.

Australian ants emerge from their nests shortly after nightfall to forage for insects. They do not return to their nests until just before dawn. Biologists believe most ant species use scent markers to navigate. As they travel above ground, ants

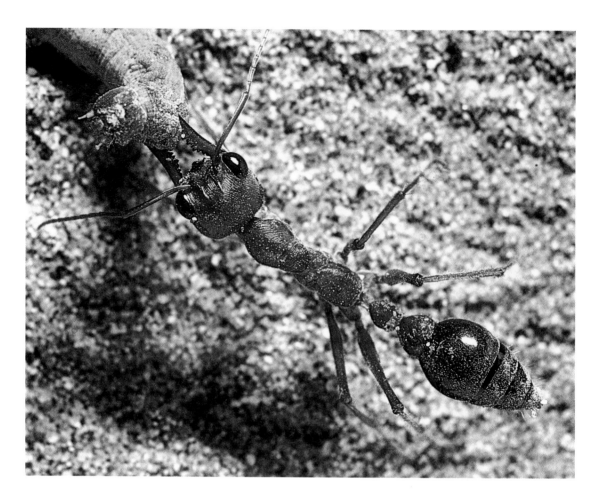

Although small in size, Australian ants are able to carry large prey, such as this caterpillar.

lay down a chemical from a gland located at the tip of their abdomen. After they have collected enough food, the ants return to their nests by following these odor trails.

An ant colony is an all–female society. Queens are winged females who produce young. Workers, soldiers, and other specialized members of a colony are all wingless, infertile females (these are the ones normally seen traveling above ground). The only function of winged males is to impregnate or fertilize virgin queens. Once they have done so, these males die. Once a queen has mated with numerous males, she stores the sperm and returns to the nest. She then lays her eggs. Those eggs that are fertilized with the sperm develop into females. Unfertilized eggs develop into males. Females become queens or workers depending on the type of food they are fed during their larval (immature) stage.

In Australian ant colonies, virgin queens and males are produced in late spring and early autumn. Although biologists have not witnessed mating activity, they believe the queens and the males leave their colonies in late summer to mate in flight.

Habitat and current distribution

Australian ants are found only in the Australian state of South Australia. They occupy several sites in an area measuring less than 0.4 square mile (1 square kilometer). Their total population number is unknown.

These ants prefer to inhabit woodlands dominated by tall eucalyptus trees. The ground in these areas is covered with a thin layer of leaf debris. Few herbs or grasses grow there. Nests are located underground and have concealed entrances.

History and conservation measures

Biologists originally believed this ant species had inhabited only Western Australia. Specimens had been collected there in 1934. In the years following, the ant could not be found. In 1977, a site was discovered in South Australia, but it was destroyed shortly afterward when workers laid an underground telephone line in the area. Since then, three other sites have been discovered nearby.

Habitat destruction is the major threat to this ant. Human populations are increasing in the Australian ant's limited range. Fire is also a concern. Bush fires at night could kill large numbers of foraging workers, thus wiping out a colony.

BEETLE, AMERICAN BURYING
Nicrophorus americanus

PHYLUM: Arthropoda

CLASS: Insecta

ORDER: Coleoptera

FAMILY: Silphidae

STATUS: Critically endangered, IUCN
Endangered, ESA

RANGE: USA (Arkansas, Massachusetts, Nebraska, Oklahoma, Rhode Island)

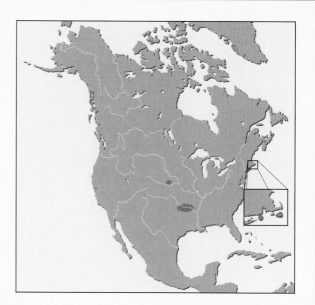

Beetle, American burying

Nicrophorus americanus

Description and biology

The American burying beetle, also known as the giant carrion beetle, is the largest of the North American carrion beetles (those that feed on carrion, or the decaying flesh of dead animals). This shiny black beetle reaches an average length of 1 to 1.4 inches (2.5 to 3.5 centimeters). It has bright orange or red spots on the plate covering its head, on the plate immediately behind, and on the plates covering its forewings.

These beetles often fight over carrion. Males fight males, and females fight females. When one male and one female remain, they form a couple. Working together, they dig out the soil beneath the carcass (dead body) until it is completely buried about 8 inches (20 centimeters) deep.

In the underground chamber, the beetles coat the carcass with secretions from their mouths and anuses. These secretions strip away the carcass's fur or feathers while preserving

468

what remains. In a passageway near the carcass, the female lays her eggs, and they hatch in a few days. The parents then feed the larvae (young) from the decomposing carcass for about 50 days, until the larvae develop into adults.

This complex parental teamwork—both in preparing the carcass and in raising the young—makes the American burying beetle unique among beetle species.

Habitat and current distribution

The American burying beetle is currently found in only four locations: on Block Island in Rhode Island, in a 14-county area of Oklahoma and Arkansas, in two counties in Nebraska, and on Nantucket Island in Massachusetts. The combined populations in Massachusetts and Rhode Island number less than 1,000. Total populations in the other areas are unknown.

American burying beetles have developed a unique method of parental teamwork in which both the male and female help to feed and care for the young.

These beetles inhabit grasslands, pastures, shrub thickets, and oak–hickory forests.

History and conservation measures

The American burying beetle had a range that once extended throughout the eastern and midwestern United States and eastern Canada. Since the 1960s, however, its numbers have been rapidly declining. The beetle has disappeared from 99 percent of its former range.

Scientists are unable to explain exactly why the beetle is vanishing. They believe it might be due to changes in its habitat and food supply. Small animals the beetle uses for food and reproduction, such as mice, are fewer in number. Meanwhile, competitors such as foxes, skunks, and raccoons have increased in number. Pesticides and insecticides, used primarily on farmland, may have also played a role in the decline of the American burying beetle, but no one is sure exactly how.

Scientists are currently studying the ecology and reproductive habits of the American burying beetle. Efforts to reintroduce the beetle into suitable habitat have begun. The population of American burying beetles on Nantucket Island is a reintroduced one.

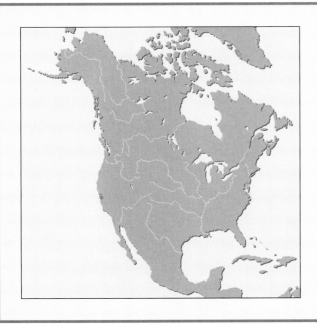

BUTTERFLY, BAY CHECKERSPOT
Euphydryas editha bayensis

PHYLUM: Arthropoda
CLASS: Insecta
ORDER: Lepidoptera
FAMILY: Nymphalidae
STATUS: Threatened, ESA
RANGE: USA (California)

Butterfly, bay checkerspot
Euphydryas editha bayensis

Description and biology

The bay checkerspot butterfly is a medium–sized butterfly with a maximum wingspan of 2.25 inches (5.72 centimeters). Females are slightly larger than males. The butterfly's black upper surface is checkered with bright red and yellow markings. Its yellow underside has sharp black and red patterns.

The life cycle of a bay checkerspot butterfly takes about a year to complete. The insect undergoes four stages: egg, larva, pupa (cocoon), and adult. This four–stage cycle is referred to as a complete metamorphosis (pronounced met–a–MORE–fa–sis) or change.

After mating in early spring, females lay eggs on host plants in batches of 20 to 95. Some females may lay as many as 1,200 eggs in a season, but the normal maximum is 600 to 700. The eggs soon hatch and the larvae or caterpillars begin feeding on their host plants. By late summer, if the larvae have

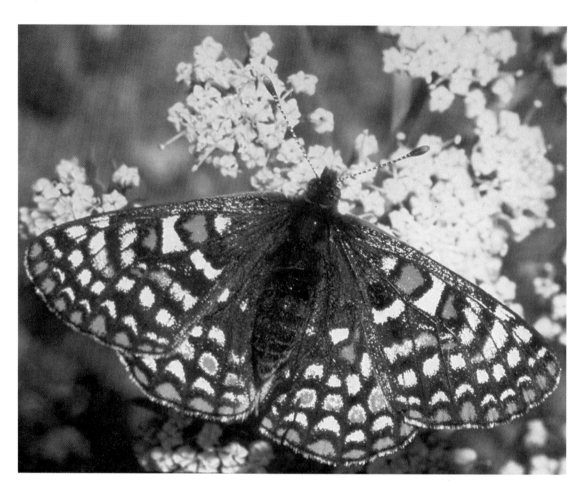

Much of the remaining bay checkerspot butterfly habitat is on property owned by a landfill corporation in California. An agreement between the corporation, the local city government, and conservationists established a butterfly preserve on the property.

developed enough or if the plants have begun to dry up from the summer heat, the larvae enter a dormant or resting stage. When winter rains revive the dry plants, the larvae become active again. In late winter, they enter the pupal, or cocoon, stage, transforming in two weeks into adult bay checkerspot butterflies. The adults feed on the nectar of several plants.

Habitat and current distribution

Bay checkerspot butterflies are known to exist only in San Mateo and Santa Clara counties in California. Because the number of butterflies alive each year changes dramatically, the total population size has never been estimated.

This butterfly inhabits grasslands where species of plantain and owl's clover—the butterfly's host plants—grow in high numbers.

History and conservation measures

Bay checkerspot butterflies once inhabited numerous areas around the San Francisco Bay, including the San Francisco peninsula, the mountains near San Jose, the Oakland hills, and several spots in Alameda County. All of these habitat areas were lost as urban development exploded in the region in the twentieth century. The butterflies are currently threatened with the loss of their host plants to animal grazing, brush fires, and introduced grassland plants.

In Santa Clara County, much of the remaining butterfly habitat is on property owned by a landfill corporation. An agreement between the corporation, the San Jose city government, and conservationists (people protecting the natural world) established a butterfly preserve on the property. Other habitat areas are currently being managed to provide protection for the bay checkerspot butterfly.

BUTTERFLY, CORSICAN SWALLOWTAIL
Papilio hospiton

PHYLUM: Arthropoda
CLASS: Insecta
ORDER: Lepidoptera
FAMILY: Papilionidae
STATUS: Endangered, IUCN
Endangered, ESA
RANGE: France (Corsica) and
Italy (Sardinia)

Butterfly, Corsican swallowtail

Papilio hospiton

Description and biology

The Corsican swallowtail butterfly has an average wingspan of just under 3 inches (7.6 centimeters). Its coloring is primarily black and yellow. Its hind wings are each marked by a small red "eye spot" located near the back of the wings. A row of small blue spots highlights the edges of these wings. The butterfly's tails are small and tapered.

The caterpillar or larval stage of this butterfly eats various plants of a plant family that includes fennel, giant fennel, and wild carrots. It is often preyed on by wasps. The caterpillar enters the pupal, or cocoon, stage in late spring to transform into an adult butterfly. It emerges from the pupa between May and June and remains active until early August.

474

Habitat and current distribution

Corsican swallowtail butterflies are found only on the islands of Corsica and Sardinia in the Mediterranean Sea. Corsica, belonging to France, lies about 100 miles (161 kilometers) southeast of the southern coast of France. Sardinia, belonging to Italy, lies just south of Corsica.

These butterflies inhabit open mountainous country at altitudes between 2,000 and 4,900 feet (610 and 1,494 meters).

History and conservation measures

The chief threats to the Corsican swallowtail butterfly are the loss of its food source and its habitat. The plants eaten by the butterfly when it is in its caterpillar stage are burned by shepherds on the islands. The shepherds claim these plants are poisonous to their sheep. Human development on these islands, such as the building of ski resorts, has also destroyed much butterfly habitat.

Like many other butterfly species, the Corsican swallowtail butterfly is further threatened by amateur and commercial butterfly collectors. Although protected under international treaty, this butterfly is still illegally captured. It is then sold for large sums of money to collectors around the world.

The French government has passed laws protecting this butterfly on the island of Corsica, but the laws are not well enforced and the butterfly has continued to suffer. The Italian government has yet to pass any laws guarding the Corsican swallowtail butterfly on the island of Sardinia.

BUTTERFLY, QUEEN ALEXANDRA'S BIRDWING
*Ornithoptera alexandrae
(or troides alexandrae)*

PHYLUM: Arthropoda
CLASS: Insecta
ORDER: Lepidoptera
FAMILY: Papilionidae
STATUS: Endangered, IUCN
Endangered, ESA
RANGE: Papua New Guinea

Butterfly, Queen Alexandra's birdwing

Ornithoptera alexandrae (or Troides alexandrae)

Description and biology

Many biologists (people who study living organisms) believe the Queen Alexandra's birdwing butterfly is the world's largest butterfly. It has an average head and body length of 3 inches (7.6 centimeters). Females of the species have wingspans measuring more than 10 inches (25.4 centimeters). Males, which are smaller, have wingspans of about 7 inches (17.8 centimeters). Females and males also differ in color. In females, the upper surfaces of the wings have cream markings on a dark, chocolate–brown background. In males, the upper surfaces have iridescent yellow, pale blue, and pale green markings on a black background. In both sexes, the abdomen is yellow and the lower surface of the wings where they attach to the butterfly's body are bright red.

The Queen Alexandra's birdwing butterfly has a seven–month life span. Females lay large eggs, which measure about

0.16 inch (0.41 centimeter) in diameter, on the leaves of a particular vine. The eggs hatch quickly, and the larvae or caterpillars emerge to begin feeding on these leaves. The caterpillars exist for four months before entering the pupal, or cocoon, stage to transform into an adult butterfly. After it has metamorphosed (pronounced met–a–MORE–fozed) or changed into an adult, the butterfly may live for another three months.

The adult butterfly has few predators, but its eggs are often eaten by ants. Caterpillars are preyed on by snakes, lizards, toads, and birds such as cuckoos and crow pheasants.

Habitat and current distribution

This butterfly species is found in a few sites in Papua New Guinea, but mainly on the Popondetta Plain in the northern part of the island. Because the Queen Alexandra's birdwing

Many biologists believe the Queen Alexandra's birdwing butterfly is the world's largest butterfly. Females of the species have wingspans measuring more than 10 inches, and males have wingspans of about 7 inches.

DID YOU KNOW?

The 1951 eruption of Mt. Lamington in Oro Province was the worst natural disaster ever to hit Papua New Guinea. Over 2,940 people were killed by lava flows. One dome of the volcano grew 1,600 feet (488 meters) above the crater before it collapsed. The volcano was active for six days before it finally erupted, covering most of Oro Province in ash and producing mudflows that continued until 1956. Some biologists believe the volcano's destruction of a large amount of prime habitat was the beginning of the decline of the Queen Alexandra's birdwing butterfly.

butterfly flies high and is rarely seen, biologists have been unable to determine any population totals.

Queen Alexandra's birdwing butterflies inhabit primary and secondary lowland rain forests at elevations up to 1,300 feet (396 meters). Biologists have reported seeing male butterflies swarm around large Kwila trees when they are bearing flowers. Those males that do not visit these flowers are not accepted by females to mate. Biologists cannot explain the reason for this.

History and conservation measures

The Queen Alexandra's birdwing butterfly was identified in 1906, when a female specimen was first collected. During the twentieth century, the butterfly's habitat was broken up by logging operations and farming. In 1951, the Mt. Lamington volcano erupted, destroying about 100 square miles (259 square kilometers) of prime butterfly habitat.

Large tracts of butterfly habitat in the Popondetta region have been converted into cocoa and rubber plantations. Currently, the Queen Alexandra's birdwing butterfly is threatened by the area's expanding oil palm industry. Growing human populations in the region pose a further threat as forests are cleared to create urban areas.

The Queen Alexandra's birdwing butterfly is protected by international treaties, but illegal capture remains a threat. Collectors around the world will pay large amounts of money to own a specimen of the world's largest butterfly.

The Papua New Guinea government has passed legislation safeguarding this and other butterfly species on the island. These laws are strictly enforced. A Wildlife Management Area, covering approximately 27,000 acres (10,800 hectares) of grassland and forest, has been established north of the Popondetta region. Plans to establish more reserves for the Queen Alexandra's birdwing butterfly are in progress.

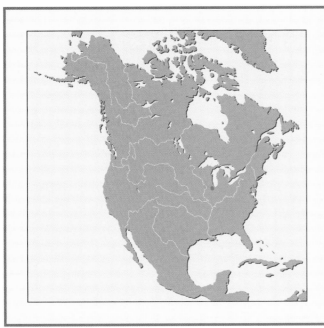

DRAGONFLY, HINE'S EMERALD
Somatochlora hineana

PHYLUM: Arthropoda

CLASS: Insecta

ORDER: Odonata

FAMILY: Corduliidae

STATUS: Endangered, IUCN
Endangered, ESA

RANGE: USA (Illinois, Michigan,
Wisconsin)

Dragonfly, Hine's emerald

Somatochlora hineana

Description and biology

The Hine's emerald dragonfly, also known as the Ohio emerald dragonfly, is a fairly large dragonfly. It has a yellow labrum (pronounced LAY–brum; upper part of the mouth), metallic green frons (front of the head capsule), and black leg segments. On its dark thorax (body segment between the head and abdomen) are two yellow stripes. The second of these stripes is slightly wider and shorter than the first.

Biologists (people who study living organisms) have very little information about this insect's feeding and breeding habits.

Habitat and current distribution

In 1997, the Hine's emerald dragonfly was discovered in three separate locations in Mackinac County in the upper peninsula of Michigan. Prior to this discovery, the dragonfly

Habitat destruction is the primary cause for the decline of the Hine's emerald dragonfly. The draining of wetlands remains a major threat to the species.

had been sighted at two sites in Illinois and six sites in Wisconsin.

This dragonfly prefers to inhabit bogs, which are areas of wet spongy ground composed chiefly of peat (soil made up mainly of decaying plant matter). In Michigan, this dragonfly was found inhabiting fen meadows, low–lying grassy areas covered wholly or partially with water.

History and conservation measures

The Hine's emerald dragonfly was originally discovered in Ohio, where it inhabited Logan, Lucas, and Williams counties in the northwestern part of the state. It was also known to inhabit northwest Indiana's Lake County. Biologists have not collected specimens from any of these areas since 1953, and they now believe the dragonfly has disappeared completely from this former range.

Habitat destruction is the primary cause for the decline of this species. Wetlands throughout the dragonfly's former range were drained to create urban and commercial areas. The draining of wetlands remains a major threat to the Hine's emerald dragonfly.

DID YOU KNOW?

Dragonflies are ancient insects, dating back before the beginning of the reign of the dinosaurs some 225 million years ago. Other than being smaller, present–day dragonflies do not differ very much from their ancestors. In fact, modern dragonflies are descendants of the very first winged insects, which were unable to flex their wings flat over their backs. Because of this, dragonflies are grouped in the subclass Paleoptera, meaning "with ancient wings."

EARWIG, SAINT HELENA GIANT
Labidura herculeana

PHYLUM: Arthropoda
CLASS: Insecta
ORDER: Dermaptera
FAMILY: Labiduridae
STATUS: Critically endangered, IUCN
RANGE: Saint Helena

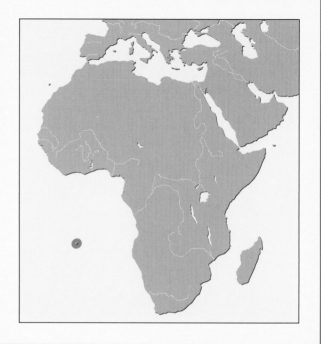

Earwig, Saint Helena giant
Labidura herculeana

Description and biology

Of the 900 classified species of earwigs in the world, the Saint Helena giant earwig is the largest, with an average body length of 1.4 to 2.1 inches (3.6 to 5.3 centimeters). Males are larger than females. The horny, forceplike pincers extending from the rear of the body measure between 0.6 and 0.9 inch (1.5 and 2.3 centimeters). Males use their pincers to battle each other over the right to mate with a female. The pincers in females are shorter but more serrated. Both males and females have black bodies and reddish legs. This earwig species is wingless.

The largest Saint Helena giant earwig ever collected is housed in a Belgium museum. It is a male with a total body and pincher length of more than 3 inches (7.6 centimeters).

Mating between males and females seems to take place between December and February.

Habitat and current distribution

The Saint Helena giant earwig is found only on the island of Saint Helena, a British dependency (territory) located in the southern Atlantic Ocean about 1,200 miles (1,931 kilometers) off the southwest coast of Africa. On Saint Helena, the earwig is restricted to Horse Point Plain in the extreme northeast portion of the island.

Horse Point Plain is dry and barren. Small bushes and tufts of grass are the main types of vegetation in the area. The earwig prefers to live under stones or in the soil near burrows that it uses as escape routes. During the summer rainy season, the insect is active. When the dry season begins, the earwig seeks shelter underground.

History and conservation measures

The Saint Helena giant earwig was discovered on Saint Helena in 1789. Until 1965, the insect was considered quite common on the island.

However, recent searches on Saint Helena have failed to find a single earwig. The reason is that much of its habitat has been altered or destroyed. Soil erosion is widespread because native plants have been cleared from large areas. Surface rocks in these areas have been removed for use in building human dwellings. As a result, the earwig has been left with an open, barren habitat that affords little protection.

In addition to the loss of its habitat, the Saint Helena giant earwig is further threatened by a number of introduced predators, particularly mice and centipedes.

Unless conservation measures are taken soon, the critically endangered Saint Helena giant earwig faces the real possibility of extinction.

DID YOU KNOW?

Further attention was brought to the plight of the St. Helena giant earwig on January 4, 1982, when the Philatelic (stamp collecting) Bureau of the St. Helena Post Office issued a commemorative postage stamp depicting the insect. The stamp carried a postage price of £1 (one pound British sterling).

FLY, DELHI SANDS FLOWER–LOVING

Rhaphiomidas terminatus abdominalis

PHYLUM: Arthropoda
CLASS: Insecta
ORDER: Diptera
FAMILY: Apioceridae
STATUS: Endangered, ESA
RANGE: USA (California)

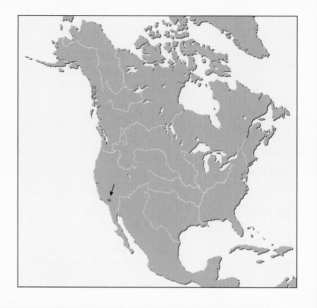

Fly, Delhi Sands flower-loving

Rhaphiomidas terminatus abdominalis

Description and biology

The Delhi Sands flower–loving fly is a very large fly, about 1 inch (3.9 centimeters) long. It is orange and brown with bands or dark brown spots on its abdomen. The fly has a long tubular–shaped proboscis (a long, flexible snout). Unlike common houseflies, the Delhi Sands flower–loving fly extracts nectar from flowers. In this way it has a pollinating function (transferring pollen from one flower's male parts to another flower's female parts), like a hummingbird or a honeybee. It is also like the hummingbird in its strong flying, whether it is soaring rapidly up into the air or hovering over a flower while feeding.

The Delhi Sands flower–loving fly goes through a complete metamorphosis (pronounced met–uh–MORE–fuh–sis) in its life cycle, which means it undergoes four stages: egg, larva, pupa (cocoon), and adult. It exists as an adult fly for only a few weeks in August and September, during which it feeds, mates, lays eggs, and then dies. Before her death, the mother will lay as many as 40 eggs an inch or two beneath the soil in a shady area. The eggs hatch in about twelve days. The offspring will then spend the majority of their life under the surface of the sand in the larval and pupa stages. It is not known what the larva eats. The life span of the species is about two years.

Habitat and current distribution

The Delhi Sands flower–loving fly is currently found only in tiny areas in San Bernardino and Riverside counties, California. The habitat is characterized by fine sandy soil, known as Delhi series sands. There are 11 or 12 known populations of the flies in these sand dunes.

History and conservation measures

Before southern California became so densely populated, the Colton Sand Dune system encompassed about 40 square miles (104 square kilometers) in the Delhi Sands region. It was the largest inland sand dune system in southern California, and the Delhi Sands flower–loving fly probably occurred throughout the system. In the nineteenth century, citrus and grape farming was introduced to the area, and large areas were cleared of their native plants. In the twentieth century, urban sprawl (the spreading of houses, shopping centers, and other city facilities through previously undeveloped land) reached out to the area. After widespread construction, the Colton Sand Dune ecosystem had virtually been eliminated. At most, about 1,200 acres (485 hectares) of the original habitat remain; about 98 percent of the ecosystem is gone. All of the 11 or 12 populations of the Delhi Sands flower–loving fly live in tiny, fragmented pieces of their former habitat, and most of their native plant foods are gone. Estimates of the existing population are in the low hundreds.

In 1993, the Delhi Sands flower–loving fly became the first fly (and the seventeenth insect) to be listed as endangered under the Endangered Species Act (ESA). The U.S. Fish and Wildlife Service proposed establishing three recovery units

> **DID YOU KNOW?**
>
> There were once two subspecies of *Rhaphiomidas terminatus*: the El Segundo flower–loving fly and the Delhi Sands flower–loving fly. The El Segundo fly lived in the El Segundo, California, sand dunes ecosystem (the ecological community, including plants, animals, and microorganisms, considered together with their environment), which was completely destroyed in the 1960s when the Los Angeles International Airport was built. The El Segundo flower–loving fly, with the loss of its habitat, became extinct.

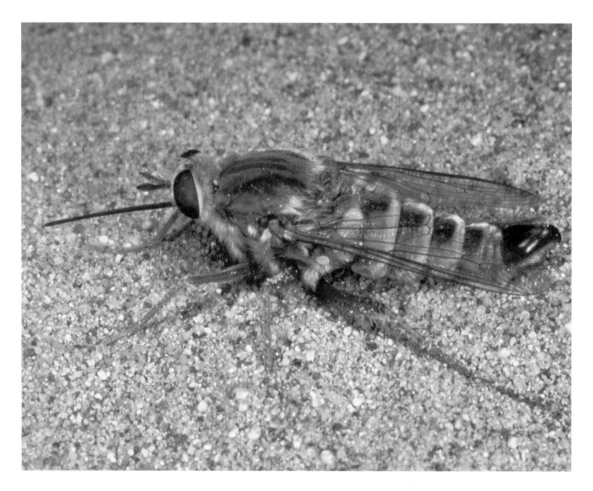

In 1993, the Delhi Sands flower–loving fly became the first fly to be listed as endangered under the Endangered Species Act (ESA).

within the remaining ecosystem to protect eight of the existing populations. But the fly's habitat is within privately owned lands, and the pressures from developing communities in the area, which want to clear more land for development, have remained very strong. The federal courts, working under ESA, have stopped some urban development, notably an emergency route for a medical center, in order to protect the fly's remaining habitat, but more construction is expected. There has been some political uproar over the idea that a fly's fate should be placed above the pursuits of humans. Conservationists, however, have argued that the loss of the Delhi Sands flower–loving fly is not all that is at stake: the loss of this species, should it come to pass, would signal the loss of an entire unique ecosystem, with all its biodiversity (variety of life forms).

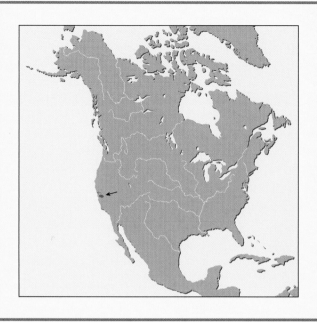

GRASSHOPPER, ZAYANTE BAND–WINGED
Trimerotropis infantilis

PHYLUM: Arthropoda
CLASS: Insecta
ORDER: Orthoptera
FAMILY: Acrididae
STATUS: Endangered, IUCN
Endangered, ESA
RANGE: USA (California)

Grasshopper, Zayante band-winged

Trimerotropis infantilis

Description and biology

The Zayante band–winged grasshopper is a small brownish–gray grasshopper with blue hind legs. It has dark bands on its front wings, pale yellow hind wings, and bands around its eyes. Males have an average body length of about half an inch (13.7 to 17.2 millimeters). Females are larger than males, with body lengths of .75 to .85 inch (19.7 to 21.6 millimeters).

Adult Zayante band–winged grasshoppers are active between May and October. When this grasshopper is flushed out of a thicket, it has been observed to fly three to seven feet into the air. It then lands on bare ground. It is particularly noticeable when it flies because its hind wings are yellow and produce a buzzing sound. Little is known about the life cycle of the species.

Habitat and current distribution

The Zayante band–winged grasshopper is found in Santa Cruz County, California, in the Zayante sand hills habitat, which is a sand parkland comprised of a combination of chaparral (low thickets of shrubs and small trees) and ponderosa pine forests. Within the Zayante sand hills habitat, the grasshopper is concentrated on ridges and hills in areas where plant life is sparse and much of the ground is made up of the loose sand called Zayante soils.

History and conservation measures

The Zayante sand hills ecosystem (the ecological community made up of plants, animals, and microorganisms within their environment) has been severely reduced by human activities such as sand mining, construction of homes and commercial properties, and recreation. While there was once about 500 to 600 acres (200 to 240 hectares) of the sand parkland, now only about 250 acres (40 hectares), an estimated 40 percent of the former habitat, remains intact. Another threat to the species is the introduction of nonnative plants to the area, particularly because forest fires, which formerly stopped alien plants from invading, are no longer allowed to occur in the area. Apparently the shade from new species of trees reduces the usable space for the grasshoppers, while other invading plants move into the space the grasshoppers would otherwise inhabit. Pesticides (chemicals used to kill pests) have also damaged the habitat.

Since the Zayante band–winged grasshopper was listed as endangered under the Endangered Species Act (ESA), restrictions have been placed upon sand miners in the area, and the construction of homes and businesses has been minimized. Research is underway to learn more about the habitat needs of the Zayante band–winged grasshopper. In 2001, the U.S. Fish and Wildlife Service designated 10,560 acres of land in Santa Cruz County, California, as critical habitat for the endangered Zayante band–winged grasshopper. Critical habitat is an area that the Fish and Wildlife Service deems essential to the physical and biological needs of the species, providing the appropriate space for population growth and normal behavior. The designation does not mean that the land will become a reserve or be managed by the government, but the owners will receive education on the conservation of the Zayante band–winged grasshopper.

LOUSE, PYGMY HOG SUCKING
Haematopinus oliveri

PHYLUM: Arthropoda

CLASS: Insecta

ORDER: Anoplura

FAMILY: Haematopinidae

STATUS: Critically endangered, IUCN

RANGE: Bhutan, India, Nepal

Louse, pygmy hog sucking

Haematopinus oliveri

Description and biology

The pygmy hog sucking louse is a parasite, or an organism that lives on or in another organism (called a host) and gets its nourishment from that host. The louse lives only on the pygmy hog, the smallest of all pig species. Because it lives on the hog's body surface, the louse is known as an ectoparasite.

Biologists (people who study living organisms) have not yet been able to collect a male louse specimen. Female pygmy hog sucking louses measure about 0.15 inch (0.38 centimeter) in length. They are wingless and have flat, leathery bodies. Their legs are strong with powerful claws for clinging to the hairs on the pygmy hog's body. These louses feed only on the hog's blood, and their mouths are specially developed for piercing and sucking.

Biologists do not know exactly how the louses reproduce. Mating seems to take place between males and females on a host hog. Females attach their eggs to the hairs on the hog's body, and the eggs hatch in about two weeks.

Habitat and current distribution

The pygmy hog sucking louse cannot survive apart from the pygmy hog. Therefore, it is found only where pygmy hogs are found. The primary habitat for these hogs is dense, tall grasslands. The greatest number of hogs is found mainly in Manas Wildlife Sanctuary and Barnadi Wildlife Sanctuary, both located in northwestern Assam (a state in far eastern India). Biologists estimate that less than 300 pygmy hogs currently exist.

History and conservation measures

The greatest threat to the pygmy hog sucking louse is the loss of its host, and the pygmy hog is one of the most endangered mammals in the world.

Hunting has reduced the number of pygmy hogs, but destruction of the animal's habitat is the main reason for its decline. The upland savannas of northern India are fertile, and farmers routinely set fires to these grassland areas to clear them to create farms. The extensive fires often kill many pygmy hogs because they cannot escape in time. Those that do escape are forced onto very small grassland areas where they are sometimes killed by unexpected fires or by hunters.

In 1985, the International Union for Conservation of Nature and Natural Resources (IUCN) placed the pygmy hog on its first list of the 12 most threatened species in the world. The following year, the United Nations Educational, Scientific, and Cultural Organization (UNESCO) designated the Manas Wildlife Sanctuary as a World Heritage Site. In India, the pygmy hog has been granted the maximum legal protection allowed.

Despite these protective measures, pygmy hog habitat continues to be destroyed. If nothing is done to stem this destruction, the pygmy hog—and with it the pygmy hog sucking louse—will disappear.

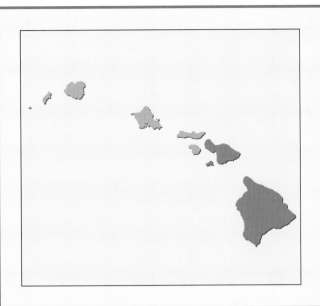

MOTH, BLACKBURN'S SPHINX
Manduca blackburni

PHYLUM: Arthropoda
CLASS: Insecta
ORDER: Lepidoptera
FAMILY: Sphingidae
STATUS: Endangered, ESA
RANGE: USA (Hawaii)

Moth, Blackburn's sphinx

Manduca blackburni

Description and biology

The Blackburn's sphinx moth, called *pulelehua* in Hawaiian (meaning "flying lehua flower that lasts a short time"), is the largest insect in Hawaii. Its wingspan is 5 inches (12 centimeters). It is grayish brown and has black bands across the top of its rear wings and orange spots along its abdomen. The forewings are long and narrow and the body is like a rounded stick with tapered ends.

Because the Blackburn's sphinx moth is very rare, little is known about its habits. However, it is a member of the sphinx moth family and shares many traits with better–known members of this family. These moths are often called "hummingbird" or "hawk" moths because they are so bird–like in looks and behavior. Like hummingbirds, they are strong fliers notable for the rapid movements of their wings. They feed like hummingbirds by hovering over a flower to sip the nectar.

491

Sphinx moths usually mate quickly after reaching adulthood. The female sphinx moth may lay as many as 1,000 eggs, usually on the surface of an 'aiea, a native Hawaiian plant that is its preferred host plant. A few days later, the eggs hatch. The male and female die after reproducing. In its larval (caterpillar) stage, the Blackburn's sphinx moth is a 3.5– to 4–inch (9– to 10–centimeter) caterpillar, almost the size of a hot dog. The caterpillars can be either bright green or gray with white spots or lines. They are usually called "hornworms" because they have a red or black horn on their abdomen. The caterpillars feed on plants from the nightshade family, particularly the 'aiea plant, from which they eat the leaves, stems, and flowers. However, this plant is becoming rare—two of the four 'aiea species are listed as endangered. Blackburn's sphinx moths also eat plants that have been introduced to Hawaii, such as a variety of tobacco plants, as well as eggplant and tomato. After the larval stage, the insect goes through the pupal (cocoon) stage, for which it goes underground. In this stage, it transforms, to eventually rise up to the surface as an adult moth.

Habitat and current distribution

The Blackburn's sphinx moth occurs from sea level to 2,500 feet (763 meters) in dry coastal forests. No one knows the number of adult or larval Blackburn's sphinx moths, but it is believed that there are currently four populations on the Hawaiian Islands of Maui, Kaho'olawe, and Hawaii. The main population is in Maui at Kanaio, a natural reserve. This population resides in an area that is both publicly and privately owned. Part of the public area is a natural reserve, while another part of the public area is training ground for the Hawaiian National Guard.

History and conservation measures

At one time the Blackburn's sphinx moth occurred throughout the Hawaiian Islands on Kauai, Oahu, Molokai, Maui, and Hawaii. It was most common in Maui. After the 1940s, very few of the species were observed. In the 1970s, after an extensive search for the species failed to turn up any specimens, it was thought to be extinct. Then, in 1984, a population of Blackburn's sphinx moth was discovered at Kanaio. Since then, three other populations have been discovered.

The primary threat to the Blackburn's sphinx moth is the destruction of its habitat by deer and by feral animals (animals that were once domesticated but have become wild), particularly goats. The animals eat the native plants and trample their roots and seedlings. The native 'aiea plant, which is important to the moth's survival, is being destroyed rapidly. Because these moths have become so rare, they have become valuable in the international market for insect specimens. Humans hunt them for trade. Military maneuvers by the National Guard within the moth's core habitat pose a threat, as do accidental fires in the arid region. Ants and parasitic wasps prey on the eggs and caterpillars.

The Blackburn's sphinx moth was the first Hawaiian insect to be placed on the U.S. Fish and Wildlife Service's endangered species list. In the early 2000s, research into captive breeding and conservation of the sphinx moth is ongoing. Work is being done to restore the dry forests that are home to the remaining populations. The 'aiea is being planted in the Kanaio habitat. The military groups that use the training grounds within the habitat are being educated about the moth and its preservation.

WETAPUNGA
Deinacrida heteracantha

PHYLUM: Arthropoda
CLASS: Insecta
ORDER: Orthoptera
FAMILY: Stenopelmatidae
STATUS: Vulnerable, IUCN
RANGE: New Zealand

Wetapunga
Deinacrida heteracantha

Description and biology

Wetas are nocturnal (active at night) grasshoppers with extremely long antennae. The giant wetas are among the largest insects in the world, and the wetapunga is the heaviest of the eleven giant weta species. It can weigh up to 2.5 ounces (70.9 grams), making it the heaviest insect in the world. The body of an adult female wetapunga may measure 4 inches (10 centimeters) long. With its armored, spiny legs spread out, the insect may reach 7 inches (17.8 centimeters) in length. Males are smaller in size.

Wetapungas have rounded bodies that are various shades of brown in color. They lack wings. Behind their head lies a broad protective shield. This anatomical detail, which was present in some dinosaur species, indicates how primitive these insects are.

Like other weta species, the life cycle of a wetapunga lasts a little over two years. Wetapungas mate and lay eggs during all but the winter months. Mating and egg–laying are usually repeated many times over a period of several days. The male dies soon after the final mating. After laying all of her eggs, sometimes up to 400 in total, the female also dies.

The eggs are approximately 0.27 inch (0.69 centimeter) long and 0.08 inch (0.2 centimeter) wide. They are laid at a depth of up to 0.78 inch (1.98 centimeters) beneath the soil surface. During midsummer, some eggs hatch within three weeks. Most eggs remain undisturbed in the ground through the winter, hatching after nine or ten months. The newly hatched wetapungas, called nymphs, are pale, mottled miniature versions of the adults. During the two years it takes them to reach adulthood, nymphs molt (shed) their skins about 10 times.

Wetapungas are primarily vegetarian. They venture out at dusk to feed on the leaves of a variety of trees, shrubs, herbs, and grasses. They are preyed on by many animals, including cats, rats, pigs, hedgehogs, birds, tuataras, and lizards.

Habitat and current distribution

Wetapungas once inhabited the main New Zealand islands. Now, they are found only on Little Barrier Island, a small island lying off the northeast coast of North Island (of the main New Zealand islands). They are arboreal (tree–dwellers). They spend most of their time in kauri, pohutukawa, kanuka, and other broadleaf trees, seldom coming down to the ground.

History and conservation measures

Before humans began settling on New Zealand islands, bats were the only warm–blooded mammals in the New Zealand ecosystem. All species of wetas thrived in safety. Sometime between 1,000 and 2,000 years ago, native people from Polynesian islands (Maoris) first traveled to the New Zealand islands. They brought with them the kiore, or Polynesian rat. It quickly became a predator of wetas.

When European settlers began arriving in the eighteenth century, they brought to the islands an enormous array of other animals. They cut down the forests for timber and to create farmland, and the whole shape of the New Zealand landscape changed. Those lands that were not cleared were quickly overrun with rodents, deer, goats, pigs, and opossums. In the 200 years since the arrival of European settlers, over 80 percent of New Zealand's natural vegetation has disappeared.

All eleven weta species are protected by New Zealand law and their limited habitats have been designated as reserves. However, predators remain in these habitats. Although domestic cats that had been living in the wild on Little Barrier Island have been exterminated, the wetapunga is still threatened by the kiore.

CONCH, QUEEN
Strombus gigas

PHYLUM: Mollusca

CLASS: Gastropoda

ORDER: Archaeogastropoda

FAMILY: Strombidae

STATUS: No special status

RANGE: Bahamas, Bermuda, Cuba, Dominican Republic, Haiti, Jamaica, Leeward Islands, Puerto Rico, Trinidad and Tobago, USA (Florida), Virgin Islands (British), Virgin Islands (US), Windward Islands

Conch, queen
Strombus gigas

Description and biology

The queen conch (pronounced KONGK), also called the pink conch, has a heavy, solid, spiral shell with a broad, flaring lip. At maturity, the conch can weight up to 5 pounds (2.3 kilograms) and its shell can reach a length of 8 to 12 inches (20 to 30.5 centimeters). The shell's exterior is light pink to white in color. The inside is a glossy pink, yellow, or peach. A row of blunt spines line the upper portion of the shell below the apex (top). Queen conchs are "right–handed"; that is, the shell coils to the right when one looks down on the apex of the shell.

When just a young mollusk, the conch has no bone structure, just a soft body. This body consists of a long and narrow foot, a head with yellow eyes on the end of two

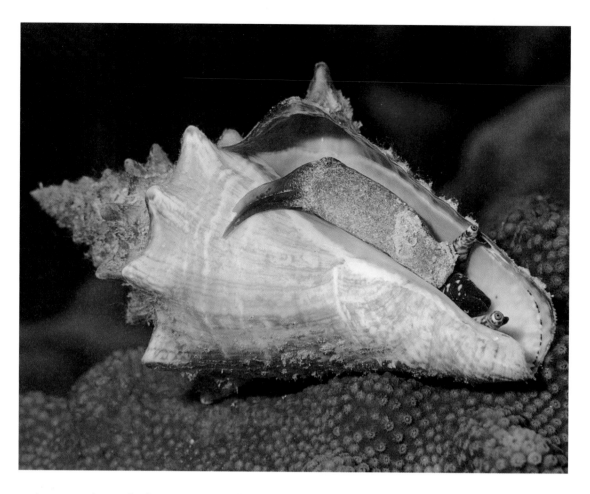

A queen conch emerging from its shell.

protruding stalks, and a snout–like mouth between them. A pair of slender tentacles also appear on the head. A fleshy covering of yellow or orange skin, called the mantle, encloses the foot and head.

At the end of the conch's foot is a sickle–shaped claw called an operculum (pronounced o–PER–cue–lum). The conch uses its operculum to dig into the sea floor to pull its body forward in short hops and to right itself when turned over.

The shell of a young conch does not have the flaring lip of an adult. It is very delicate. The spines are pointed and not yet blunted. The shell is composed mainly of calcium carbonate. The mantle of the conch excretes this material as a fluid, which quickly hardens to a crystal form. As the conch ages, it continues to build its shell, increasing the thickness. The shell can grow as much as 3 inches (7.6 centimeters) per year. The lip begins to develop after two to three years.

Queen conchs are primarily nocturnal, emerging at night to feed on a variety of algae species and sea grasses. Young conchs are preyed on by crabs, sharks, loggerhead turtles, groupers, snappers, and octopi. Adult conchs are preyed on mainly by humans.

Female queen conchs breed during the summer months in shallow waters in sandy areas behind reefs. After mating with a male, the female stores the sperm for several weeks until she is ready to release her eggs. A female can lay eight or more egg masses each season. An egg mass consists of a single continuous sticky tube that contains between 400,000 and 750,000 eggs. The tube folds back on itself, producing a slightly curved mass. Once the eggs are laid, the female releases the stored sperm to fertilize them. The eggs hatch after three to five days, and the shelled larvae emerge to begin their period of development. Queen conchs have an estimated life span of six to ten years. Some may live longer.

Habitat and current distribution

The queen conch is found in Bermuda, southeast Florida, and the West Indies. Actual population numbers are currently unknown. The queen conch has declined near areas inhabited by humans, but it may still be common in more remote areas.

The species inhabits sandflats, gravel, and coral rubble in shallow warm water near islands and coral reefs where sea grass is abundant. As they mature, the conchs move from shallow, inshore sands to deeper offshore sites. Although they have been found in water at depths up to 400 feet (122 meters), it is rare for conchs to inhabit water deeper than 70 feet (21 meters).

History and conservation measures

The queen conch has always served as an important food source for people in the Caribbean. The protein–rich meat of the conch makes a nutritious meal. But rising human populations throughout the Caribbean have brought increased pressures on the conch. Not only is it eaten, it is also sought out by fishermen for use as bait. And its shell is highly prized by tourists from around the world. The queen conch is now rare in areas where it formerly was common, such as the Florida Keys.

Captive–breeding programs have so far proved useless. Although the conch is easy to raise in captivity, it does not fare well when placed back in its ocean habitat. Predators quickly eat captive–bred young conchs.

The queen conch is protected by international treaties. The International Union for Conservation of Nature and Natural Resources placed the species in a commercially threatened status in the 1990s, but later removed it. Greater enforcement of these restrictions is necessary to ensure the survival of the species.

FANSHELL
Cyprogenia stegaria

PHYLUM: Mollusca

CLASS: Bivalvia

ORDER: Unionoida

FAMILY: Unionidae

STATUS: Critically endangered, IUCN
Endangered, ESA

RANGE: USA (Kentucky, Tennessee, Virginia)

Fanshell
Cyprogenia stegaria

Description and biology

A medium–sized freshwater mussel, the fanshell measures about 3.2 inches (8.1 centimeters) long. Its shell is yellowish–green with fine green lines across the surface. The inside of the shell is gray–white. It feeds on plant material it removes from the water through a tube called a siphon. Muskrats are known predators of this mussel.

The reproductive cycle of the fanshell is complex. In the spring, a male releases sperm that is carried away by stream currents. A female takes in this sperm as she is feeding, and the eggs stored in her gills are fertilized. When the eggs hatch, the glochidia (pronounced glow–KID–ee–a; larval forms of the mussel) develop in the female's gills.

After a while, the glochidia are released from the gills into the stream and they attach themselves to the gills of a passing fish (those glochidia that do not attach themselves to a

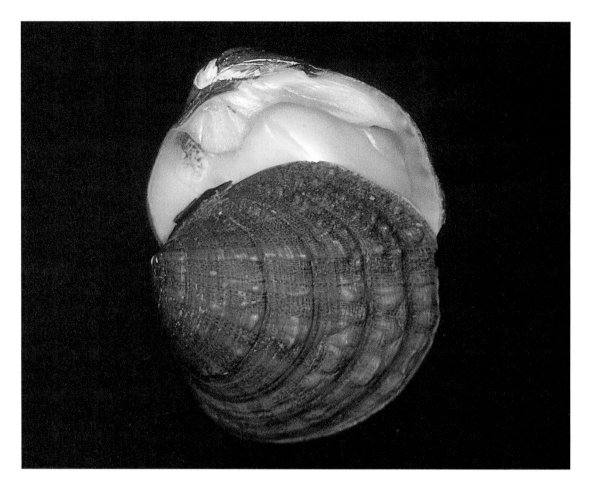

One of the most endangered mussel species in North America, fanshells can survive only if their habitat is left undisturbed and unpolluted.

host fish sink to the bottom of the stream and die). The glochidia remain attached to the fish until they begin to develop a shell and are large enough to survive on their own. They detach from the fish and fall to the stream bottom, burying themselves until only their shell margins (edges) and feeding siphons are exposed.

Habitat and current distribution

Populations of breeding fanshells are found in only three locations: in Clinch River in Tennessee and Virginia, in Green River in Kentucky, and in Licking River in Kentucky. Additional populations are scattered throughout eight other rivers, but these fanshells are older and are no longer reproducing.

Like other North American freshwater mussels, fanshells need clean, undisturbed stream habitats. Any silt (mineral particles) or sediment (sand and stones) in the water can pose a serious threat. It can clog their siphons and ultimately kill them.

History and conservation measures

The fanshell was once found in 26 rivers running through 7 states. It has declined in number because of major, harmful changes to its habitat. The construction of dams on rivers and the mining of sand and gravel from river bottoms have combined to destroy much of the fanshell's habitat. Pollution has become another serious threat. In Clinch River, coal mining operations and toxic spills from a power plant have killed a considerable number of fish and mussels.

The fanshell will survive only if its remaining habitat is protected.

MUSSEL, DWARF WEDGE
Alasmidonta heterodon

PHYLUM: Mollusca
CLASS: Bivalvia
ORDER: Unionoida
FAMILY: Unionidae
STATUS: Endangered, ESA
RANGE: USA (Maryland, New Hampshire, North Carolina, Vermont)

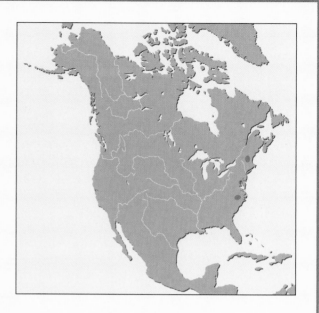

Mussel, dwarf wedge

Alasmidonta heterodon

Description and biology

The dwarf wedge mussel is a very small mussel species. It does not grow any longer than 1.5 inches (3.8 centimeters). The outer side of its shell is dark in color; the inner part is much lighter. The mussel feeds on plankton (microscopic plants and small animals) and other plant matter it removes from the water through a tube called a siphon.

Like other mussels, the dwarf wedge mussel reproduces in a unique way. Males release sperm, which is carried by currents downstream. As they feed, females take in the sperm, which fertilizes the eggs stored in their gills. When the eggs hatch, the glochidia (pronounced glow–KID–ee–a; larval forms of the mussel) continue to develop in the gills.

After a certain time, the glochidia are released and attach themselves to the gills or fins of a particular fish species (those glochidia unable to attach themselves to a fish sink to the

mm 0   10   20   30
in 0   1

The dwarf wedge mussel is a very small mussel species. It does not grow any longer than 1.5 inches, as seen here.

river bottom and die). In a few weeks, after having developed a shell, the young mussels detach from the fish and sink to the riverbed. Here, they bury themselves, leaving only their shell margins (edges) and siphons exposed.

Habitat and current distribution

Dwarf wedge mussels inhabit sandy and muddy bottoms of rivers where there is not much current and very little silt (mineral particles). Too much silt or sediment (sand and stones) in the water can clog a mussel's siphon and kill it. Major populations of this mussel are found in only four states: Maryland (in the McIntosh Run and Tuckahoe Creek), New Hampshire (Ashuelot and Connecticut Rivers), North Carolina (Little and Tar Rivers), and Vermont (Connecticut River).

History and conservation measures

The dwarf wedge mussel's total population size is currently unknown, but it is obviously in decline. Previously, it was found as far north as New Brunswick, Canada. Its range extended from there south through North Carolina. The populations that remain are isolated and contained in a relatively small region that is growing smaller.

As with other North American freshwater mussels, dams and water pollution have destroyed much of the dwarf wedge mussel's habitat. When dams are built, the water upstream becomes filled with silt. Downstream, water levels, currents, and temperature change often. Industrial wastes and pesticide runoff from farms are the main pollutants of the mussel's habitat. If these pollutants do not kill the mussel immediately, they accumulate in its tissues and will eventually kill it.

Saving the dwarf wedge mussel habitat is the only way to ensure the survival of this species.

MUSSEL, FAT POCKETBOOK PEARLY
Potamilus capax

PHYLUM: Mollusca

CLASS: Bivalvia

ORDER: Unionoida

FAMILY: Unionidae

STATUS: Critically Endangered, IUCN
Endangered, ESA

RANGE: USA (Arizona, Illinois, Indiana, Iowa, Kentucky, Minnesota, Missouri, Mississippi, New York, Texas, Wisconsin)

Mussel, fat pocketbook pearly

Potamilus capax

Description and biology

The fat pocketbook pearly mussel is a fresh water mussel that grows to about 4 to 5 inches (10 to 13 centimeters) long. It has a smooth and shiny yellow, tan, or brown outer shell that is round and inflated. In young mussels, the shell is thin, but in adults it is thick. The inside of the shell is pink at the center and bluish white toward the shell edges.

The fat pocketbook lives at the bottoms of large rivers in places where the water is less than eight feet deep. It buries itself in the sand or mud at the bottom of the river with only its feeding siphons (tubular organs used to draw in fluids) exposed to the water. It then feeds by pumping water through its siphon, gathering nutrition from the tiny plant and animal life in the water.

The fat pocketbook lives at the bottoms of large rivers in places where the water is less than eight feet deep. It buries itself in the sand or mud at the bottom of the river with only its feeding siphons exposed to the water.

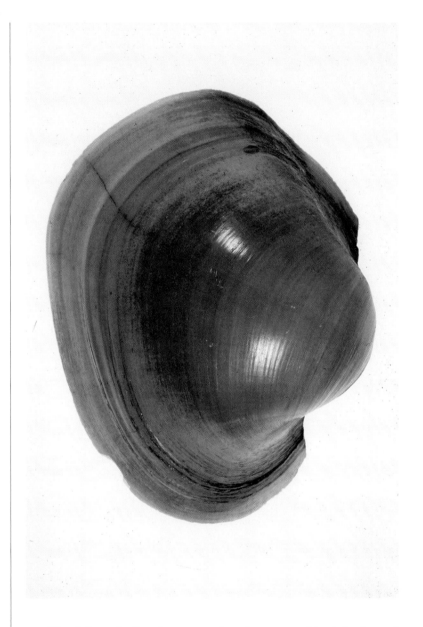

The fat pocketbook spawns (produces eggs) in late August or September. To breed, the male fat pocketbook discharges his sperm into the river's current. The female, located downstream from the male, siphons the sperm to fertilize her eggs. The eggs are then kept in the female's gill (the organ used for obtaining oxygen from the water) pouches, where they develop into larvae (an immature stage of development, like the caterpillar stage of an insect). The larvae, called the glochidia (pronounced glow–KID–ee–), hatch in June or July, and the female fat pocketbook expels them into the water. In order to survive, each larva must find a host fish and clamp onto it with its tiny clasping valves. Only certain fish, such as fresh-water drum and white crappie, are suitable hosts for fat pocketbooks, and if the larva does not find a host fish, it will fall to the bottom of the river and die. The larva that finds a host will remain attached to the fish for about two to four weeks, until it has grown its own shell. At that point, it unclasps itself from the fish and, if it is lucky enough to be in an appropriate habitat, buries itself in the sand or mud at the bottom of the river or stream. There it will probably remain for its long life. The life span of a fat pocketbook may be up to 50 years.

Habitat and current distribution

The fat pocketbook is found in drainage ditches or in sand, gravel, or muddy streams with flowing water. It is known to occur in the upper Mississippi River, the lower Wabash and Ohio rivers, the Cumberland River, and the White River and St. Francis River in Arizona.

History and conservation measures

The fat pocketbook has ceased to exist in much of its former range. For instance, the species inhabited the Mississippi River in Missouri up until the 1960s, but it has not been seen there for several decades. Elsewhere the population is declining, mainly due to severe loss of habitat.

Human efforts to change the course or nature of the waterways in which the fat pocketbook lives are responsible for most of the reduction in population. The construction of dams and channels and the practice of dredging (digging up the river bottom) for navigation and flood control present major threats to the fat pocketbook. These practices destroy the habitat at the bottom of the rivers and also result in siltation—filling the water with too much mud or sediment. When fat pocketbooks siphon in silt, it can block up their feeding organs and it can also suffocate them. All changes in water temperature, water flow, and water quality are potentially harmful to these mussels. Pollution from farming and industry has also caused their decline. The fat pocketbook is a filter–feeder, and chemicals or contaminants in the water will eventually poison it. The destruction of the river habitat may also be reducing the number of the host fish that are essential to the fat pocketbook's life cycle.

The U.S. Fish and Wildlife Service has put together a recovery plan for the fat pocketbook. It is working to protect and preserve the population of the species that is currently living in the St. Francis River in Arizona, particularly by protecting this habitat from dredging and other destructive practices. There is ongoing research into the habits of the mussel and a search for other populations in the wild. Fat pocketbook populations are being reintroduced into the former habitats of the species, by releasing both adult fat pocketbooks and fish with fat pocketbook larvae attached into rivers where the habitat is deemed stable.

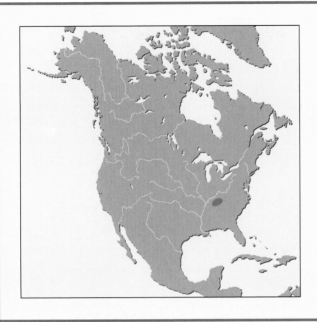

MUSSEL, RING PINK
Obovaria retusa

PHYLUM: Mollusca

CLASS: Bivalvia

ORDER: Unionoida

FAMILY: Unionidae

STATUS: Critically endangered, IUCN
Endangered, ESA

RANGE: USA (Kentucky and Tennessee)

Mussel, ring pink
Obovaria retusa

Description and biology

The ring pink mussel, also known as the golf stick pearly mussel, is a medium–sized mussel. The outer surface of its shell is yellow–green to brown in color. Inside, its shell is dark purple with a white border.

Like other freshwater mussels, the ring pink mussel breeds in a unique way. In the spring, males of the species release sperm, which is carried downstream by currents. As they are feeding, females take in this sperm, which fertilizes the eggs stored in their gills. Once the eggs hatch, the glochidia (pronounced glow–KID–ee–a) or larval forms of the mussel continue to develop in the gills.

After a while, the glochidia are released from the female's gills. They then attach themselves to the gills of a host fish (those glochidia that are unable to attach themselves sink to the river's bottom and die). The glochidia remain on the host

Although the outside of the ring pink mussels' shell is yellow–green to brown it color, its name was derived from the pink interior of the shell.

fish until they have grown and developed a shell. Once they have, the young mussels detach from the fish and sink to the riverbed where they bury themselves in the sand, leaving only their shell margins (edges) and siphons exposed.

A siphon is a tube through which the mussel feeds, removing plankton (microscopic plants and small animals) and other plant matter from the water. Because this is the only way it feeds, a mussel requires a river environment where there is not much current and very little silt. Too much silt (mineral particles) or sediment (sand and stones) in the water can clog a mussel's siphon and kill it.

Habitat and current distribution

The ring pink mussel is the most endangered of all North American freshwater mussels. It inhabits sections of the silt–free, sandy bottoms of the Tennessee, Cumberland, and Green Rivers in Tennessee and Kentucky. Biologists (people who study living organisms) are unaware of the total number of these mussels still in existence.

History and conservation measures

The ring pink mussel was once found in several major tributaries of the Ohio River. These stretched into Alabama, Illinois, Indiana, Ohio, Pennsylvania, and West Virginia. As indicated by its current small range, this mussel is in grave danger of extinction. Biologists believe the known remaining populations are all too old to reproduce.

As is the case with many other freshwater mussels, the ring pink mussel is disappearing because humans have tampered with its habitat. Dams built on rivers have caused upstream sections to become filled with silt. Downstream areas are subject to constantly changing currents, water levels, and water temperature.

Water pollution is another major threat, especially to remaining populations. Industrial wastes and pesticide runoff from farms are the main pollutants of the mussel's habitat.

Unless biologists discover new populations of the ring pink mussel in the wild, the future of this species is in doubt.

PEARLYMUSSEL, LITTLE–WING
Pegias fabula

PHYLUM: Mollusca
CLASS: Bivalvia
ORDER: Unionoida
FAMILY: Unionidae
STATUS: Critically endangered, IUCN
Endangered, ESA
RANGE: USA (Kentucky, Tennessee, Virginia)

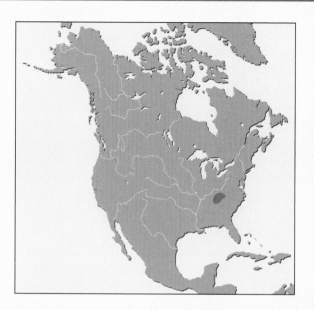

Pearlymussel, little-wing
Pegias fabula

Description and biology

The shell of the little–wing pearlymussel measures up to 1.5 inches (3.8 centimeters) long and 0.5 inch (1.3 centimeters) wide. The outer side is light green or yellow–brown in color; the inner side is much lighter. Dark rays run along the shell's front edge. A white, chalky film often flakes off its surface. Like other freshwater mussels, the little–wing pearlymussel feeds on plankton (microscopic plants and small animals) and other plant matter it removes from the water through a siphon or tube.

The little–wing pearlymussel breeds in the spring in a unique way. A male releases sperm that is carried downstream by currents. While eating, a female takes in this sperm, which fertilizes eggs stored in her gills. The eggs hatch, and the glochidia (pronounced glow–KID–ee–a) or larval forms of the mussel continue to develop in her gills.

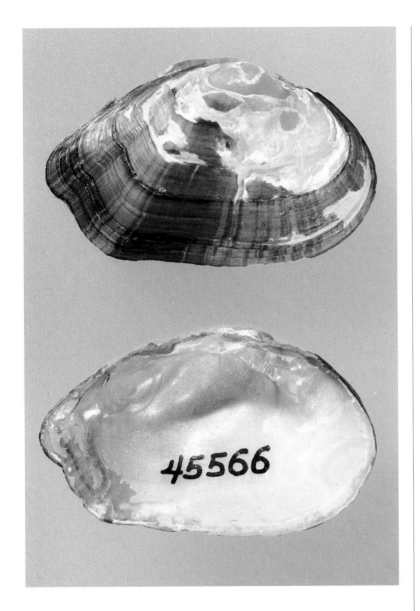

The only way to save the little–wing pearlymussels' water habitat is to implement measures preventing water pollution.

After a certain period, the glochidia are released. Floating away, they attach themselves to the gills of a host fish (those glochidia unable to attach themselves sink to the bottom of the river and die). When they have grown and developed a shell, the young pearlymussels detach and fall to the riverbed. Here, they bury themselves, leaving only their shell margins (edges) and siphons exposed.

Habitat and current distribution

In the mid–1980s, biologists (people who study living organisms) conducted a survey of this pearlymussel's habitat. They found this species in only five locations: Horse Lick Creek, the Big South Fork Cumberland River, and the Little South Fork Cumberland River in Kentucky; Great Falls Lake in Tennessee; and the North Fork Holston River in Virginia. During this study, biologists found only 17 live pearlymussels.

Little–wing pearlymussels inhabit rivers with cool waters and moderately to steeply inclined riverbeds. Because of the way the pearlymussel feeds, these rivers must have a low current and very little silt (mineral particles). Too much silt in the water can plug the pearlymussel's siphon and kill it.

History and conservation measures

The little–wing pearlymussel once existed in at least 27 cool water tributaries of the Tennessee and Cumberland Rivers. Biologists believe the pearlymussel is now extinct in North Carolina and Alabama. A total of 18 populations have disappeared in Kentucky, Tennessee, and Virginia.

Water pollution has been the main reason for the pearlymussel's decline. Toxic (poisonous) runoff from farms, strip mining operations, and industries has clouded many rivers that were once clear. Increased amounts of sediment (sand and stones) have also built up in these rivers, settling on the riverbeds and suffocating the pearlymussels.

In Kentucky, Tennessee, and Virginia, laws have passed banning the harvesting (gathering) of freshwater mussels without a permit. In Kentucky, part of the pearlymussels' remaining habitat is bounded by the Daniel Boone National Forest. Despite these conservation measures, pollution from coal exploration threatens to pollute the little–wing pearlymussels' habitat in unprotected areas.

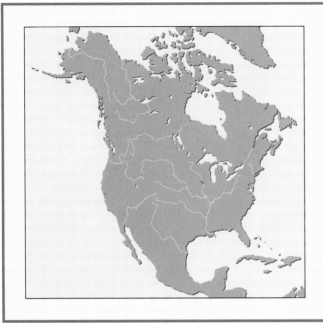

SNAIL, IOWA PLEISTOCENE
Discus macclintocki

PHYLUM: Mollusca
CLASS: Gastropoda
ORDER: Stylommatophora
FAMILY: Discidae
STATUS: Data deficient, IUCN
Endangered, ESA
RANGE: USA (Illinois and Iowa)

Snail, Iowa Pleistocene

Discus macclintocki

Description and biology

The Iowa Pleistocene (pronounced PLICE–ta–seen) snail is a small forest snail measuring 0.3 inch (0.8 centimeter) wide. Its domed shell is brown or off–white with a greenish cast. The shell is marked by tightly coiled whorls (spirals), usually six.

These snails eat tree leaves, including those of maples, white and yellow birches, willows, and dogwoods. After the first hard freeze in late fall, they burrow in the soil and hibernate through the winter. They are active in the spring and summer, but become sluggish in late summer when their habitat begins to dry out.

Like all land snails, Iowa Pleistocene snails are hermaphroditic (pronounced her–ma–fra–DI–tick). This means that each snail has both male and female reproductive organs. They can each lay eggs and also fertilize the eggs laid by other snails.

The Iowa Pleistocene snail inhabits cool, moist areas found around the entrances to caves or fissures (long narrow cracks or openings in the ground).

Between March and August, the snails lay two to six eggs apiece under logs or bark, in the soil, or in moist rock crevices. After the eggs are fertilized, they incubate (develop) for 28 days before hatching. On average, Iowa Pleistocene snails live for five years.

Habitat and current distribution

The Iowa Pleistocene snail is found only in one county in Illinois (Jo Davies County) and two in Iowa (Dubuque and Clayton Counties). Biologists (people who study living organisms) estimate that the total snail population, scattered over 18 locations, numbers about 60,000.

This snail lives in a very specific habitat. It inhabits cool, moist areas found around the entrances to caves or fissures (long narrow cracks or openings in the ground). Underground ice, formed by water bubbling up from underground, cools the surface where the snail lives in deep, moist, deciduous (shedding trees) leaf debris.

History and conservation measures

The Iowa Pleistocene snail has existed as a species for more than 300,000 years. It receives its name from the geologic time period in which it arose, the Pleistocene epoch, which covers the period from 2,000,000 to 11,000 years ago. The Pleistocene is the best known glacial period (Ice Age) of Earth's history.

The Iowa Pleistocene snail's present–day habitat recreates the conditions of the environment inhabited by its ancestors. If glacial conditions returned to the midwestern United States, it is likely that the number of Iowa Pleistocene snails would increase and their range would expand. During cooler periods in Earth's history, the snail's range extended over the present–day states of Nebraska, Iowa, Missouri, Illinois, Indiana, and Ohio.

Humans pose the greatest threat to this snail. Over the last 150 years, almost 75 percent of its habitat has been converted into farms and stone quarries (excavation sites where stone is dug, cut, or blasted out of the ground).

In 1986, the Nature Conservancy, the Iowa Conservation Commission, and the U.S. Fish and Wildlife Service established the Driftless Area Project in northeastern Iowa. The aim of this voluntary project is to protect any remaining Iowa Pleistocene snail habitat. Private landowners have been asked to conserve any such habitat on their land. So far, more than 65 percent of the landowners contacted have agreed to take part in the project.

DID YOU KNOW?

Ice ages were periods in Earth's history when average annual temperatures dropped low enough to allow glaciers and vast sheets of ice to spread and cover large portions of the planet's surface. Over the last 2.5 million years, about two dozen ice ages have occurred.

Scientists do not know exactly what causes ice ages or periods of glaciation, but they have offered many theories. Some scientists believe that changes in the geometry of Earth's orbit around the sun affects the amount of solar radiation reaching the planet, making it warmer or cooler. Others believe changes on Earth are responsible. They point out that volcanic eruptions may have contributed to significant temperature variations on the planet. Dust particles thrown into the air during an eruption can reflect sunlight back into space, reducing the amount of heat reaching Earth's surface.

SNAIL, MANUS ISLAND TREE
Papustyla pulcherrima

PHYLUM: Mollusca

CLASS: Gastropoda

ORDER: Stylommatophora

FAMILY: Camaenidae

STATUS: Data deficient, IUCN
Endangered, ESA

RANGE: Papua New Guinea

Snail, Manus Island tree

Papustyla pulcherrima

Description and biology

The brilliant color of the Manus Island tree snail makes it easily recognizable. Its shell, which is approximately 1.6 inches (4 centimeters) long, is intense pea–green in color. A yellow band runs along the suture, the point where the shell attaches to the snail's body. The brilliant green color of the shell is contained in its outer layer. As the snail ages and the shell wears away, a yellow layer underneath begins to show. Within the shell, the snail is tan in color with brown stripes running down both sides.

Biologists (people who study living organisms) know very little about the Manus Island tree snail's feeding and reproductive habits.

Habitat and current distribution

This snail is found in the rain forests of Manus Island, the largest of the Admiralty Islands (an island group north of

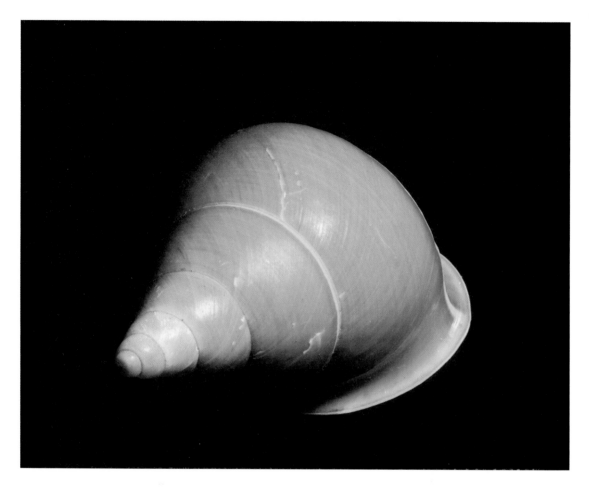

Papua New Guinea, of which it is a part). Biologists do not know how many of these snails currently exist.

The Manus Island tree snail prefers to inhabit the high canopy of the rain forests. During the day, it is mainly inactive. It is usually found about 16 feet (4.9 meters) above the ground attached to the underside of leaves of Dillenia and Astronia trees. It is also found on the leaves of large climbing plants.

History and conservation measures

The Manus Island tree snail's shell has been traditionally used by Manus Islanders in decorations, and it is currently used in jewelry. In the past, large numbers of shells were either purchased by tourists or shell collectors.

The primary threat to the Manus Island tree snail is believed to be logging. The trees the snail inhabits are valued for their timber.

Despite this, the primary threat to the snail is believed to be logging. The trees the snail inhabits are valued for their timber. Manus Island is still largely covered in natural forest, but approximately 11 percent of that is now open to logging operations. If the cutting down of trees in the Manus Island tree snail's range continues, reserves will have to be set aside to ensure the survival of this species.

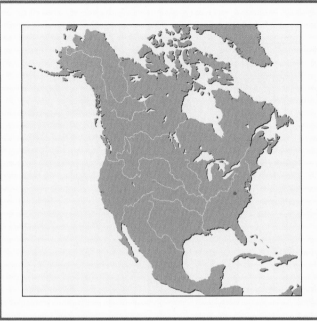

SPINYMUSSEL, JAMES RIVER
Pleurobema collina

PHYLUM: Mollusca

CLASS: Bivalvia

ORDER: Unionoida

FAMILY: Unionidae

STATUS: Critically endangered, IUCN
Endangered, ESA

RANGE: USA (Virginia and West Virginia)

Spinymussel, James River
Pleurobema collina

Description and biology

The James River spinymussel, also known as the Virginia spinymussel, is one of only three known freshwater spiny-mussels. These mussels are so–named because juveniles, or young, have one to three spines on each valve or shell. These spines are usually lost by the time the spinymussel reaches adulthood. An average adult has a shell length between 2 and 3.5 inches (5 and 8.9 centimeters). Spinymussels feed on plankton (microscopic plants and small animals) and other plant matter they strain from the water through a tube called a siphon.

Like other mussels, the James River spinymussel breeds in a unique way every spring. Males release sperm, which is car-ried away by river currents. Downstream, females take in this sperm while feeding. The eggs stored in their gills are then fertilized. When the eggs hatch, the glochidia (pronounced

The James River spinymussel prefers clean, slow–flowing freshwater streams. Too much silt or sediment in the water can clog a spinymussel's siphon, eventually killing it.

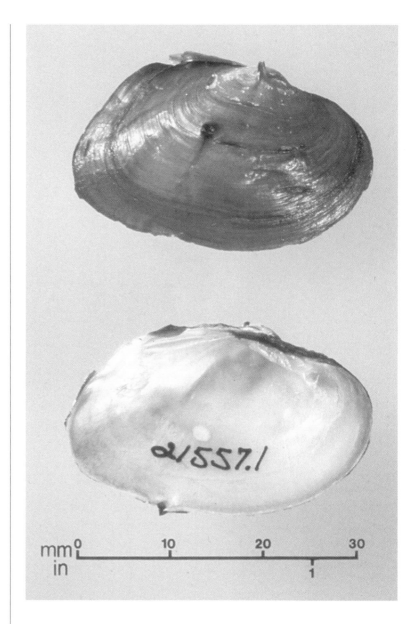

glow–KID–ee–a) or larval forms of the mussel stay in the gills and continue to develop.

After a while, the glochidia are released into the river. They then attach themselves to the gills of a host fish (those glochidia that are unable to attach themselves float to the bottom of the river and die). When they have developed a shell and grown large enough to care for themselves, the young spinymussels detach from the host fish and sink to the riverbed. They bury themselves in the gravel or sand, leaving only their shell margins (edges) and siphons exposed.

Habitat and current distribution

This species of mussel is found in four headwater streams (streams that form the source of a river) of the James River. In Craig and Botetourt Counties in Virginia, it inhabits Craig, Catawba, and Johns Creeks. In Monroe County in West Virginia, it inhabits Potts Creek.

The James River spinymussel prefers clean, slow–flowing freshwater streams. Too much silt (mineral particles) or sediment (sand and stones) in the water can clog a spinymussel's siphon, eventually killing it.

History and conservation measures

The James River spinymussel was discovered in 1836 in the Calfpasture River in Rockbridge County, Virginia. At the time, the spinymussel inhabited most of the area drained by the James River. Its current range is less than 10 percent of that original range.

A primary factor in the spinymussels' decline has been habitat destruction. Land adjacent to rivers and streams throughout its range has been developed into farms and urban areas. Runoff from those farms, which includes pesticides, herbicides, and silt, has poisoned much of the spinymussels' habitat. It continues to do so.

The James River spinymussel is further threatened by the Asiatic clam. This introduced species has taken over much of the spinymussel's former habitat. The Asiatic clam eats the majority of phytoplankton (microscopic aquatic plants) in the water, robbing the James River spinymussel and other native mussels of the nutrients they need.

STIRRUPSHELL
Quadrula stapes

PHYLUM: Mollusca
CLASS: Bivalvia
ORDER: Unionoida
FAMILY: Unionidae
STATUS: Critically endangered, IUCN
Endangered, ESA
RANGE: USA (Alabama)

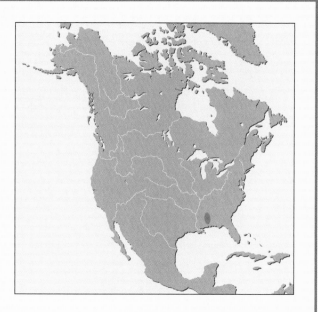

Stirrupshell
Quadrula stapes

Description and biology

The stirrupshell is a small freshwater mussel with a shell measuring 2.2 inches (5.6 centimeters) long. Its yellowish–green shell is marked with a pattern of zig–zag lines. These lines are light green on young stirrupshells and dark brown on older ones. The inner surface of the shell is silvery white.

Like other North American freshwater mussels, the stirrupshell must have a river habitat that is clean and undisturbed. The stirrupshell eats plant material it removes from the water by a feeding tube called a siphon. Any silt (mineral particles) or sediment (sand and stone) in the water can pose a serious threat to the stirrupshell. Its siphon can become clogged, causing it to suffocate to death.

A stable habitat is also necessary for the stirrupshell to reproduce, which, like other mussels, it does in a unique way. In the spring, males release sperm, which is carried away by

Like other mussels, it is important that stirrupshells have an undisturbed habitat in which to reproduce.

34332.3

mm | 10 | 20 | 30
in | | | 1

river currents. Females feeding downstream take in this sperm, which then fertilizes the eggs stored in their gills. When the eggs hatch, the glochidia (pronounced glow –KID–ee–a) or larval forms of the mussel continue to develop in the gills.

After some time, the glochidia are released and attach themselves to the gill of a host fish (those glochidia unable to attach to a host fish drift to the bottom of the river and die). The glochidia remain attached to the host fish until they become young stirrupshells, meaning they have developed a shell and are large enough to survive on their own. The young stirrupshells detach from the host fish and fall to the riverbed, burying themselves with only their shell margins (edges) and feeding siphons exposed.

Habitat and current distribution

The stirrupshell is found only in Alabama in areas of the Sispey River and the Gainsville Bendway (a part of the East Fork Tombigbee River cut off by the construction of the Tennessee–Tombigbee Waterway). Its total population number is unknown, but the U.S. Fish and Wildlife Service noted in the Endangered Species database in the early 2000s that this species may well be extinct in the wild, as no populations have been found for some time.

History and conservation measures

This species of mussel was once found in the Tombigbee River from Columbus, Mississippi, to Epes, Alabama. It was also found in the Alabama and Black Warrior Rivers.

The stirrupshell has declined mainly because of the construction of the Tennessee–Tombigbee Waterway (a series of channels, locks, and impoundments or reservoirs built to provide a link for barge traffic between these two rivers). The dredging (digging out) of river bottoms to create channels destroyed many mussel beds. To maintain these channels, this dredging continues periodically. Dams and locks built for the waterway caused mussel beds to become flooded. The water flowing over these areas was also slowed, causing silt to build up. Many stirrupshells suffocated as a result.

Where to Learn More

Books

Ackerman, Diane. *The Rarest of the Rare: Vanishing Animals, Timeless Worlds.* New York: Random House, 1995. Naturalist and poet Ackerman travels from the Amazon rain forests to a remote Japanese island in search of endangered creatures and their habitats, revealing the factors that are contributing to their endangerment and describing preservation efforts.

Baskin, Yvonne. *The Work of Nature: How the Diversity of Life Sustains Us.* Washington, DC: Island Press, 1997. Science writer Baskin examines the practical consequences of declining biodiversity on ecosystem health and functioning, highlighting examples from around the world.

Chadwick, Douglas W., and Joel Sartore. *The Company We Keep: America's Endangered Species.* Washington, DC: National Geographic Society, 1996. Wildlife biologist Chadwick chronicles past and current conservation efforts, profiling dozens of birds and animals on the top ten endangered list. The book, for readers aged ten and above, also includes rich photographs by photojournalist Sartore, range maps, habitat descriptions, population counts, and current status for all endangered North American species.

Cohen, Daniel. *The Modern Ark: Saving Endangered Species.* New York: Putnam, 1995. Aimed at young adult readers, this work explains the problems faced by endangered species and the solutions—such as the Species Survival Plan—to help protect their futures.

Dobson, David. *Can We Save Them? Endangered Species of North America.* Watertown, MA: Charlesbridge, 1997. For students aged seven to ten, Dobson's work introduces readers to twelve species of endangered animals and plants in North America and suggests ways to restore each one's natural environment.

Earle, Sylvia. *Sea Change: A Message of the Oceans.* New York: Putnam, 1995. Marine biologist and leading deep-sea explorer Earle writes about her three decades of undersea exploration and makes an urgent plea for the preservation of the world's fragile and rapidly deteriorating ocean ecosystems.

Endangered Wildlife of the World. New York: Marshall Caven-
   dish, 1993. Developed for young adults, this 11-volume reference set presents 1,400 alphabetical entries focusing on the
   plight of endangered species, with a special emphasis placed
   on the species of North America.

Galan, Mark. *There's Still Time: The Success of the Endangered
   Species Act.* Washington, DC: National Geographic Society,
   1997. For young readers, this photo-essay work features plants
   and animals that have been brought back from the brink of
   extinction, primarily because of the Endangered Species Act.

Harris, Michael. *Lament for an Ocean: The Collapse of the Atlantic
   Cod Fishery: A True Crime Story.* Toronto, Ontario: McClelland
   and Stewart, 1998. A gripping journalistic exposé about the
   overfishing that caused the collapse of the Atlantic Cod fishery in Canada, despite the clear warnings of marine scientists.

Hoff, Mary King, and Mary M. Rodgers. *Our Endangered Planet:
   Life on Land.* Minneapolis, MN: Lerner, 1992. For young adult
   readers, Hoff's work describes the delicate ecological balance
   among all living things on land, the damage done by human-
   ity in contributing to the extinction of various species, and
   ways of preventing further harm.

Hoyt, John Arthur. *Animals in Peril: How "Sustainable Use" Is
   Wiping Out the World's Wildlife.* New York: Avery Publishing
   Group, 1995. Hoyt, executive officer of the U.S. Humane Society, contends that conservation agencies are destroying many
   animal species by cooperating with local governments in a
   conservation policy that actually promotes slaughter, suffering, and extinction.

Liittschwager, David, and Susan Middleton, in association with
   the Environmental Defense Organization. *Remains of a Rain-
   bow: Rare Plants and Animals of Hawaii.* National Tropical
   Botanical Garden and Nature Conservancy of Hawaii, con-
   tributers. Washington, D.C.: National Geographic, 2001. A
   collection of photographs of the endangered species of
   Hawaii, capturing the delicate balance of Hawaii's lush and
   rapidly deteriorating ecosystems.

Mackay, Richard. *The Penguin Atlas of Endangered Species.* New
   York: Penguin, 2002. A resource suitable for young adults and
   older, this atlas provides vital information on ecosystems,
   identifying wildlife, the importance of biodiversity, the transplanting of plants and animals across continents, and more.
   Also included in its 128 pages are case studies illustrating the
   major threats to biodiversity and the measures being taken to
   conserve the species.

Mann, Charles, and Mark Plummer. *Noah's Choice: The Future
   of Endangered Species.* New York: Knopf, 1995. Mann and
   Plummer examine the controversy over the Endangered

Species Act and call for a new set of principles to serve as a guideline for choosing which endangered species to save.

Matthiessen, Peter. *Wildlife in America.* Rev. ed. New York: Penguin Books, 1995. Acclaimed naturalist-writer Matthiessen first published this classic work on the history of the rare, threatened, and extinct animals of North America in 1959.

McClung, Robert. *Last of the Wild: Vanished and Vanishing Giants of the Animal World.* Hamden, CT: Linnet Books, 1997. For readers aged 12 and above, McClung's work profiles threatened animals around the world and discusses why they are in danger and what is being done to save them.

McClung, Robert. *Lost Wild America: The Story of Our Extinct and Vanishing Wildlife.* Hamden, CT: Shoe String Press, 1993. McClung traces the history of wildlife conservation and environmental politics in America to 1992, and describes various extinct or endangered species.

Meacham, Cory J. *How the Tiger Lost Its Stripes: An Exploration into the Endangerment of a Species.* New York: Harcourt Brace, 1997. Journalist Meacham offers a probing analysis of the endangerment of the world's pure species of tigers and the role of zoos, scientists, and politics in stopping it.

Middleton, Susan, and David Liittschwager. *Witness: Endangered Species of North America.* San Francisco, CA: Chronicle Books, 1994. Through a series of 200 color and duotone portraits, photographers Middleton and Liittschwager capture 100 species of North American animals and plants on the brink of extinction.

Patent, Dorothy Hinshaw. *Back to the Wild.* San Diego, CA: Gulliver Books, 1997. For readers aged ten and above, Patent's work describes efforts to save endangered animals from extinction by breeding them in captivity, teaching them survival skills, and then releasing them into the wild.

Pollock, Stephen Thomas. *The Atlas of Endangered Animals.* New York: Facts on File, 1993. For younger readers, Pollock's work uses maps, pictures, symbols, and text to focus on areas of the world in which human activity is threatening to destroy already endangered animal species.

Quammen, David. *The Song of the Dodo: Island Biogeography in an Age of Extinctions.* New York: Scribner, 1996. In a work for adult readers, Quammen interweaves personal observation, scientific theory, and history to examine the mysteries of evolution and extinction as they have been illuminated by the study of islands.

Schaller, George. *The Last Panda.* Chicago, IL: University of Chicago Press, 1993. Noted biologist Schaller presents an account of the four years he spent in China's Sichuan Province working to protect both panda habitat and the few pandas that remained.

Threatened Birds of the World: The Official Source for Birds on the IUCN Red List. Alison Stattersfield and David R. Capper, eds. Barcelona, Spain: Birdlife International/Lynx Editions, 2000. A comprehensive encyclopedia of endangered, threatened, or vulnerable bird species worldwide, this 852-page reference is illustrated with charts, illustrations, and photographs. Each of the 1,186 threatened birds listed in this comprehensive source receives a half-page, illustrated entry, including a range map, photos or illustrations, a discussion of why the bird is listed as threatened, and information on identification, range and population, ecology, threats, conservation, and action plans.

Tudge, Colin. *Last Animals at the Zoo: How Mass Extinctions Can Be Stopped.* Washington, DC: Island Press, 1992. Zoologist Tudge details the grim conditions many animals must overcome in their natural habitats and the bleak prospects for recovery by those already on the brink of extinction.

Weidensaul, Samuel. *The Ghost with Trembling Wings: Science, Wishful Thinking, and the Search for Lost Species.* New York: North Point Press, 2003. In a series of suspenseful stories set all over the world, the author chronicles the reappearance of some supposedly extinct animals, such as the ivory-billed woodpecker and the coelacanth. In some cases, the reappearances have actually occurred, but in others it has been wishful thinking, and many of the searches have been fruitless. The book discusses both the science and the ethics of such wishful thinking.

Wilson, Edward Osborne. *The Future of Life.* New York: Knopf, 2002. A Pulitzer-prize winning naturalist's overview of the dire problems facing the natural world today, including fascinating stories of struggling species and an imagined conversation with Henry David Thoreau at Walden Pond. Wilson makes and impassioned plea for the future, providing global strategies to save the planet.

Periodicals

Endangered Species Bulletin
Division of Endangered Species
U.S. Fish and Wildlife Service, Washington, DC 20240

Endangered Species UPDATE
School of Natural Resources and Environment
The University of Michigan, Ann Arbor, MI 48109-1115

Sierra Magazine (bimonthly)
Sierra Club
85 Second Street
San Francisco, CA 94105-3441

Web Sites

Birdlife International
http://www.birdlife.net/

Convention on International Trade in Endangered Species
http://www.wcmc.org.uk:80/CITES/english/index.html

EcoNet: Habitats and Species
http://www.igc.apc.org/igc/issues/habitats

EE-Link: Endangered Species, University of Michigan
http://www.nceet.snre.umich.edu/EndSpp/Endangered.html

Endangered! Exploring a World at Risk: The American Museum
of Natural History
http://www.amnh.org/nationalcenter/Endangered

Endangered Species Act (brief history), University of Oregon
http://gladstone.uoregon.edu/~cait/

Endangered Species Home Page, U.S. Fish and Wildlife Service
http://www.fws.gov/~r9endspp.endspp.html

Endangered Species Protection Program, U.S. Environmental
Protection Agency
http://www.epa.gov/espp

Endangered Species Study Web: General Resources
http://www.studyweb.com/animals/endang/endanger.htm

Endangered Species Update, University of Michigan
http://www.umich.edu/~esupdate/

EnviroLink: Largest online environmental information resource
http://www.envirolink.org/

Environmental Education (EE) Link: Endangered Species
http://eelink.net/EndSpp/specieshighlights-mainpage.html

Environmental Organization Web Directory: Wildlife and endangered species focus
http://www.webdirectory.com/Wildlife/General_Endangered
_Species

Green Nature
http://greennature.com

IUCN Red List of Threatened Animals
http://www.wcmc.org.uk/data/database/rl_anml_combo.html

IUCN Red List of Threatened Plants
http://www.wcmc.org.uk/species/plants/plant_redlist.html

SeaWorld Education Department: Endangered Species
http://www.seaworld.org/infobooks/Endangered/home.html

Society for the Protection of Endangered Species (group of
endangered species-related weblinks)
http://pubweb.ucdavis.edu/Documents/GWS/Envissues
/EndSpes/speshome.htm

Terra's Endangered Species Tour (includes range maps)
http://www.olcommerce.com/terra/endanger.html

Organizations Focusing on Endangered and Threatened Species (selected list)

African Wildlife Foundation
1717 Massachusetts Ave., NW
Washington, DC 20036
(202) 265-8393; Fax: (202) 265-2361
Internet: http://www.awf.org
Organization that works to craft and deliver creative solutions for the long-term well-being of Africa's remarkable species and habitats.

American Cetacean Society
P.O. Box 1319
San Pedro, CA 90733-0391
(310) 548-6279; Fax: (310) 548-6950
Internet: http://www.acsonline.org
Nonprofit organization that works in the areas of conservation, education, and research to protect marine mammals, especially whales, dolphins, and porpoises, and the oceans in which they live.

Animal Welfare Institute
P.O. Box 3650
Washington, DC 20007
(202) 337-2332; Fax: (202) 338-9478
Organization active in the protection of endangered species, among other issues, related to animal welfare.

Center for Biological Diversity
P.O. Box 710
Tucson AZ 85702-0710
(520) 623-5252; Fax: (520) 623-9797
Internet: http://www.center@biologicaldiversity.org
A nonprofit regional conservation organization with over 7,500 members, dedicated to protecting biological diversity through science, policy, education, and environmental law. The Center has been a premier endangered species advocate. It has obtained, often by filing lawsuits in the federal courts, ESA protection for 280 species and the designation of over 38 million acres of critical habitat, helping to protect U.S. coasts, oceans, deserts, forests, rivers and grasslands for threatened species.

Center for Marine Conservation, Inc.
1725 DeSales St., NW, Suite 500
Washington, DC 20036
(202) 429-5609; Fax: (202) 872-0619

Nonprofit organization dedicated to protecting marine wildlife and their habitats and to conserving coastal and ocean resources.

Center for Plant Conservation, Inc.
P.O. Box 299
St. Louis, MO 63166
(314) 577-9450; Fax: (314) 577-9465
Internet: http://www.mobot.org/CPC/
National network of 25 botanical gardens and arboreta dedicated to the conservation and study of rare and endangered U.S. plants.

The Conservation Agency
6 Swinburne Street
Jamestown, RI 02835
(401) 423-2652; Fax: (401) 423-2652
Organization that conducts research and gathers data specifically aimed to preserve rare, endangered, and little-known species.

Defenders of Wildlife
1101 14th St., NW, Suite 1400
Washington, DC 20005
(202) 682-9400; Fax: (202) 682-1331
Internet: http://www.defenders.org/
Nonprofit organization that works to protect and restore native species, habitats, ecosystems, and overall biological diversity.

Earthjustice Legal Defense Fund
426 17th Street, 5th Floor
Oakland, CA 94612-2820
(510) 550-6725; Fax: (510) 550-6749
Internet: http://www.eajusca@earthjustice.org
Founded in 1971 as Sierra Club Legal Defense Fund, Earthjustice is a nonprofit law firm dedicated to protecting nature by working through the courts. Earthjustice has played a leading role in shaping the development of environmental law in the courtrooms and also in Washington, D.C. where it is influential in shaping policies and legislation. The organization also runs environmental law clinics at Stanford University and the University of Denver, educating students in public interest environmental law.

Endangered Species Coalition
666 Pennsylvania Ave., SE
Washington, DC 20003
(202) 547-9009
Coalition of more than 200 organizations that seeks to broaden and mobilize public support for protecting endangered species.

Environmental Investigation Agency (EIA)
P.O. Box 53343
Washington D.C. 20009
(202) 483-6621; Fax: (202) 986-8626
Internet: http://www.EIAgency@email.msn.com
An international campaigning organization formed in 1984, committed to investigating and exposing environmental crime by using advanced investigative techniques. EIA often works undercover to expose international crimes such as illegal trade in wildlife and illegal logging. The organization has brought about changes in international and national laws and policies.

International Union for Conservation of Nature and Natural Resources (IUCN-The World Conservation Union)
U.S. Office: 1400 16th St., NW
Washington, DC 20036
(202) 797-5454; Fax: (202) 797-5461
Internet: http://www.iucn.org
An international independent body that promotes scientifically based action for the conservation of nature and for sustainable development. The Species Survival Commission (SSC) of the IUCN publishes biennial Red List books, which describe threatened species of mammals, birds, reptiles, amphibians, fish, invertebrates, and plants.

International Wildlife Coalition
70 East Falmouth Highway
East Falmouth, MA 02536
(508) 548-8328; Fax: (508) 548-8542
Internet: http://www.webcom.com/-iwcwww
Nonprofit organization dedicated to preserving wildlife and their habitats. IWC's Whale Adoption Project preserves marine mammals.

International Wildlife Education and Conservation
1140 Westwood Blvd., Suite 205
Los Angeles, CA 90024
(310) 208-3631; Fax: (310) 208-2779
Internet: http://www.iwec.org/iwec.htm
Nonprofit organization that seeks to ensure the future of endangered animals and to promote animal welfare through public education and conservation of habitats.

Marine Environmental Research Institute
772 West End Ave.
New York, NY 10025
(212) 864-6285; Fax (212) 864-1470
Nonprofit organization dedicated to protecting the health and biodiversity of the marine environment, addressing such problems as global marine pollution, endangered species, and habitat destruction.

National Audubon Society
700 Broadway
New York, NY 10002
(212) 979-3000
Internet: http://www.audubon.org
A national network of community-based nature centers dedicated to the conservation and restoration of natural resources
with emphasis on wildlife, habitats, soil, water, and forests,
particularly emphasizing advocacy on behalf of areas sustain-
ing important bird populations.

National Wildlife Federation
Laurel Ridge Conservation Education Center
8925 Leesburg Pike
Vienna, VA 22184-0001
(703) 790-4000; Fax: (703) 442-7332
Internet: http://www.nwf.org
Nonprofit organization that seeks to educate, inspire, and
assist individuals and organizations of diverse cultures to
conserve wildlife and other natural resources.

Nature Conservancy
1815 North Lynn St.
Arlington, VA 22209
(703) 841-5300; Fax: (703) 841-1283
Internet: http://www.tnc.org
International nonprofit organization committed to preserving
biological diversity by protecting natural lands and the life
they harbor.

Pacific Center for International Studies
33 University Sq., Suite 184
Madison, WI 53715
(608) 256-6312; Fax: (608) 257-0417
An international think tank specializing in the assessment
of international treaty regimes, including the Convention on
International Trade in Endangered Species (CITES) and the
International Convention for the Regulation of Whaling
(ICRW).

Save the Manatee Club
500 North Maitland Ave.
Maitland, FL 32751
(407) 539-0990; Fax: (407) 539-0871
Internet: http://www.objectlinks.com/manatee
National nonprofit organization that seeks to preserve the endangered West Indian manatee through public education, research funding, rescue, rehabilitation, and advocacy.

Wildlife Preservation Trust International, Inc.
400 West Girard Ave.
Philadelphia, PA 19104
(215) 222-3636; Fax: (215) 222-2191

Organization that supports the preservation of endangered species through hands-on field work, research, education, and training.

World Conservation Monitoring Centre
219 Huntington Rd.
Cambridge, England CB3 ODL
(01223) 277314; Fax: (01223) 277136
Internet: http://www.wcmc.org.uk
Organization that supports conservation and sustainable development through the provision of information services on issues relating to nature conservation.

World Society for the Protection of Animals
29 Perkins St.
P.O. Box 190
Boston, MA 02130
(617) 522-7000; Fax: (617) 522-7077
International organization committed to the alleviation of animal suffering and to the conservation of endangered animals.

World Wildlife Fund
1250 24th St., NW
Washington, DC 20037
(202) 293-4800; Fax: (202) 293-9211
Internet: http://www.wwf.org
The largest private U.S. organization working worldwide to protect wildlife and wildlands—especially in the tropical forests of Latin America, Asia, and Africa.

Photo Credits

Photographs appearing in Endangered Species, *2nd Edition, were received from the following sources. Every effort has been made to secure permission; if omissions have been made, please contact us.*

Abbott's booby (Papasula abbotti), illustration by Patricia Ferrer. Reproduced by permission.—Addax with lowered head, photograph by Mark Boulton. Photo Researchers, Inc. Reproduced by permission.—African elephant, photograph by Mark Boulton. Photo Researchers, Inc. Reproduced by permission.—African wild dogs, photograph by Nigel J. Dennis. Photo Researchers, Inc. Reproduced by permission.—Agave Living Rock cactus (Ariocarpus agavoides), photograph. © Rick and Nora Bowers / Visuals Unlimited. Reproduced by permission.—American burying beetle, photograph. Photo Researchers, Inc. Reproduced by permission.—American crocodile, photograph by R. Cramm. Photo Researchers, Inc. Reproduced by permission.—Anas bernieri (duck), photograph. BIOS/Peter Arnold, Inc. Reproduced by permission.—Andean flamingo, photograph by Dr. M.P. Kahl. Photo Researchers, Inc. Reproduced by permission.—Atlantic cod, photograph by Tom McHugh. Photo Researchers, Inc. Reproduced by permission.—Audouin's Gull, photograph by Jose Luis G. Grande. Photo Researchers, Inc. Reproduced by permission.—Australian ant with caterpillar prey, photograph. Planet Earth Pictures Limited. Reproduced by permission.—Aye aye, photograph by Mike Dulaney. Cincinnati Zoo. Reproduced by permission.—Bactrian camel, photograph by Renee Lynn. Photo Researchers, Inc. Reproduced by permission.—Baiji dolphin's (Lipotes vexillifer), photograph. © Thomas Jefferson/Seapics.com. Reproduced by permission.—Bald eagle, photograph by Tim & Pat Leeson. Photo Researchers, Inc. Reproduced by permission.—Baltic sturgeon, photograph by Tom McHugh. Photo Researchers, Inc. Reproduced by permission.—Bay checkerspot butterfly, photograph by Richard A. Arnold. Reproduced by permission.—Bengal tiger walking along beach, photograph by Jeff Lepore. Photo Researchers, Inc. Reproduced by permission.—Black caiman, photograph.

Cincinnati Zoo. Reproduced by permission.—Black rhinoceros, photograph by M. Philip Kahl, Jr. Photo Researchers, Inc. Reproduced by permission.—Black-capped vireo feeding babies, photograph by S. & S. Rucker. Vireo. Reproduced by permission.—Black-cheeked lovebirds, photograph by E. R. Degginger. Photo Researchers, Inc. Reproduced by permission. —Blue whale, photograph by Pieter Folkens. Planet Earth Pictures, Limited. Reproduced by permission.—Braun's rock-cress, photograph. U.S. Fish and Wildlife Service. Reproduced by permission.—Bridled nailtail wallaby, photograph by Mitch Reardon. Photo Researchers, Inc. Reproduced by permission.— Bristle fern (Trichomanes radicons), photograph by E.D. Degginger. Bruce Coleman, Inc. Reproduced by permission. —Brown hyena, photograph by Tom McHugh. Photo Researchers, Inc. Reproduced by permission.—Buffy-eared marmoset (Callithrix aurita), photograph. Claus Meyer/Minden Pictures. Reproduced by permission.—Bull trout, photograph by Wade Fredenberg, U. S. Fish and Wildlife Service. Reproduced by permission.—California condor, photograph by Kenneth W. Fink. Photo Researchers, Inc. Reproduced by permission.—California Freshwater Shrimp, photograph. © 1994 Middleton/Littschwager. Reproduced by permission.— California red-legged frog (Rana aurora draytonii), photograph by Bruce Watkins. Animals Animals/Earth Scenes. Reproduced by permission.—Captive imperial Amazon parrot (Amasona imperialis-caribbean), photograph. © Frank W. Lane; Frank Lane Picture Agency/Corbis. Reproduced by permission.— Cape vultures, photograph by Nigel Dennis. Photo Researchers, Inc. Reproduced by permission.—Cave crayfish, photograph by Smith, Ken, Arkansas Natural Heritage Commission. Reproduced by permission.—Central American River Turtle, photograph by Tom McHugh. Photo Researchers, Inc. Reproduced by permission.—Central American tapir, photograph by Thor Janson. Photo Researchers, Inc. Reproduced by permission.—Chapman's rhododendron in bloom, photograph by David & Hayes Norris. Photo Researchers, Inc. Reproduced by permission.—Chatam Island Forget-Me-Not, in bloom, photograph by Brian Enting. Photo Researchers, Inc. Reproduced by permission.—Chatham Island black robin (Petroica traversi), illustration by Emily Damstra. Reproduced by permission.—Cheer pheasant, photograph by Tom McHugh. Photo Researchers, Inc. Reproduced by permission. —Cheetah, photograph by S.R. Maglione. Photo Researchers,

Inc. Reproduced by permission.—Chimpanzee, photograph by Nigel J. Dennis. Photo Researchers, Inc. Reproduced by permission.—Chinchilla, photograph by Stephen Dalton. Photo Researchers, Inc. Reproduced by permission.—Chinese alligator, photograph by Ken King. Planet Earth Pictures, Limited. Reproduced by permission.—Chinese Egret, photograph by M. Strange. Vireo. Reproduced by permission.—Chinese giant salamander, photograph. Cincinnati Zoo. Reproduced by permission.—Ciconia boyciana, photograph. BIOS/Peter Arnold, Inc. Reproduced by permission.—Coelacanth, photograph. Planet Earth Pictures, Limited. Reproduced by permission.— Cook Strait Tuatara, photograph by Tom McHugh. Photo Researchers, Inc. Reproduced by permission.—Crested honeycreeper, photograph by Jack Jeffrey. Photo Resource Hawaii. Reproduced by permission.—Culebra Island Giant, photograph by C. Kenneth Dodd, Jr., USGS. Reproduced by permission.—Dalmation pelican, photograph by Edmund Appel. Photo Researchers, Inc. Reproduced by permission.— Dama gazelle nursing baby, photograph by Joseph Van Wormer. Photo Researchers, Inc. Reproduced by permission.— Danube salmon, photograph by Hans Reinhard. Photo Researchers, Inc. Reproduced by permission.—Delhi sands flower-loving fly, photograph by Greg Ballmer. Reproduced by permission.—Desert pupfish, photograph by Tom McHugh. Photo Researchers, Inc. Reproduced by permission.—Desert tortoise, photograph by Tim Davis. Photo Researchers, Inc. Reproduced by permission.—Dugong, photograph. © Tom McHugh/Photo Researchers, Inc. Reproduced by permission.— Elephant, Asian, photograph by Ben Simon. Stock Market/Corbis. Reproduced with permission.—European Bison or Wisent (Bison bonasus), photograph by Peter Weimann. Animals Animals/Earth Scenes. Reproduced by permission.—European mink (Mustela lutreola), photograph. BIOS/Peter Arnold, Inc. Reproduced by permission.—Fanshell, inside and outside, photograph by S. David Jenike. Cincinnati Zoo. Reproduced by permission.—Fat Pocketbook pearly mussel, photograph by A.E. Spreitzer. Reproduced by permission.—Fiji Island iguana, photograph by Joseph L. Collins. Photo Researchers, Inc. Reproduced by permission.—Florida torreya, photograph by Gary Retherford. Photo Researchers, Inc. Reproduced by permission.—Fountain darter, photograph by Roger W. Barbour. Reproduced by permission.—Galapagos Hawk, photograph by Jeanne White. Photo Researchers, Inc. Reproduced by permission.—Galapagos land iguana, photograph by Margaret Welby. Planet Earth Pictures, Limited. Reproduced by permission.—Galapagos Tortoise, photograph by Francois Gohier. Photo Researchers, Inc. Reproduced by permission.—Gavial sliding on sand, photograph by Jeffrey W. Lang. Photo Researchers, Inc. Reproduced by permission.—Giant anteater, photograph by Robert J. Huffman. Field Mark Publications. Reproduced by permission.—Giant armadillo, photograph by Paul Crum. Photo Researchers, Inc. Reproduced by permission.—Giant catfish, photograph by Roland Seitre. © Roland Seitre/Peter Arnold, Inc. Reproduced by permission.—Giant Kangaroo Rat, photograph by Susan Middleton. © 1998 Susan Middleton. Reproduced by permission.—Giant panda, photograph by Tom & Pat Leeson. Photo Researchers, Inc. Reproduced by permission.—Golden bandicoot, photograph by Jiri Lochman. Planet Earth Pictures Limited. Reproduced by permission.—Golden Lion Tamarins, photograph. Cincinnati Zoo. Reproduced by permission.—Golden parakeet, photograph by Lynx Edicions. Vireo. Reproduced by permission.—Goldenrod, photograph by John MacGregor. Reproduced by permission.—Goliath frog with gold watch near head, photograph by Paul A. Zahl. Photo Researchers, Inc. Reproduced by permission.—Gorilla, posed, photograph by Jerry L. Ferrara. Photo Researchers, Inc. Reproduced by permission.—Gray fruit bat clinging to rock, photograph by Merlin D. Tuttle. Photo Researchers, Inc. Reproduced by permission.—Gray wolf howling, photograph by Myer Bornstein. Planet Earth Pictures Limited. Reproduced by permission.—Great Phillipine Eagle, photograph by Alain Evrard. Photo Researchers, Inc. Reproduced by permission.—Green pitcher plant, photograph. Photo Researchers, Inc. Reproduced by permission.—Green sea turtle, floating in water, photograph by Dr. Paula A. Zahl. Photo Researchers, Inc. Reproduced by permission.—Grevy zebra, photograph by Leonard Lee Rue III. Photo Researchers, Inc. Reproduced by permission.—Grizzly bear, photograph by Jeff Lepore. Photo Researchers, Inc. Reproduced by permission.—Guadalupe fur seal, photograph by C. Allan Morgan. Reproduced by permission.—Harvestman, photograph. U. S. Fish and Wildlife Service. Reproduced by permission.—Hawaiian crow, photograph by R. & N. Bowers. Vireo. Reproduced by permission.—Hawaiian goose, photograph by Roger Wilmshurst. Photo Researchers, Inc. Reproduced by permission. —Hawaiian hawk, photograph by Tom McHugh. Reproduced by permission.—Hawaiian monk seal, photograph. U. S. Fish and Wildlife Service. Reproduced by permission.—Hines emerald dragonfly, photograph. Reproduced by permission.—Honeycreeper, photograph by H. Douglas Pratt. Reproduced by permission.—Hoolock gibbon, southeast Asia, photograph by Tom McHugh. Photo Researchers, Inc. Reproduced by permission.—Houston toad, photograph by Joseph T. Collins. Photo Researchers, Inc. Reproduced by permission.—Humpback whale, photograph by Francois Gohier. Photo Researchers, Inc. Reproduced by permission.—Huon tree kangaroo, photograph. © Art Wolfe/ Photo Researchers, Inc. Reproduced by permission.—Iberian lynxes at a zoo in southern Spain, photograph. © Reuters New-Media Inc./Corbis. Reproduced by permission.—Indian python, photograph by Mandal Ranjit. Photo Researchers, Inc. Reproduced by permission.—Iowa pleistocene snails, photograph. U. S. Fish and Wildlife Service. Reproduced by permission.—Island fox (Urocyon littoralis santarosae), photograph. © Kennan Ward/Corbis. Reproduced by permission.—Ivory-billed woodpecker, photograph by Ken Lucas. Planet Earth Pictures, Limited. Reproduced by permission.—Jaguar, photograph by Renee Lynn. Photo Researchers, Inc. Reproduced by permission.—James River Spinymussel, photograph. A.E. Spreitzer. Reproduced by permission.—Kakapo, photograph. Photo Researchers, Inc. Reproduced by permission.—Kentucky cave shrimp, photograph. U. S. Fish and Wildlife Service. Reproduced by permission.—Kirtland's warbler, photograph by Bill Dyer. Photo Researchers, Inc. Reproduced by permission.—Koala, photograph by Robert J. Huffman. Field Mark Publications. Reproduced by permission.—Komodo Dragon, photograph. Cincinnati Zoo. Reproduced by permission.—Laysan finch in grassy area, photograph by Karl W. Kenyon. Photo Researchers, Inc. Reproduced by permission.—Laysan Teal duck (Anas layanensis) at the Houston Zoo, photograph by Mickey Gibson. Animals Animals/Earth Scenes. Reproduced by permission.—Lear's Macaws, photograph by Kenneth W. Fink. Photo Researchers, Inc. Reproduced by permission.—Leatherback sea turtle, photograph by C. Allan Morgan. Reproduced by permission.—Leopard, photograph by Gregory G. Dimijian. Photo Researchers, Inc. Reproduced by permission.—Leopard lizard, photograph by Rod Planck. Photo Researchers, Inc. Reproduced by permission.—Little wing pearly mussel, photograph by A. E. Spreitzer. All Rights Reserved.

Reproduced by permission.—Lord Howe Wood Rail, photograph by Vincent Serventy. Planet Earth Pictures, Limited. Reproduced by permission.—Madison Cave Isopod, photograph. © 1994 Middleton/Littschwager. Reproduced by permission.—Manatee (Trichechus manatus), photograph. © Douglas Faulkner/Corbis. Reproduced by permission.—Mandrill, photograph by Gregory G. Dimijian. Photo Researchers, Inc. Reproduced by permission.—Manus Island green snail (Papustyla pulchenrima), photograph. © L. Newman & A. Flowers. Reproduced by permission.—Marbled murrelet, photograph by R. L. Pitman. Vireo. Reproduced by permission.—Marine otter (Lutra felina), photograph. © Roland Seitre/Peter Arnold, Inc. Reproduced by permission.—Markhor, photograph. Cincinnati Zoo. Reproduced by permission.—Mauna Loa, photograph by Derral Herbst. Reproduced by permission.—Mauritius kestral, photograph by Nick Garbutt. Planet Earth Pictures, Limited. Reproduced by permission.—Meadow viper (Vipera ursinii rakosiensis), photograph. © Zoltan Takacs. Reproduced by permission.—Mexican prairie dog (Cynomys mexicanus), photograph by Patricio Robles Gil. Reproduced by permission.—Mongoose lemur, photograph by Tom McHugh. Photo Researchers, Inc. Reproduced by permission.—Monito gecko, photograph by C. Kenneth Dodd, Jr., USGS. Reproduced by permission.—Mountain pygmy possum, photograph by Tom McHugh. Photo Researchers, Inc. Reproduced by permission.—Musk deer, photograph by M. K. Ranjitsinh. Photo Researchers, Inc. Reproduced by permission.—Nashville crayfish, photograph. U. S. Fish and Wildlife Service. Reproduced by permission.—Nevin's barberry, photograph by Steve Junak. Reproduced by permission.—Northern white rhinoceros, photograph by Kenneth W. Fink. Photo Researchers, Inc. Reproduced by permission.—Northern bald ibis, photograph. Cincinnati Zoo. Reproduced by permission.—Northern spotted owl, photograph by Tom & Pat Leeson. Photo Researchers, Inc. Reproduced by permission.—Numbat, photograph. Photo Researchers, Inc. Reproduced by permission.—Numenius borealis, photograph. © J. Pierre Sylvestre/BIOS/Peter Arnold, Inc. Reproduced by permission.—Orangutan, photograph by Tim Davis. Photo Researchers, Inc. Reproduced by permission.—Orinoco crocodile, photograph by Tom McHugh. Photo Researchers, Inc. Reproduced by permission.—Ornithoptera alexandrae butterfly, photograph. © Francois Gilson/BIOS/Peter Arnold, Inc. Reproduced by permission.—Pallid sturgeon, photograph. U. S. Fish and Wildlife Service. Reproduced by permission.—Peregrine falcon with wings outstretched, photograph by Tim Davis. Photo Researchers, Inc. Reproduced by permission.—Piping plover, photograph by Bill Dyer. Photo Researchers, Inc. Reproduced by permission.—Plowshare tortoise with baby, photograph by Nick Garbutt. Planet Earth Pictures, Limited. Reproduced by permission.—Prairie white fringed orchid, photograph by Jim W. Grace. Photo Researchers, Inc. Reproduced by permission.—Pristis perotteti, photograph. BIOS/Peter Arnold, Inc. Reproduced by permission.—Przewalski's horse, San Diego Zoo, photograph by J. Gordon Miller. Reproduced by permission.—Puerto Rican boa (Epicrates inornata), photograph by John Mitchell. Photo Researchers, Inc. Reproduced by permission.—Puerto Rican boa, photograph. U. S. Fish and Wildlife Service. Reproduced by permission.—Puna grebe (Podiceps taczanowskii), photograph. Peter Arnold, Inc. Reproduced by permission.—Purple-winged dove (Claravis godefrida), photograph. © Luis C. Marigo/Peter Arnold, Inc. Reproduced by permission.—Pygmy hippopotamus, photograph. Cincinnati Zoo. Reproduced by permission.—Pygmy hog, photograph by Tom McHugh. Photo Researchers, Inc. Reproduced by permission.—Pygmy sculpin, photograph by Noel Burkhead. Reproduced by permission.—Pygmy-owl, photograph by Mike Wrigley, U.S. Fish and Wildlife Service. Reproduced by permission.—Queen conch on star coral, photograph by Charles V. Angelo. Photo Researchers, Inc. Reproduced by permission.—Red panda, photograph by Toni Angermayer. Photo Researchers, Inc. Reproduced by permission.—Red wolf, photograph by Tom & Pat Leeson. Photo Researchers, Inc. Reproduced by permission.—Red-cockaded woodpecker, photograph by David & Hayes Norris. Photo Researchers, Inc. Reproduced by permission.—Relict trillium, photograph by Jeff Lepore. Photo Researchers, Inc. Reproduced by permission.—Reslendent Quetzal, photograph by Gregory G. Dimijian. Photo Researchers, Inc. Reproduced by permission.—Ring pink mussel, photograph by A. E. Spreitzer. All Rights Reserved. Reproduced by permission.—Robbin's cinquefoil, photograph. U. S. Fish and Wildlife Service. Reproduced by permission.—Rothchild's starling, photograph. Cincinnati Zoo. Reproduced by permission.—Salt water crocodile, photograph by Tom McHugh. Photo Researchers, Inc. Reproduced by permission.—San Francisco Garter snake (Thamnophis sirtalis tetrataenis), photograph by Paul Freed. Animals Animals/Earth Scenes. Reproduced by permission.—Santa Cruz salamander, photograph. Cincinnati Zoo. Reproduced by permission.—Scimitar-horned oryx, photograph by Tom McHugh. Photo Researchers, Inc. Reproduced by permission.—Seychelles Magpie Robin, photograph by Pete Oxford. Planet Earth Pictures, Limited. Reproduced by permission.—Short-tailed albatross, photograph by Gilbert S. Grant. Photo Researchers, Inc. Reproduced by permission.—Shortnose Sucker, photograph by Joseph Tomelleri. Cimarron Trading Co. Reproduced by permission.—Siberian cranes, photograph. Planet Earth Pictures, Limited. Reproduced by permission.—Sichuan hill-partridge (Arborophila rufipectus), illustration by Bruce Worden. Reproduced by permission.—Silver rice rat (Oryzomys argentatus), photograph by Numi C. Mitchell. The Conservation Agency. Reproduced by permission.—Skinheads, photograph. Corbis. Reproduced by permission.—Small whorled pogonia flower, photograph. © Hal Horwitz/Corbis. Reproduced by permission.—Snow leopards, photograph. Cincinnati Zoo. Reproduced by permission.—Somali wild ass (Equus africanus), photograph. © Steve Kaufman/Corbis. Reproduced by permission.—Spiral aloes, photograph by Robert Story. Planet Earth Pictures Limited. Reproduced by permission.—Squirrel Monkey with baby on back, photograph. Planet Earth Pictures, Ltd. Reproduced by permission.—Steller sea lion (Eumetopias jubatus), photograph by Yva/Eastcott Momatiuk, John (Eastcott/Momatiuk). Animals Animals/Earth Scenes. Reproduced by permission.—Stirrup shell, photograph by A. E. Spreitzer. All Rights Reserved. Reproduced by permission.—Sun bear, photograph by Tom McHugh. Photo Researchers, Inc. Reproduced by permission.—Swamp deer, photograph by Tom McHugh. Photo Researchers, Inc. Reproduced by permission.—Texas blind cave salamander, photograph by Charles E. Mohr. Photo Researchers, Inc. Reproduced by permission.—Texas Wildrice, photograph by Paul M. Montgomery. All Rights Reserved. Reproduced by permission.—Tooth cave spider, photograph. U. S. Fish and Wildlife Service. Reproduced by permission.—Vancouver Island Marmot, photograph by Fletcher and Baylis. © Fletcher & Baylis/Photo Researchers, Inc. Reproduced by permission.—Venus flytrap, photograph by J.H. Robinson. Photo Researchers, Inc. Reproduced by permission.—Vicunas, mother and baby, photograph. Photo Researchers, Inc. Reproduced by permission.—Volcano Rabbit, photograph. Planet Earth Pictures Limited. Reproduced by permission.—West Indian Mahogany Tree (Swietenia mahogany), photograph by Patti Murray. Animals Animals/Earth Scenes. Reproduced by pemission.—Western big-eared bat (Plecotus townsendii) hibernating in a West Virginia cave, photograph. © J. L. Lepore. Reproduced by permission.—White-breasted thrasher, photograph by Doug Wechsler. Vireo. Reproduced by permission.—Whooping crane, photograph by Tim Davis. Photo Researchers, Inc. Reproduced by permission.—Wild buffalo (Bubalus bubalus), photograph by Khalid Ghani. Animals Animals/Earth Scenes. Reproduced by permission.—Wild yak, photograph by Tom McHugh. Photo Researchers, Inc. Reproduced by permission.—Wombats (Lasiohinus krefftii), photograph. © John Cancalosi/Peter Arnold, Inc. Reproduced by permission.—Wooly spider monkeys, photograph by Andrew L. Young. Photo Researchers, Inc. Reproduced by permission.—Wyoming black-footed ferret in den, photograph by Alan D. Carey. Photo Researchers, Inc. Reproduced by permission.—Wyoming toad, photograph by E. Maruska. Cincinnati Zoo. Reproduced by permission.—Yellow-eyed penguin, photograph by George Holton. Photo Researchers, Inc. Reproduced by permission.—Yellow-shouldered blackbird, photograph by Bruce A. Sorrie. U.S. Fish and Wildlife Service. Reproduced by permission.

Index

American mink *1:* 156, 158

American peregrine falcon *2:* **318–21,** 319 (ill.), 372

Amphipod, Illinois cave *2:* **447–49,** 448 (ill.)

Amur tiger *1:* 227

Anas bernieri 2: **424–26,** 425 (ill.)

Anas laysanensis 2: **306–8,** 307 (ill.)

Andean flamingo *2:* **325–27,** 326 (ill.)

Andrias davidianus 3: **536–38,** 537 (ill.)

Angola
  cheetah *1:* **47–49,** 48 (ill.)
  dog, African wild *1:* **65–67,** 66 (ill.)
  elephant, African *1:* **75–78,** 76 (ill.), 79, 81
  gorilla *1:* **97–100,** 98 (ill.)
  hyena, brown *1:* **110–12,** 111 (ill.)
  rhinoceros, black *1:* **204–7,** 205 (ill.)

Angonoka *3:* 716

Anguilla
  mahogany, American *3:* **632–34,** 633 (ill.)

Angulated tortoise *3:* **716–18,** 717 (ill.)

Anodorhynchus leari 2: **365–67,** 366 (ill.)

Anole, Culebra Island giant *3:* **672–74,** 673 (ill.)

Anole, Roosevelt's giant *3:* 672

Anolis roosevelti 3: **672–74,** 673 (ill.)

Anoplolepis gracilipes 2: 282

Ant, Australian *2:* **465–67,** 466 (ill.)

Ant, dinosaur *2:* 465

Anteater, banded *1:* 167

Anteater, giant *1:* **4–6,** 5 (ill.)

Antelope
  addax *1:* **1–3,** 2 (ill.)
  gazelle, dama *1:* **90–92,** 91 (ill.)
  oryx, scimitar-horned *1:* **174–76,** 175 (ill.)

Antigua and Barbuda
  mahogany, American *3:* **632–34,** 633 (ill.)

Antrolana lira 2: **456–58,** 457 (ill.)

Ant, yellow crazy *2:* 282

Apes, great
  chimpanzee *1:* **50–53,** 51 (ill.)
  gorilla *1:* **97–100,** 98 (ill.)
  orangutan *1:* **170–73,** 171 (ill.)

Apes, lesser
  gibbon, hoolock *1:* **93–96,** 94 (ill.)

Appalachian Mountain Club (AMC) *3:* 613

Arabian camel *1:* 43

Arabis perstellata 3: **614–16,** 615 (ill.)

Arabis perstellata var. *ampla 3:* 614, 616

Arabis perstellata var. *perstellata 3:* 614, 616

Aratinga guarouba (Guarouba guarouba) 2: **382–84,** 383 (ill.)

Arborophila rufipectus 2: **392–95,** 393 (ill.)

Arctic char *3:* 591

Arctic peregrine falcon *2:* 318

Arctocephalus townsendi 1: **212–14,** 213 (ill.)

Argentina
  anteater, giant *1:* **4–6,** 5 (ill.)
  armadillo, giant *1:* **7–9,** 8 (ill.)
  chinchilla, short-tailed *1:* **54–56,** 55 (ill.)
  curlew, Eskimo *2:* **303–5,** 304 (ill.)
  flamingo, Andean *2:* **325–27,** 326 (ill.)
  ground-dove, purple-winged *2:* **334–36,** 335 (ill.)
  jaguar *1:* **113–15,** 114 (ill.)
  otter, marine *1:* **177–79,** 178 (ill.)
  vicuña *1:* **231–34,** 233 (ill.)

Argun palm *3:* **638–39**

Argyroxiphium kauense 3: **655–57,** 656 (ill.)

Ariocarpus agavoides 3: **604–6,** 605 (ill.)

Arizona (USA)
  cactus, Peebles Navajo *3:* **607–8**
  condor, California *2:* **285–88,** 286 (ill.)
  ferret, black-footed *1:* **83–86,** 84 (ill.)
  mussel, fat pocketbook pearly *2:* **507–10,** 508 (ill.)
  owl, cactus ferruginous pygmy *2:* **374–77,** 375 (ill.)
  tortoise, desert *3:* **719–21,** 720 (ill.)

Arkansas (USA)
  bat, gray *1:* **19–21,** 20 (ill.), *2:* 452
  bat, Ozark big-eared *1:* 24
  beetle, American burying *2:* **468–70,** 469 (ill.)
  crayfish, Hell Creek Cave *2:* **450–52,** 451 (ill.)

Armadillo, giant *1:* **7–9,** 8 (ill.)

Armenia
  pelican, Dalmatian *2:* **396–98,** 397 (ill.)
  viper, meadow *3:* **738–40,** 739 (ill.)

Asia *See* Southeastern Asia; *names of specific countries*

Asian buffalo *1:* 40

Asian elephant *1:* **79–82,** 81 (ill.)

Ass, African wild *1:* **10–13,** 11 (ill.)

Atlantic cod *3:* **554–57,** 556 (ill.)

Atlantic Ocean
  cod, Atlantic *3:* **554–57,** 556 (ill.)
  sturgeon, Baltic *3:* **580–82,** 581 (ill.)
  See also Oceanic species

Atlantic rain forest *1:* 151, 188

Attalea crassispatha 3: **640–41**

Audouin's gull *2:* **337–39,** 338 (ill.)

Australia
  ant, Australian *2:* **465–67,** 466 (ill.)

owl, northern spotted 2: **378–81,** 379 (ill.)

Brown bear 1: 25, 27

Brown-headed cowbird 2: 439

Brown hyena 1: 110–12, 111 (ill.)

Brunei
bear, sun 1: **29–31,** 30 (ill.)
crocodile, saltwater 3: **688–90,** 689 (ill.)
egret, Chinese 2: **315–17,** 316 (ill.)
elephant, Asian 1: **79–82,** 81 (ill.)
orangutan 1: **170–73,** 171 (ill.)

Bubalus bubalis 1: **40–42,** 41 (ill.)

Buffalo *1:* 32

Buffalo, Asian *1:* 40

Buffalo, Indian *1:* 40

Buffalo, wild water *1:* **40–42,** 41 (ill.)

Buffy-tufted ear marmoset *1:* 149

Bufo baxteri (hemiophrys) 3: **548–50,** 549 (ill.)

Bufo houstonensis 3: **545–47,** 546 (ill.)

Bulgaria
mink, European 1: **156–58,** 157 (ill.)
pelican, Dalmation 2: **396–98,** 397 (ill.)
viper, meadow 3: **738–40,** 739 (ill.)

Bullfinch, Azores 2: **283–84**

Bullfinch, common 2: 283

Bullfrogs 3: 531–32, 714–715

Bull trout 3: **591–94,** 592 (ill.)

Bunipithecus hoolock 1: **93–96,** 94 (ill.)

Burkina Faso
cheetah 1: **47–49,** 48 (ill.)
dog, African wild 1: **65–67,** 66 (ill.)
elephant, African 1: **75–78,** 76 (ill.), 79, 81
oryx, scimitar-horned 1: **174–76,** 175 (ill.)

Burramys parvus 1: **189–91,** 190 (ill.)

Burundi
chimpanzee 1: **50–53,** 51 (ill.)
dog, African wild 1: **65–67,** 66 (ill.)

Buteo galapagoensis 2: **340–42,** 341 (ill.)

Buteo solitarius 2: **343–45,** 344 (ill.)

Butterfly, bay checkerspot 2: **471–73,** 472 (ill.)

Butterfly, Corsican swallowtail 2: **474–75**

Butterfly, Queen Alexandra's birdwing 2: **476–78,** 477 (ill.)

C

Cabbage, Lundy 3: **602–3**

Cactus, agave living-rock 3: **604–6,** 605 (ill.)

Cactus ferruginous pygmy owl 2: **374–77,** 375 (ill.)

Cactus, Peebles Navajo 3: **607–8**

Caicos Islands *See* Turks and Caicos Islands

Caiman, black 3: **678–81,** 679 (ill.)

California (USA)
albatross, short-tailed 2: **274–76,** 275 (ill.)
barberry, Nevin's 3: **598–601,** 600 (ill.)
butterfly, bay checkerspot 2: **471–73,** 472 (ill.)
condor, California 2: **285–88,** 286 (ill.)
fly, Delhi Sands flower-loving 2: **484–86,** 486 (ill.)
fox, island gray 1: **87–89,** 88 (ill.)
frog, California red-legged 3: **529–32,** 531 (ill.), 714–715
grasshopper, Zayante band-winged 2: **487–88**
lizard, blunt-nosed leopard 3: **703–4,** 704 (ill.)
murrelet, marbled 2: **371–73,** 372 (ill.)
owl, northern spotted 2: **378–81,** 379 (ill.)
pupfish, desert 3: **564–66,** 565 (ill.)

rat, giant kangaroo 1: **198–200,** 199 (ill.)
salamander, Santa Cruz long-toed 3: **539–41,** 540 (ill.)
seal, Guadalupe fur 1: **212–14,** 213 (ill.)
sea lion, Steller's 1: **218–20,** 219 (ill.)
shrimp, California freshwater 2: **459–61,** 460 (ill.)
snake, San Francisco garter 3: **713–15,** 715 (ill.)
sucker, shortnose 3: **586–88,** 587 (ill.)
tortoise, desert 3: **719–21,** 720 (ill.)

California chaparral, defined 3: 599

California condor 2: **285–88,** 286 (ill.)

California freshwater shrimp 2: **459–61,** 460 (ill.)

California red-legged frog 3: **529–32,** 531 (ill.), 714–715

California vulture 2: 285

Callithrix aurita 1: **149–52,** 150 (ill.)

Cambarus zophonastes 2: **450–52,** 451 (ill.)

Cambodia
bear, sun 1: **29–31,** 30 (ill.)
catfish, giant 3: **551–53,** 552 (ill.)
crocodile, saltwater 3: **688–90,** 689 (ill.)
dugong 1: **71–74,** 73 (ill.)
elephant, Asian 1: **79–82,** 81 (ill.)
kouprey 1: **125–27**
python, Indian 3: **710–12,** 711 (ill.)
tiger 1: **227–30,** 228 (ill.)

Cambodian forest ox 1: 125

Camel, Arabian 1: 43

Camel, bactrian 1: **43–46,** 44 (ill.)

Camel family (Camelidae)
camel, bactrian 1: **43–46,** 44 (ill.)
vicuña 1: **231–34,** 233 (ill.)

Camelus bactrianus 1: **43–46,** 44 (ill.)

tiger *1:* **227–30,** 228 (ill.)

yak, wild *1:* **257–59,** 258 (ill.)

Indiana (USA)
bat, gray *1:* **19–21,** 20 (ill.), *2:* 452
mussel, fat pocketbook pearly *2:* **507–10,** 508 (ill.)

Indian buffalo *1:* 40

Indian elephant *1:* 79

Indian mynah *2:* 370

Indian Ocean *See* Oceanic species

Indian python *3:* **710–12,** 711 (ill.)

Indian tiger *1:* 227

Indicator species, defined *1:* 179

Indigo macaw *2:* 365

Indo-Chinese tiger *1:* 227, 229

Indonesia
bear, sun *1:* **29–31,** 30 (ill.)
crocodile, saltwater *3:* **688–90,** 689 (ill.)
dugong *1:* **71–74,** 73 (ill.)
egret, Chinese *2:* **315–17,** 316 (ill.)
elephant, Asian *1:* **79–82,** 81 (ill.)
monitor, Komodo Island *3:* **707–9,** 708 (ill.)
orangutan *1:* **170–73,** 171 (ill.)
python, Indian *3:* **710–12,** 711 (ill.)
sawfish, freshwater *3:* **570–72,** 571 (ill.)
shark, Borneo *3:* **577–79**
starling, Rothchild's *2:* **418–20,** 419 (ill.)
tiger *1:* **227–30,** 228 (ill.)

Indopacific crocodile *3:* 688

Insectivorous, defined *3:* 663

International Union for Conservation of Nature and Natural Resources (IUCN) *See specific IUCN status designations*

Invasive plants *3:* 623

Io *2:* 343

Iowa (USA)
mussel, fat pocketbook pearly *2:* **507–10,** 508 (ill.)

orchid, eastern prairie fringed *3:* 637

snail, Iowa Pleistocene *2:* **517–19,** 518 (ill.)

Iowa Pleistocene snail *2:* **517–19,** 518 (ill.)

Iran
cheetah *1:* **47–49,** 48 (ill.)
crane, Siberian *2:* **293–95,** 294 (ill.)
dugong *1:* **71–74,** 73 (ill.)
pelican, Dalmation *2:* **396–98,** 397 (ill.)
viper, meadow *3:* **738–40,** 739 (ill.)

Iraq
dugong *1:* **71–74,** 73 (ill.)
pelican, Dalmation *2:* **396–98,** 397 (ill.)

Ireland
fern, bristle *3:* **621–23,** 622 (ill.)
sturgeon, Baltic *3:* **580–82,** 581 (ill.)

Island gray fox *1:* **87–89,** 88 (ill.)

Isoodon auratus 1: **17–18,** 18

Isopod, Madison Cave *2:* **456–58,** 457 (ill.)

Isotria medeoloides 3: **647–49,** 648 (ill.)

Israel
dugong *1:* **71–74,** 73 (ill.)
oryx, scimitar-horned *1:* **174–76,** 175 (ill.)

Italian cypress *3:* 620

Italy
butterfly, Corsican swallowtail *2:* **474–75**
fern, bristle *3:* **621–23,** 622 (ill.)
gull, Audouin's *2:* **337–39,** 338 (ill.)
sturgeon, Baltic *3:* **580–82,** 581 (ill.)
viper, meadow *3:* **738–40,** 739 (ill.)

Ivory-billed woodpecker *2:* **440–43,** 441 (ill.)

J

Jacaranda *3:* 653

Jaguar *1:* **113–15,** 114 (ill.)

Jamaica
conch, queen *2:* **497–500,** 498 (ill.)
crocodile, American *3:* **682–84,** 683 (ill.)
mahogany, American *3:* **632–34,** 633 (ill.)
manatee, West Indian *1:* **140–42,** 141 (ill.)
plover, piping *2:* **405–7,** 406 (ill.)

James River spinymussel *2:* **523–25,** 524 (ill.)

Japan
albatross, short-tailed *2:* **274–76,** 275 (ill.)
dugong *1:* **71–74,** 73 (ill.)
egret, Chinese *2:* **315–17,** 316 (ill.)
sea lion, Steller's *1:* **218–20,** 219 (ill.)
stork, Oriental white *2:* **421–23,** 422 (ill.)

Japanese honeysuckle *3:* 662

Japanese white stork *2:* 421

Javan tiger *1:* 227, 230

Jefferson, Thomas *2:* 457

Jordan
cheetah *1:* **47–49,** 48 (ill.)
dugong *1:* **71–74,** 73 (ill.)

Junín grebe *2:* 331

Juniper, Bermuda *3:* 609

Juniper scale *3:* 610

Juniperus bermudiana 3: **609–10**

K

Kabal markhor *1:* 148

Kakapo *2:* **356–58,** 357 (ill.)

Kangaroo family (Macropodidae)
kangaroo, Matschie's tree *1:* **116–19,** 118 (ill.)
wallaby, brindled nail-tailed *1:* **235–37,** 236 (ill.)

Kangaroo, Huon tree *1:* 116

Kangaroo, Matschie's tree *1:* **116–19,** 118 (ill.)

Kansas (USA)
bat, gray *1:* **19–21,** 20 (ill.), *2:* 452

Kauai cave wolf spider *1:* 166

Parakeet, golden *2:* **382–84**, 383 (ill.)

Parasite, defined *2:* 489

Parasitism, defined *2:* 432, 439

Parrot family (Psittacidae)
 kakapo *2:* **356–58**, 357 (ill.)
 lovebird, black-cheeked *2:* **362–64**, 363 (ill.)
 macaw, Lear's *2:* **365–67**, 366 (ill.)
 parakeet, golden *2:* **382–84**, 383 (ill.)
 parrot, imperial *2:* **385–87**, 386 (ill.)
 parrot, thick-billed *2:* **388–91**, 389 (ill.)

Parrot, imperial *2:* **385–87**, 386 (ill.)

Parrot, thick-billed *2:* **388–91**, 389 (ill.)

Partridge, Sichuan *2:* 392

Partridge, Sichuan hill *2:* **392–95**, 393 (ill.)

Peale's peregrine falcon *2:* 318

Pearlymussel, little-wing *2:* **514–16**, 515 (ill.)

Pediocatus peeblesianus 3: **607–8**

Peebles Navajo cactus *3:* **607–8**

Pegias fabula 2: **514–16**, 515 (ill.)

Pelecanus crispus 2: **396–98**, 397 (ill.)

Pelican, Dalmation *2:* **396–98**, 397 (ill.)

Penguin, yellow-eyed *2:* **399–401**, 400 (ill.)

Pennsylvania (USA)
 pogonia, small whorled *3:* 649

Percina tanasi 3: 562

Peru
 anteater, giant *1:* **4–6**, 5 (ill.)
 armadillo, giant *1:* **7–9**, 8 (ill.)
 caiman, black *3:* **678–81**, 679 (ill.)
 chinchilla, short-tailed *1:* **54–56**, 55 (ill.)
 crocodile, American *3:* **682–84**, 683 (ill.)

flamingo, Andean *2:* **325–27**, 326 (ill.)
 grebe, Puna *2:* **331–33**, 332 (ill.)
 jaguar *1:* **113–15**, 114 (ill.)
 otter, marine *1:* **177–79**, 178 (ill.)
 vicuña *1:* **231–34**, 233 (ill.)

Petit coco (little coconut) *3:* 640

Petroica traversi 2: **414–17**, 415 (ill.)

Phalacrocorax harrisi 2: **289–92**, 290 (ill.)

Pharomachrus mocinno 2: **408–10**, 409 (ill.)

Phascolarctus cinerus 1: **120–24**, 123 (ill.)

Pheasant, cheer *2:* **402–4**, 403 (ill.)

Philippine eagle *2:* **313–14**, 314 (ill.)

Philippines
 crocodile, saltwater *3:* **688–90**, 689 (ill.)
 dugong *1:* **71–74**, 73 (ill.)
 eagle, Philippine *2:* **313–14**, 314 (ill.)
 egret, Chinese *2:* **315–17**, 316 (ill.)
 shark, Borneo *3:* **577–79**
 stork, Oriental white *2:* **421–23**, 422 (ill.)

Phoenicoparrus andinus 2: **325–27**, 326 (ill.)

Picoides borealis 2: **444–46**, 445 (ill.)

Pigeon, prairie *2:* 303

Pineal eye, defined *3:* 726

Pine, bigcone pinyon *3:* **642–43**

Pink conch *2:* 497

Pinus maximartinezii 3: **642–43**

Piolo *2:* 283

Piping plover *2:* **405–7**, 406 (ill.)

Pitcher plant, green *3:* **644–46**, 645 (ill.)

Pithecophaga jefferyi 2: **313–14**, 314 (ill.)

Plains bison *1:* 32–33, 34

Platanthera leucophaea 3: **635–37**, 636 (ill.)

Plecotus townsendii 1: **22–24**, 23 (ill.)

Plecotus townsendii ingens 1: 22, 23, 24

Plecotus townsendii virginianus 1: 22, 23, 24

Pleurobema collina 2: **523–25**, 524 (ill.)

Plover, piping *2:* **405–7**, 406 (ill.)

Podiceps taczanowskii 2: **331–33**, 332 (ill.)

Pogonia, small whorled *3:* **647–49**, 648 (ill.)

Poland
 bison, European *1:* **36–39**, 37 (ill.)
 mink, European *1:* **156–58**, 157 (ill.)
 salmon, Danube *3:* **567–69**, 568 (ill.)
 sturgeon, Baltic *3:* **580–82**, 581 (ill.)

Polynesian rat *3:* 727

Pongo pygmaeus 1: **170–73**, 171 (ill.)

Po'ouli honeycreeper *2:* **349–52**, 350 (ill.)

Porcupine, bristle-spined *1:* 187

Porcupine, thin-spined *1:* **187–88**

Portugal
 bullfinch, Azores *2:* **283–84**
 fern, bristle *3:* **621–23**, 622 (ill.)
 lynx, Iberian *1:* **137–39**, 138 (ill.)
 sturgeon, Baltic *3:* **580–82**, 581 (ill.)

Possum, mountain pygmy *1:* **189–91**, 190 (ill.)

Potamilus capax 2: **507–10**, 508 (ill.)

Potentilla robbinsiana 3: **611–13**, 612 (ill.)

Prairie dog, Mexican *1:* **192–94**, 193 (ill.)

Prairie pigeon *2:* 303

rhinoceros, black *1:* **204–7,**
205 (ill.)
vulture, Cape *2:* **433–36,** 434
(ill.)

Zizania texana 3: **666–68,** 667
(ill.)

Edgewood Public Montessori LMC
Okemos, MI